35⁰⁰

GRAPHIS POSTERS 88

The International Annual of Poster Art

Das Internationale Jahrbuch der Plakatkunst

Le Répertoire International de l'Art de l'Affiche

Edited by/Herausgegeben von/Réalisé par

B. Martin Pedersen

Publisher and Creative Director: B. Martin Pedersen

Assistant Editor: Annette Crandall

Designers: Marino Bianchera, Martin Byland

Photographer: Walter Zuber

Graphis Press Corp, Zurich (Switzerland)

GRAPHIS PUBLICATIONS

GRAPHIS, International bi-monthly journal of graphic art and photography
GRAPHIS DESIGN ANNUAL, The international annual on design and illustration
PHOTOGRAPHIS, The international annual of photography
GRAPHIS POSTERS, The international annual on poster art
GRAPHIS PACKAGING, An international survey of packaging design
GRAPHIS DIAGRAMS VOL. 2, The graphic visualization of abstract, technical and statistical facts and functions
GRAPHIS COVERS, An anthology of all GRAPHIS covers with artists' short biographies and indexes of all GRAPHIS issues
GRAPHIS ANNUAL REPORTS, An international compilation of the best designed annual reports
FILM + TV GRAPHICS 2, An international survey of the art of film animation

GRAPHIS-PUBLIKATIONEN

GRAPHIS, Die internationale Zweimonatszeitschrift für Graphik und Photographie
GRAPHIS DESIGN ANNUAL, Das internationale Jahrbuch über Design und Illustration
PHOTOGRAPHIS, Das internationale Jahrbuch der Photographie
GRAPHIS POSTERS, Das internationale Jahrbuch der Plakatkunst
GRAPHIS PACKUNGEN, Internationaler Überblick der Packungsgestaltung
GRAPHIS DIAGRAMS BAND 2, Die graphische Darstellung abstrakter, technischer und statistischer Daten und Fakten
GRAPHIS COVERS, Eine Sammlung aller GRAPHIS-Umschläge mit Informationen über die Künstler und
    Inhaltsübersichten aller Ausgaben der Zeitschrift GRAPHIS
GRAPHIS ANNUAL REPORTS, Ein internationaler Überblick der Gestaltung von Jahresberichten
FILM + TV GRAPHICS 2, Ein internationaler Überblick über die Kunst des Animationsfilms

PUBLICATIONS GRAPHIS

GRAPHIS, La magazine bimestrielle internationale d'arts graphiques et de la photographie
GRAPHIS DESIGN ANNUAL, L'annuel international du design et de l'illustration
PHOTOGRAPHIS, L'annuel international de la photographie appliquée
GRAPHIS POSTERS, L'annuel international de l'affiche
GRAPHIS PACKAGING, Panorama international de l'art de l'emballage
GRAPHIS DIAGRAMS VOL. 2, La représentation graphique de faits et donnés abstraits, techniques et statistiques
GRAPHIS COVERS, Recueil de toutes les couvertures de GRAPHIS avec des notices biographiques des artistes
    et récapitulatif des index annuels du magazine GRAPHIS.
GRAPHIS ANNUAL REPORTS, Panorama international du design de rapports annuels d'entreprises
FILM + TV GRAPHICS 2, Panorama international du cinéma d'animation

PUBLICATION No. 188 (ISBN 3 85709 388 9)
© Copyright under Universal Copyright Convention
Copyright 1988 by Graphis Press Corp., 107 Dufourstrasse, 8008 Zurich, Switzerland
No part of this book may be reproduced in any form without written permission of the publisher
Printed in Japan by Toppan
Typeset in Switzerland by Setzerei Heller, Zurich

CULTURE

KULTUR

CULTURE

ADVERTISING

WERBUNG

PUBLICITÉ

SOCIETY

GESELLSCHAFT

SOCIÉTÉ

ABBREVIATIONS

Australia .... AUS

Austria .... AUT

Belgium .... BEL

Bulgaria .... BUL

Canada .... CAN

Czechoslovakia .... CSR

Denmark .... DEN

Finland .... FIN

France .... FRA

Germany (West) .... GER

Great Britain .... GBR

Greece .... GRE

Hong Kong .... HKG

Hungary .... HUN

Ireland .... IRL

Italy .... ITA

Japan .... JPN

Korea .... KOR

Netherlands .... NLD

Norway .... NOR

Poland .... POL

Portugal .... POR

Soviet Union .... USR

Spain .... SPA

Sweden .... SWE

Switzerland .... SWI

Turkey .... TUR

USA .... USA

ABKÜRZUNGEN

Australien .... AUS

Belgien .... BEL

Bulgarien .... BUL

Dänemark .... DEN

Deutschland (BRD) .... GER

Finnland .... FIN

Frankreich .... FRA

Griechenland .... GRE

Grossbritannien .... GBR

Hongkong .... HKG

Irland .... IRL

Italien .... ITA

Japan .... JPN

Kanada .... CAN

Korea .... KOR

Niederlande .... NLD

Norwegen .... NOR

Österreich .... AUT

Polen .... POL

Portugal .... POR

Schweden .... SWE

Schweiz .... SWI

Sowjetunion .... USR

Spanien .... SPA

Tschechoslowakei .... CSR

Türkei .... TUR

Ungarn .... HUN

USA .... USA

ABRÉVIATIONS

Allemagne occidentale .... GER

Australie .... AUS

Autriche .... AUT

Belgique .... BEL

Bulgarie .... BUL

Canada .... CAN

Corée .... KOR

Danemark .... DEN

Espagne .... SPA

Etats-Unis .... USA

Finlande .... FIN

France .... FRA

Grande-Bretagne .... GBR

Grèce .... GRE

Hongkong .... HKG

Hongrie .... HUN

Irlande .... IRL

Italie .... ITA

Japon .... JPN

Norvège .... NOR

Pays-Bas .... NLD

Pologne .... POL

Portugal .... POR

Suède .... SWE

Suisse .... SWI

Tchécoslovaquie .... CSR

Turquie .... TUR

Union Soviétique .... USR

REMARKS

■ Our sincere thanks are extended to all contributors throughout the world who have made it possible for us to publish a broad international spectrum of outstanding work.

■ Entry instructions may be requested at: Graphis Press Corp., Dufourstrasse 107, 8008 Zurich, Switzerland

ANMERKUNGEN

■ Unser herzlicher Dank gilt Einsendern aus aller Welt, die es uns möglich gemacht haben, ein breites, internationales Spektrum der besten Arbeiten zu veröffentlichen.

■ Teilnahmebedingungen: Graphis Verlag AG, Dufourstrasse 107, 8008 Zurich, Schweiz

AVERTISSEMENT

■ Nos sincères remerciements vont à tous les collaborateurs du monde entier, qui nous ont permis de publier un vaste panorama international des meilleurs travaux.

■ Demande de participation: Editions Graphis SA, Dufourstrasse 107, 8008 Zurich, Suisse

We just can't escape the poster. There it is, bold and brazen, facing us on every street corner, plastered over every scrap of wall, mounted on all the billboards, meeting our gaze through bus and train windows. Whether we think of it as a sprinkling of common-place culture or a dastardly act of environmental pollution makes no difference. Yet, in spite of, or perhaps because of, its ubiquity, the poster has to cope with quite a few problems of its own. First of all it's got to engage in active combat to attract the observer's attention, and this is harder than it sounds. The poster is right there in the field competing against the clutter of myriad life-essential and information-giving environmental signs, pointers and notices. And that great visual world out there is screaming its head off for attention.

Media and market researchers have established that only about 25 to 30% of the population who rush past the poster take any notice of it! The poster designer's task is to increase this percentage of so-called "poster-affinitive" people. And they've got to get their message across amongst this mad, mad jumble of gaudy, giant pictures. This is the second, and usually more difficult task to fulfill.

Almost one hundred years have gone by since the first great flourishing period of poster creation. It was a period when artists such as Toulouse Lautrec, Théophile-Alexandre Steinlen, Jules Cheret and Aubrey Beardsley (to mention only the most famous) designed posters that put all their predecessors into the shadows. They proved that advertising could not only put forth works of art, but could at the same time produce art that would have an immense advertising effect. The favorite topics, by the way, of these early poster artists were the circus and variety – and always beautiful women of course. In the latter case this has continued to be true.

Much has happened in the history of the poster medium since those early golden days. Great pinnacle periods of inspiration and powerful design followed times in which the poster had precious little in common with "art". And there were plenty of opinion-makers ready to pronounce the imminent death of the poor poster – only to find themselves proved wrong when the following generation resuscitated it.

The good poster arouses the greatest respect and here again nothing much has changed over the last century. But the number of true poster geniuses has wavered, and so has the resonance that their posters have found with public and clients alike. Naturally the poster's popularity varies from country to country but to contemporaries the study of the diversity of impressions is obstructed. It's far better to defer judgement on the great directions and accomplishments until they can be viewed from a further distance in time. Nevertheless it is possible to utter a few statements on the poster status quo:

1. The technical spectrum has never been so great. In fact, there are, at present especially, many directions of style and graphic techniques. Large-format photographs and illustrations, purely typographic posters, naive collages, and computer images appear next to each other. And this variety, incidentally, is present worldwide. In the seventies, there emerged a flood of posters in which the photograph was the focal point. This innovation was caused by the new developments in reproduction and print techniques. This situation has now balanced out; the photographic poster is taken for granted and is therefore less of a sensation. New paths of design are emerging, without the "tried and true" disappearing from the billboards.

Of course there are still national differences. Those who have the opportunity to visit poster exhibitions in which productions from East and West Europe are shown – at the Biennale in Lahti, Finland, or in Brno, Czechoslovakia, for example – find this particularly noticeable. However, the contrast is not so blatant as it was ten or fifteen years ago.

Poster creation in Japan too represents an exotic wonderworld to Western eyes, although countless adaptations on the part of East and West can be seen. A lively exchange of creative ideas and talents ensures that there is an increase in internationalism, which is certainly not to the disadvantage of the medium. In fact, it is this interchange that keeps it on its toes.

2. The poster is finding new customers. A new trend (which can be traced over the past few years and will evidently continue unbroken) is that the medium is no longer limited to the "classic" poster products, such as cigarettes, cars, household goods, and public events. Other sectors and sub-sectors – luxury goods, cosmetics, banking and insurance services – now are among regular poster patrons on the street. This too has its impact on design. Outdoor advertising is not only increasingly

HERBERT LECHNER

applied as an effective means for the possibilities of image use, but also allows greater creative freedom.

On the other hand, the poster as a promotional vehicle is getting more recognition as a vital component of a comprehensive media mix. This leads to its integration in an already existing design line (catchphrase: Corporate Design) and resets limits on this newly won freedom. In the case of the cultural poster, there are seldom such problems. As in the past, designers of theater, concert and exhibition posters (and in many countries of film posters too) are allowed the freedom to work out their own concepts. (They sometimes lack an adequate budget, but that's another story.)

3. Outdoor advertising is coming indoors. Increasingly outdoor poster art is such that it is not intended for exposure to the vagaries of the winds and weather at all. Expensively produced and limited in distribution, these posters serve as self-promotion for creative designers and agencies. The poster reissues with motifs by the old masters now have rivals.

Many proprietary brand producers are also aware of the promotional effects of such "noble" and elegant posters and use them for their own public relations. Companies steeped in tradition revive old poster motifs for their firm's anniversaries – and this is now all part and parcel of a company's good image. Newcomers to the trade draw attention to themselves by mailing poster scrolls to their potential target groups. The poster as an extravagant, but higly effective, direct mailing piece has changed from being a message-bearer for many to being a gift for the few.

Such targeted posters are naturally not as subject to stringent poster rules. Reduction to the essential, omission of all details, message elucidated to exaggeration point – these characteristics of a powerful outdoor advertising are not necessary if its message has to appeal to someone within the four walls of his office or studio. Many of these interior posters are similar in their complex design to Chinese wall newspapers. It goes without saying though that such posters still possess a great visual stimulus.

4. The typographical content of posters is becoming more important. A striking tendency in recent years that has been confirmed in-ternationally is the truly unconventional association with the works of earlier advertising and cultural epochs. Symbols, techniques, "signatures" of past experts are wittily interpreted. This genre counts equally on the viewer's joy at recognition of an old master and on his amusement at the new twist. This is not limited to today's poster design. You only have to think of the countless Marilyn Monroe or Humphrey Bogart imitators, or of the remakes of film classics. A shot of nostalgia is part of the success: "Play it again, Sam!"

5. Poster design is becoming more and more a team effort. And I don't only mean those great creative collaborative teams like the Germans Rambow, Lienemeyer, and van de Sand, or the Grapus group in France. It's more a question of the poster becoming a combined operations task: photographer, illustrator, typographer, and layout person all contribute their expert knowledge. Should the motifs originate from the graphic computer then machines are in the game too. The Hohlweins and Cassandres, the Savignacs, Leupins and Müller-Brockmanns created a poster from A to Z: Lettering was still written or drawn, logotypes incorporated, and they often supervised the printing. Now the specialists are involved. From the heyday of the great soloist we've come to the era of the whole orchestra. This is all well and good – even necessary. Does a poster creator really have to be a master photographer, super illustrator and inspired lettering artist all at once? Not really. His accomplishment is not one bit lessened if he takes on the assistance of others with relevant talents. And often a jointly created poster is still an unmistakable expression of a single personality.

What about the future of the poster? The discussions on the often quoted "new media" and the new-fangled forms of addressing today's consumers occasionally leave us thinking that the "old" posters are dragging their feet in the background. This point of view is quite unjustified. As the following pages emphatically prove, the poster has not suffered any loss in vitality, power of statement, topicality or modernity.

HERBERT LECHNER (b. 1952) was chief editor of the trade magazine "Graphik visuelles Marketing" for five years and is now engaged as a freelance writer in Munich. He is the author of several books, including "The History of Modern Typography" and "Cartoons and Caricatures in Advertising".

Dem Plakat entgeht man nicht. Wer sich im öffentlichen Raum bewegt, und das tun wir schliesslich fast alle tagtäglich, der wird laufend mit unübersehbaren Aussenwerbemitteln konfrontiert. Ob «Alltagskultur» oder «Umweltverschmutzung» sei zunächst dahingestellt. Doch das Plakat hat es auch schwer. Denn der Kampf um die Aufmerksamkeit des Betrachters ist ungleich härter als bei Anzeige oder Prospekt, TV-Spot oder Werbefilm. Stehen doch die Bilder und Aussagen auf den Plakatwänden und Litfasssäulen in direkter Konkurrenz mit unzähligen, teilweise lebenswichtigen Signalen der Umwelt.

Die Medien- und Marktforscher haben deshalb festgestellt: Gerade 25–30% der Passanten nehmen die Plakate, an denen sie vorübereilen, überhaupt wahr! Diese – immer noch erstaunlich grosse – Gruppe der sogenannten «Plakat-Affinen» mit jedem einzelnen Blatt noch weiter zu vergrössern, ist eine Aufgabe des Plakatkünstlers. Aus dem wilden Jahrmarkt der bunten Grossbilder dann auch noch die eigene Botschaft herauszuheben, ist die zweite, meist noch schwerer zu erfüllende.

Rund 100 Jahre sind seit der ersten grossen Blütezeit des Plakatschaffens vergangen, als Künstler wie Toulouse-Lautrec, Théophile-Alexandre Steinlen, Jules Cheret, Aubrey Beardsley (um nur die bekanntesten hervorzuheben) Plakate entwarfen, die alles bisher Dagewesene in den Schatten stellten. Sie beweisen, dass Werbung Kunstwerke hervorbringen kann, die dennoch unübersehbare Werbewirkung haben. Die bevorzugten Themen dieser frühen Blätter scheinen Zirkus und Varieté und immer wieder schöne Frauen gewesen zu sein. Wenigstens das letztere hat sich bis heute nicht sehr verändert.

Wechselvoll war der Lebenslauf des Mediums seit jenen Goldenen Tagen. Höhepunkten an Einfallsreichtum und gestalterischer Kraft folgten Perioden, in denen von Plakat-«Kunst» nicht die Rede sein konnte. Immer wieder wurde das Plakat totgesagt – um dann von der nächsten Generation wiederentdeckt zu werden!

Das gute Plakat erregt Aufsehen, auch daran hat sich in den letzten hundert Jahren nichts geändert. Aber die Zahl der wirklichen Plakat-Genies schwankt, ebenso wie die Resonanz, die ihre Blätter bei Publikum und bei Auftraggebern finden. Natürlich ist der Stellenwert des Plakates auch von Land zu Land verschieden. Dem Zeitgenossen ist der Blick durch die Vielfalt der Eindrücke verstellt. Die grossen Linien und

Tendenzen lassen sich nun mal am besten aus der Distanz erkennen. Dennoch seien nachstehend einige Aussagen zum plakativen Status quo gewagt:

1. Das technische Spektrum war nie so gross. Tatsächlich existieren augenblicklich besonders viele Stilrichtungen und graphische Techniken. Vom Grossphoto über die Illustration bis zum rein typographischen Plakat, von der naiven Collage bis zum Computerausdruck erscheint alles nebeneinander – und das eigentlich weltweit. In den 70er Jahren entstand – begründet durch die Fortschritte der Repro- und Drucktechnik – eine Flut von Plakaten, bei denen das Photo im Mittelpunkt stand. Heute ist die Situation ausgeglichener, das Photoplakat ist selbstverständlich geworden – und dadurch weniger auffällig. Neue gestalterische Wege werden beschritten, ohne dass deshalb Bewährtes von den Anschlagstellen verschwindet.

Natürlich gibt es noch nationale Unterschiede. Wer Gelegenheit hat, Plakatausstellungen zu besuchen, in denen die Produktion aus West- und Osteuropa aufeinandertrifft – beispielsweise auf den Biennalen im finnischen Lahti oder in Brno (Tschechoslowakei) –, dem wird das besonders augenfällig vorgeführt. Trotzdem erscheint der Kontrast heute nicht mehr so krass wie noch vor 10 oder 15 Jahren.

Auch das Plakatschaffen Japans stellt für europäische Augen immer noch eine exotische Wunderwelt dar – obwohl mittlerweile zahlreiche Adaptionen auf beiden Seiten feststellbar sind. Ein reger Austausch kreativer Ideen und kreativer Talente sorgt für zunehmende Internationalität, sicher nicht zum Nachteil des Mediums, das dadurch selbst in Bewegung bleibt.

2. Das Plakat findet neue Kunden. Ein Trend, der sich schon seit einer Reihe von Jahren abzeichnet, sich aber offenbar ungebrochen fortsetzt: Nicht nur die «klassischen» Plakatofferten – wie Zigaretten, Autos, Haushaltswaren, Veranstaltungen – zeigen sich auf der Strasse. Immer häufiger präsentieren sich auch andere Wirtschaftszweige via Grossfläche: Luxusgüter, Kosmetik, Banken und Versicherungen gehören mittlerweile zum festen Stamm der Plakatkunden. Das bleibt auch für die Gestaltung nicht ohne Folgen.

Immer häufiger wird zudem die Aussenwerbung als wirksames Mittel zur Imageprofilierung eingesetzt. Damit sind nicht nur die Ein-

HERBERT LECHNER

satzmöglichkeiten vervielfacht, es herrscht beim Warenplakat auch grössere kreative Freiheit.

Auf der anderen Seite wird das Werbemittel Plakat zunehmend als Bestandteil eines umfassenden Media-Mix erkannt. Das führt zur Einbindung in eine bereits bestehende Gestaltungslinie (Stichwort: Corporate Design) und schränkt diese gerade gewonnene Freiheit wieder ein. Solche Probleme ergeben sich für das Kulturplakat nur selten. Nach wie vor können Graphiker bei Theater-, Konzert- und Ausstellungsplakaten (in manchen Ländern auch beim Filmplakat) ihre Vorstellungen am unmittelbarsten realisieren. Allerdings fehlt es dann nicht selten am ausreichenden Etat. Doch das ist ein anderes Thema.

3. Die Aussenwerbung wendet sich nach innen. Immer häufiger ist das Aussenwerbemittel Nr. 1 gar nicht für den Einsatz in Wind und Wetter vorgesehen. Aufwendig produziert und in beschränkter Auflage gestreut, dienen diese Plakate zur Eigenwerbung von Kreativen und Agenturen. Die Posternachdrucke mit Motiven der Altmeister haben Konkurrenz bekommen.

Doch nicht nur sie. Viele Markenartikler haben die Werbewirkung solcher Edel-Blätter erkannt und nutzen sie für die eigene PR. Dass traditionsreiche Unternehmen zum Firmenjubiläum alte Plakatmotive wieder aufleben lassen, gehört inzwischen schon zum guten Ton. Und die Branchen-Newcomer machen auf sich aufmerksam, indem sie Plakatrollen an ihre potentiellen Zielgruppen verschicken. Das Plakat als kostspieliges, aber wirksames Direct Mailing – aus der Botschaft für alle wird ein Geschenk für wenige.

Solche Zielgruppen-Plakate sind natürlich nicht so strikt den plakativen Gestaltungsregeln unterworfen. Reduktion auf das Wesentliche, Weglassen aller Details, Verdeutlichen bis zur Überzeichnung – diese Merkmale einer wirkungsvollen Aussenwerbung sind nicht nötig, wird der Angesprochene im eigenen Büro oder Atelier mit der Botschaft konfrontiert. Manche dieser Innen-Plakate ähneln in ihrem komplexen Design schon fast chinesischen Wandzeitungen. Dass solche Plakate natürlich trotzdem einen grossen Bildreiz haben, versteht sich von selbst.

4. Die Bild-Zitate werden häufiger. Eine auffallende Tendenz der letzten Jahre, die sich durchaus auch international bestätigt, ist ein recht

unkonventioneller Umgang mit den Werken früherer Werbe- und Kulturepochen. Symbole, Techniken, «Handschriften» verflossener Grössen werden in einen neuen Kontext eingepasst und auf witzige Weise interpretiert. Dabei wird wohl gleichermassen mit der Wiedererkennung wie mit dem Amüsement des Betrachters spekuliert. Allerdings ist dieses Vorgehen keineswegs auf das aktuelle Plakatschaffen beschränkt. Man denke nur an die unzähligen Marilyn Monroe- oder «Bogey»-Nachahmer oder an die Remakes einst erfolgreicher Filmklassiker. Ein Schuss Nostalgie mag da mitspielen: «Do it again, Sam!»

5. Die Plakatgestaltung wird zum Teamwork. Damit sind nicht nur jene kreativen Arbeitsgemeinschaften angesprochen wie etwa die Bundesdeutschen Rambow, Lienemeyer, van de Sand oder die Gruppe «Grapus» in Frankreich. Vielmehr ist das Plakat in vielen Fällen zur Gemeinschaftsaufgabe geworden. Photodesigner, Illustrator, Typograph und Layouter tragen ihre Fachkenntnisse bei. Kommen dann noch Motive aus dem Graphikcomputer dazu, dann spielt auch noch die Maschine mit. Die Hohlweins und Cassandres, die Savignacs, Leupins und Müller-Brockmanns schufen noch das plakative Gesamtkunstwerk. Schriften wurden noch geschrieben oder gezeichnet, Markenzeichen umgesetzt, nicht selten sogar noch der Druck überwacht. Heute sind die Spezialisten tätig, aus dem Solisten ist in manchen Fällen ein wahres Orchester geworden. Das ist legitim, ja notwendig. Muss der Plakatentwerfer zugleich Meisterphotograph und begnadeter Schriftkünstler sein? Wohl kaum, seine Leistung ist sicher nicht geringer, wenn er sich entsprechender Lieferanten bedient. Und oftmals ist auch so ein «zusammengetragenes» Blatt ganz unverkennbar Ausdruck einer Persönlichkeit.

Und die Zukunft des Plakats? Die Diskussionen um die vielberufenen «Neuen Medien» und um neuartige Anspracheformen des Konsumenten lassen gelegentlich das «alte» Plakat etwas in den Hintergrund treten. Völlig zu Unrecht, wie die folgenden Seiten nachdrücklich beweisen: Das Plakat hat nichts von seiner Lebendigkeit, Aussagekraft und Modernität eingebüsst!

HERBERT LECHNER (geb. 1952) war fünf Jahre Chefredakteur der Fachzeitschrift «Graphik visuelles Marketing». Er arbeitet heute als freier Autor und Texter in München. Buchveröffentlichungen u.a. über «Die Geschichte der modernen Typographie» und über «Cartoons und Karikatur in der Werbung».

On n'échappe pas l'affiche. Quiconque se déplace dans un espace public – et c'est bien ce que nous faisons, jour pour jour – est confronté en permanence à des moyens publicitaires extérieurs par trop visibles. «Culture du quotidien» ou «pollution de l'environnement» – les arguments ne manquent pas pour trancher dans un sens ou dans l'autre. Pourtant, l'affiche n'a pas la vie facile. C'est qu'elle doit livrer un plus rude combat que l'annonce ou le prospectus, le spot télévisé ou le film publicitaire pour capter l'attention du passant. La raison: les images et messages des panneaux et des colonnes Morris ont à soutenir la concurrence directe d'innombrables signaux, parfois d'importance vitale, qui peuplent notre environnement.

C'est ainsi que les spécialistes des médias et des marchés ont constaté qu'à peine 25 à 30% des passants perçoivent les affiches longeant leur route. Si l'on y réfléchit bien, cette proportion d'individus ayant une affinité pour l'affiche est importante; or, la tâche de l'affichiste est précisément de l'augmenter encore. Plus malaisée est sa seconde mission: faire ressortir un message déterminé du kaléidoscope d'images couleur au grand format qu'affronte le passant.

Un siècle nous sépare de la première grande floraison de l'affiche, parée d'un statut nouveau grâce aux efforts d'artistes du renom d'un Toulouse-Lautrec, d'un Théophile-Alexandre Steinlen, d'un Jules Chéret, d'un Aubrey Beardsley, pour ne citer que les plus connus. Ces créateurs démontrèrent que la publicité peut générer des œuvres d'art investies d'une réelle efficacité publicitaire. Les sujets préférés de ces anciens lithos semblent avoir été le cirque et le music-hall, sans compter les jolies filles qui sont heureusement devenues un invariant de la création affichiste même moderne!

L'évolution de ce média depuis son Age d'Or a connu des hauts et des bas. De moments exaltants où l'inventivité et la puissance créatrice s'en donnaient à cœur joie, on est passé à des périodes sombres où il valait mieux ne pas parler de «l'art» de l'affiche. A intervalles réguliers, on en vint à proclamer la mort de l'affiche, Phénix qui renaissait pourtant de ses cendres à la génération suivante!

La bonne affiche fait sensation, aujourd'hui comme il y a cent ans. Mais le nombre des affichistes de génie varie tout comme l'écho qu'ils rencontrent auprès du grand public et la satisfaction qu'ils procurent à leurs clients. Et puis, la valeur reconnue à l'affiche varie de pays en pays.

Pour un contemporain, il peut être difficile d'apprécier des affiches données, tant l'afflux de stimuli visuels peut être contradictoire. Ce n'est qu'avec un certain recul que l'on arrive à dégager les grandes lignes et tendances. Tentons toutefois quelques affirmations au sujet du statu quo en matière d'affichisme:

1. La gamme des moyens techniques utilisés n'a jamais été aussi vaste. On relève actuellement un nombre particulièrement important de tendances stylistiques et de techniques graphiques. De la photo au grand format à l'affiche purement typographique en passant par l'illustration, du collage naïf au produit d'imprimante, toutes les formes créatives se côtoient, en principe dans toutes les zones du globe. Les progrès des techniques de reproduction et d'impression expliquent la forte augmentation, dans les années 70, d'affiches centrées sur la photographie. De nos jours, la situation est plus équilibrée; l'affiche-photo est devenue monnaie courante – et se signale donc moins à l'attention. De nouvelles voies conceptuelles sont explorées sans pour autant que les approches traditionnelles disparaissent des panneaux d'affichage.

Les différences nationales subsistent, bien entendu. Quiconque a l'occasion d'aller voir des expositions d'affiches au point de rencontre de l'Europe de l'Ouest et des pays de l'Est – à Lahti en Finlande ou à Brno en Tchécoslovaquie, par exemple – s'en rend aisément compte. Pourtant, les contrastes, encore prononcés il y a 10 ou 15 ans, ont tendance à s'atténuer.

La création affichiste du Japon représente toujours aux yeux des Européens une monde exotique et merveilleux, avec cependant un nombre élevé d'adaptations dans un sens ou dans l'autre.

Un échange continu d'idées créatrices et de talents créatifs assure l'internationalisation croissante de l'art de l'affiche, d'où un avantage certain pour le média même, qui ne risque pas de si figer.

2. L'affiche conquiert de nouveaux clients. Une tendance s'affirme depuis un certain nombre d'années sans faiblir: c'est le recrutement de l'affiche non seulement pour la publicité classique – cigarettes, automobiles, électroménager, manifestations –, mais aussi pour d'autres branches de l'économie. C'est ainsi que les articles de luxe, les cosmétiques, les banques et les assurances avides d'un impact visuel sur grande surface font désormais partie de la clientèle régulière des affichistes, ce qui n'est pas sans conséquence pour la forme donnée à cette publicité.

HERBERT LECHNER

La publicité extérieure sert de plus en plus de support aux campagnes institutionnelles. On élargit ainsi le champ d'application de l'affiche tout en accordant aux créateurs une marge de manœuvre plus satisfaisante par rapport à la publicité commerciale.

Par ailleurs, l'affiche en tant que moyen publicitaire est davantage considérée comme un élément intégrant du média-mix. Il en résulte un certain alignement sur une ligne conceptuelle prédéterminée (celle de l'image de marque globale) et, partant, une nette restriction de la liberté de création. Seule l'affiche culturelle est rarement affectée par des problèmes de ce genre. Les graphistes peuvent se réaliser à fond dans l'affiche de théâtre, de concert et d'exposition. Cette liberté va souvent de pair avec un budget limité, ce qui est une autre histoire.

3. La publicité extérieure «s'intériorise» en ce sens que nombreux sont les cas où l'affiche n'est pas de tout conçue pour affronter le vent et les intempéries. Réalisé à grands frais, ce genre d'affiches au tirage limité sert à l'autopromotion des artistes et des agences. Les rééditions des posters des vieux maîtres ont désormais de la concurrence.

Il n'y a pas qu'eux. Nombreux sont les fabricants d'articles de marque à comprendre l'efficacité publicitaire de telles «planches nobles», qu'ils font servir à leurs relations publiques. Il est aujourd'hui b.c.b.g. de commémorer les jalons importants dans l'histoire d'une entreprise établie en rééditant une affiche de jadis. Les nouveaux venus dans le commerce et l'industrie aiment de surcroît se signaler à l'attention de leur clientèle potentielle en diffusant des rouleaux d'affiches soigneusement ciblés. Ce qui fait de l'affiche un élément de publicité directe coûteux, certes, mais combien efficace. Le message pour tous se mue en cadeau pour quelques-uns.

Ces affiches destinées à des cibles déterminées ne sont évidemment pas soumises aux strictes règles affichistes: la réduction du message à l'essentiel, l'omission des détails, la mise en vedette parfois excessive – toutes ces caractéristiques d'une publicité extérieure efficace peuvent être ignorées dès lors que le prospect est censé recevoir le message dans son bureau ou dans son atelier. Certaines de ces affiches intérieures évoquent par leur complexité les affiches murales chinoises, les fameux dazibaos. Reste qu'elles revêtent un intérêt visuel incontestable.

4. Les références iconographiques se multiplient. Ces dernières années ont vu se confirmer au plan international la tendance de recourir sans conformisme aux œuvres des périodes révolues de l'histoire des civilisations et de la publicité. Les symboles, techniques et «signatures» particulières des maîtres du passé sont insérés dans un nouveau contexte et interprétés avec esprit. On fait ainsi puiser le passant dans ses souvenirs tout en lui procurant de l'amusement. Inutile de rappeler que ce mode de faire rétro n'est pas limité à l'art de l'affiche. Il suffit de penser aux innombrables imitations de Marilyn Monroe ou de Humphrey Bogart, ou aux remakes des grands classiques du cinéma. Clin d'œil nostalgique au bon vieux temps...

5. La création d'une affiche devient un travail d'équipe. Nous ne pensons pas seulement à ces communautés de travail créatif qui ont pour nom Rambow, Lienemeyer, van de Sand en RFA ou «Grapus» en France. C'est que, dans de nombreux cas, l'affiche est devenue la tâche de toute une équipe, le photo-designer, l'illustrateur, le typo, le maquettiste contribuant chacun sa part. Ajoutez-y des motifs CAO (conception assistée par ordinateur), et vous avez un cinquième coéquipier, la machine. Les Hohlwein, les Cassandre, les Savignac, les Leupin et les Müller-Brockmann ont encore réalisé des œuvres affichistes complètes en dessinant ou en calligraphiant les caractères en transposant des marques déposées, allant souvent jusqu'à surveiller l'impression. Ils ont aujourd'hui cédé la place aux spécialistes; dans certains cas, le soliste s'est mué en orchestre. Cette évolution est légitime, voire nécessaire. Le créateur de l'affiche doit-il aussi être passé maître dans l'art de la photographie ou avoir le génie de l'invention de caractères? Cela n'est guère possible, et sa performance ne souffrira pas des services de sous-traitants qu'il s'assure. Une affiche ainsi «assemblée» garde souvent la marque indiscutable d'une personnalité unique.

Et l'avenir de l'affiche? Les débats en cours sur les «nouveaux médias» à venir et dont on fait si grand cas, ou sur les formes nouvelles de la communication avec les consommateurs relèguent parfois la «vieille» affiche à l'arrière-plan. A tort cependant, comme le démontreront aisément les pages qui suivent. C'est que l'affiche n'a pas cédé un pouce sur le terrain de la vitalité, de l'expressivité et du modernisme!

HERBERT LECHNER (né en 1952) a été cinq ans rédacteur en chef du magazine spécialisé «Graphik visuelles Marketing». Il est aujourd'hui écrivain et rédacteur indépendant à Munich. Il a publié entre autres une histoire de la typographie moderne, «Die Geschichte der modernen Typographie», et une étude sur l'emploi de la B.D. et de la caricature dans la publicité, «Cartoons und Karikatur in der Werbung».

CULTURE

KULTUR

CULTURE

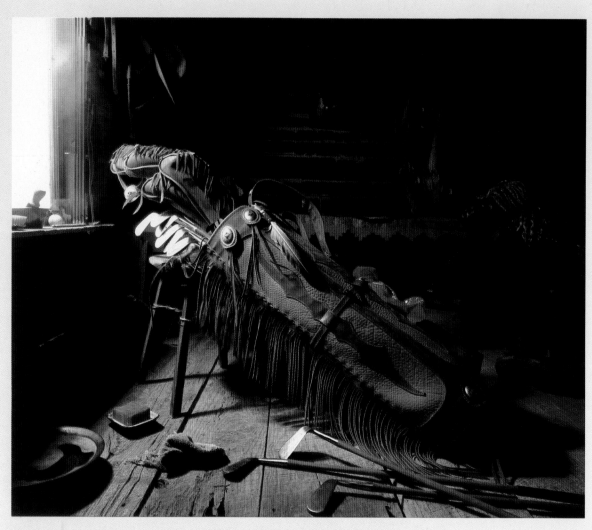

US WEST WELCOMES YOU TO THE INTERNATIONAL PGA GOLF TOURNAMENT,
AUGUST 11-17, 1986 AT CASTLE PINES GOLF CLUB, DENVER, COLORADO.

ART DIRECTOR:
Pat Burnham
PHOTOGRAPHER:
Dennis Manarchy
AGENCY:
Fallon McElligott
CLIENT:
US West
∎1

ART DIRECTOR:
Logan Broussard
DESIGNER:
Logan Broussard
PHOTOGRAPHER:
John Katz
AGENCY:
Levenson & Hill
CLIENT:
Walt Disney Productions
∎2

∎1 Announcement of an international golf tournament for professional golf players in Denver, Colorado. (USA)

∎2 For an ice revue to mark the occasion of Donald Duck's 50th birthday. (USA)

∎1 Ankündigung eines internationalen Golfturniers für professionelle Golfspieler in Denver, Colorado. (USA)

∎2 Für eine Eisrevue der Holiday on Ice anlässlich des 50. Geburtstages der Walt-Disney-Figur Donald Duck. (USA)

∎1 Annonce d'un tournoi international de golf pour golfeurs professionnels organisé à Denver, dans le Colorado. (USA)

∎2 Pour une revue sur glace de Holiday on Ice à l'occasion du 50e anniversaire du Donald Duck de Walt Disney. (USA)

■ **3** Poster for the dance/theater festival weeks held in Wuppertal theaters, directed by Pina Bausch. (GER)

■ **4** Announcement of the comedy *Servant of two Masters* by Carlo Goldoni at the Schauspielhaus Frankfurt. (GER)

■ **5** For ballet performances by Igor Stravinski at the International June Festival '87 at the Opera House in Zürich. (SWI)

■ **3** Plakat für Tanz-Theater-Wochen der Wuppertaler Bühnen unter der Leitung von Pina Bausch. (GER)

■ **4** Ankündigung der Komödie *Der Diener zweier Herren* von Carlo Goldoni am Schauspielhaus Frankfurt. (GER)

■ **5** Für Ballettaufführungen von Igor Strawinski an den Internationalen Junifestwochen '87 am Opernhaus in Zürich. (SWI)

■ **3** Affiche pour des semaines de ballets dans les théâtres de Wuppertal (RFA) sous la direction de Pina Bausch. (GER)

■ **4** Annonce de la comédie *Le Serviteur de deux maîtres* de Carlo Goldoni au Schauspielhaus de Francfort. (GER)

■ **5** Pour une série de ballets d'Igor Stravinski créés lors des Semaines internationales de juin 87 à l'Opéra de Zurich. (SWI)

ART DIRECTOR:
UTE SEIFERT
DESIGNER:
UTE SEIFERT
PHOTOGRAPHER:
ULLI WEISS
CLIENT:
WUPPERTALER BÜHNEN
■ **3**

ART DIRECTOR:
WOLFGANG HEFFE
DESIGNER:
WOLFGANG HEFFE
PHOTOGRAPHER:
WOLFGANG HEFFE
CLIENT:
SCHAUSPIEL FRANKFURT
■ **4**

▶ **ART DIRECTOR:**
K. DOMENIC GEISSBÜHLER
DESIGNER:
K. DOMENIC GEISSBÜHLER
ARTIST:
K. DOMENIC GEISSBÜHLER
CLIENT:
OPERNHAUS ZÜRICH
■ **5**

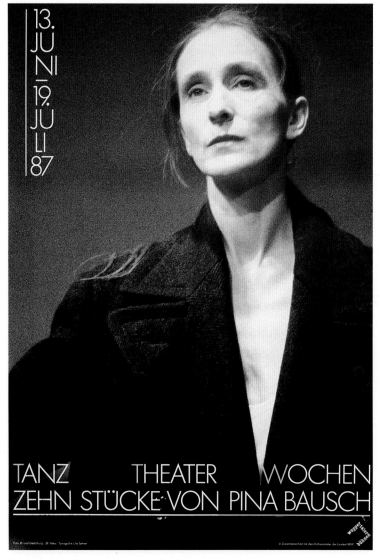

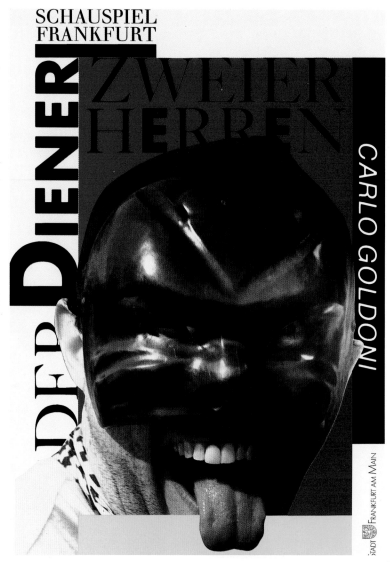

IGOR STRAWINSKI PETRUSCHKA

FEUERVOGEL

UR- UND ERSTAUFFÜHRUNGEN
AB 27. SEPTEMBER '86

SYMPHONIE IN DREI SÄTZEN

OPERNHAUS ZÜRICH

MUSIKALISCHE LEITUNG ANDRÉ PRESSER
AUSSTATTUNG DIETER SCHORAS ROSALIE JAN SKALICKY

PLAKATSPONSOR DRESDNER BANK (SCHWEIZ) AG

Gestaltung Geissbühler

CHOREOGRAPHIEN UWE SCHOLZ

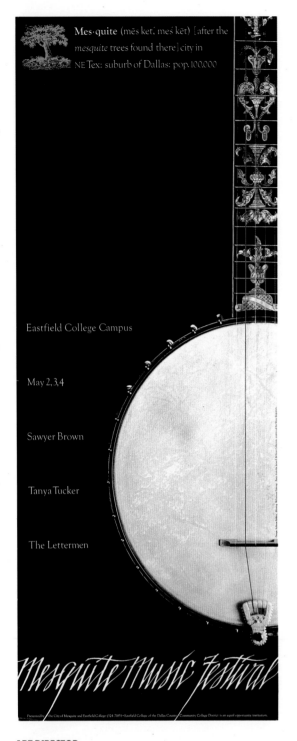

ART DIRECTOR:
Ron Sullivan

DESIGNER:
Ron Sullivan

AGENCY:
Sullivan Perkins

CLIENT:
City of Mesquite

■ 6

ART DIRECTOR:
Bob Barrie

ARTIST:
Bob Barrie

AGENCY:
Fallon McElligott

CLIENT:
Minnesota Zoo

■ 7

▶ **DESIGNER:**
Nancy Walker

ARTIST:
Bill Mayer

CLIENT:
Town Point Jazz Festival

■ 8

■ 6 Announcement of a music festival in the Texan town of Mesquite. (USA)

■ 7 For a jazz festival held at the Minnesota zoo. (USA)

■ 8 Poster for a benefit jazz festival at Town Point Park in Norfolk, Virginia. (USA)

■ 6 Ankündigung für ein Musikfestival in der texanischen Stadt Mesquite. (USA)

■ 7 Für ein Jazzfestival im Zoo von Minnesota. (USA)

■ 8 Plakat für ein Benefiz-Jazzfestival im Town Point Park in Norfolk, Virginia. (USA)

■ 6 Annonce d'un festival de musique organisé dans la ville de Mesquite, au Texas. (USA)

■ 7 Pour un festival du jazz au zoo du Minnesota. (USA)

■ 8 Affiche pour un festival de jazz de bienfaisance organisé au Town Point Park de Norfolk, en Virginie. (USA)

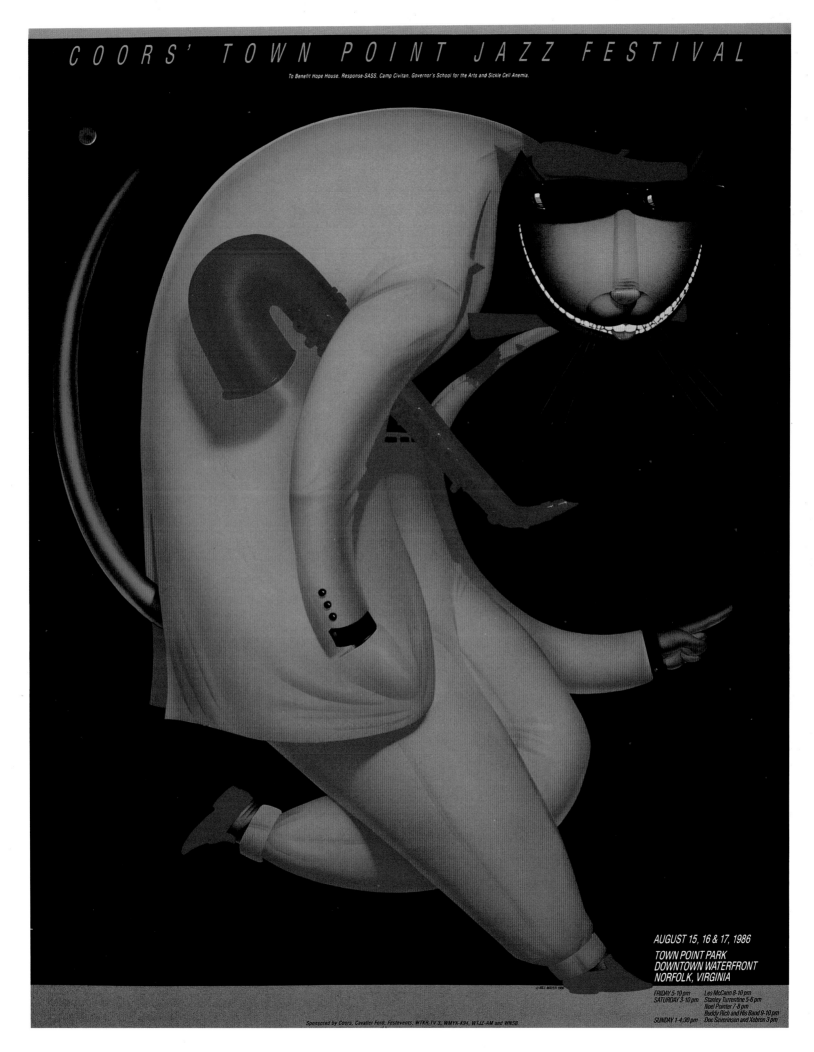

ART DIRECTOR:
S. & J. Jupin
DESIGNER:
S. & J. Jupin
ARTIST:
S. & J. Jupin
AGENCY:
S. & J. Jupin
CLIENT:
Cine Poche, Le Mans
■ **9–12**

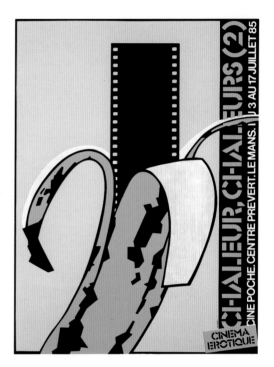

■ **9–12** Announcement of various film cycles. *9:* Films from socialistic countries, *10:* Films about youth in the eighties and *11, 12:* erotic films. (FRA)

■ **9–12** Ankündigung verschiedener Filmzyklen. *9:* Filme aus sozialistischen Ländern, *10:* Filme über die Jugend der achtziger Jahre und *11, 12:* erotische Filme. (FRA)

■ **9–12** Annonce de divers cycles cinématographiques: *9:* cinéma des pays socialistes, *10:* films consacrés à la jeunesse des années 80; *11, 12:* œuvres du cinéma érotique. (FRA)

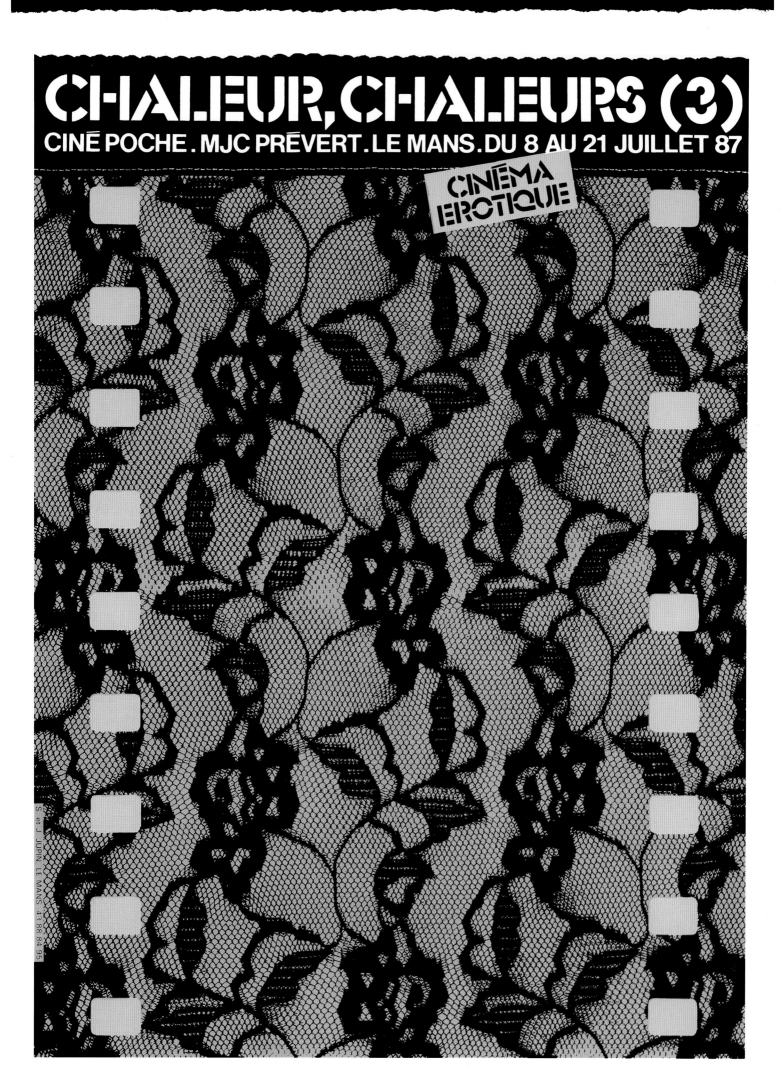

CHALEUR, CHALEURS (3)
CINÉ POCHE . MJC PRÉVERT . LE MANS . DU 8 AU 21 JUILLET 87

CINÉMA EROTIQUE

S et J JUPIN LE MANS 43 88 84 95

ART DIRECTOR:
Joe Duffy
DESIGNER:
Joe Duffy
ARTIST:
Joe Duffy
STUDIO:
The Duffy Design Group
CLIENT:
First Tennessee Bank
■ 13

ART DIRECTOR:
Charles Spencer Anderson
DESIGNER:
Charles Spencer Anderson
ARTIST:
Charles Spencer Anderson
STUDIO:
The Duffy Design Group
CLIENT:
Synergistic Design
■ 14

■ **13** Announcement of the training schedule of the Memphis Chicks baseball team. The monthly illustrations are perforated and give calendar details on the back. (USA)

■ **14** "The Survival of the Fastest" – poster for the America's Cup sailing regatta. (USA)

■ **13** Ankündigung der Trainingstage für die Baseball-Mannschaft Memphis Chicks. Die Monatsbilder sind perforiert und tragen auf der Rückseite kalendarische Angaben. (USA)

■ **14** «Überleben der Schnellsten» – Plakat für die Segelregatta des America's Cup. (USA)

■ **13** Annonce des sessions d'entraînement de l'équipe de base-ball Memphis Chicks. Les illustrations relatives aux mois sont perforées et donc détachables (calendrier au verso). (USA)

■ **14** «La survie des plus rapides» – affiche pour la régate de la Coupe America. (USA)

THE FIFTIETH

MANCHESTER

ROADRACE

ART DIRECTOR:
Robert Appleton
DESIGNER:
Robert Appleton
AGENCY:
Appleton Design Inc.
CLIENT:
*Pratt & Whitney
Aircraft*
■ 15

ART DIRECTOR:
JULIUS FRIEDMAN/
DONNA LAWRENCE

DESIGNER:
JULIUS FRIEDMAN

PHOTOGRAPHER:
JOHN BECKMAN/
MICHAEL BROHM/
GREG GORFKLE

AGENCY:
IMAGES/
DONNA LAWRENCE PRODUCTIONS

CLIENT:
DONNA LAWRENCE
PRODUCTIONS
■ **16**

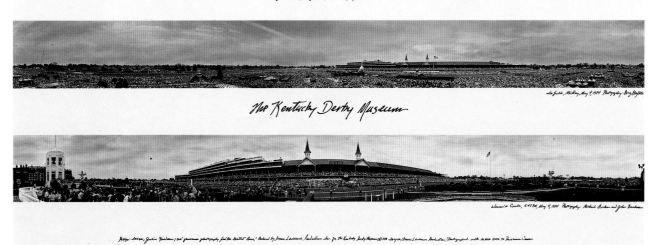

ART DIRECTOR:
JACKSON BOELTS/
ERIC BOELTS

DESIGNER:
ERIC BOELTS

ARTIST:
JACKSON BOELTS

AGENCY:
BOELTS BROS. DESIGN

CLIENT:
20–30 CLUB OF
TUCSON
■ **17**

■ **15** Calling for participants in the 50th Manchester (Connecticut) Road Race. (USA)

■ **16** Poster for the Kentucky Derby Museum with panorama photographs from various positions on the racecourse. (USA)

■ **17** Announcement of a polo game in Tucson, Arizona. It was a charity match, the proceeds going to benefit United Cerebral Palsy and other Tucson charities. (USA)

■ **15** Aufforderung zur Teilnahme am 50. Strassenlauf von Manchester, Connecticut. (USA)

■ **16** Für das Kentucky Derby Museum mit Panoramaaufnahmen von verschiedenen Standorten auf dem Renngelände. (USA)

■ **17** Ankündigung eines Polospiels in Tucson, Arizona. Es handelt sich um eine Wohltätigkeitsveranstaltung u.a. zugunsten zerebral Gelähmter. (USA)

■ **15** Invitation à participer à la 50e course sur route organisée à Manchester, dans le Connecticut. (USA)

■ **16** Affiche pour le Kentucky Derby Museum: vues panoramiques de divers sites sur le champ de courses. (USA)

■ **17** Affiche annonçante un match de polo à Tucson, en Arizona. Il s'agit d'une manifestation de bienfaisance en faveur des I.M.C. notamment. (USA)

■ **18** Construction company's invitation to "cut loose and party" – in celebration of the completion of work. (USA)

■ **19** To announce a summer picnic given by the Fort Worth Society of Creative Communications. (USA)

■ **20** Invitation to a "cool" music celebration on the 5th anniversary of the Fallon McElligott agency. (USA)

■ **18** Einladung einer Baufirma, um das Ende der Bauarbeiten zu feiern. (USA)

■ **19** Ankündigung eines Sommerpicknicks der Fort-Worth-Gesellschaft für kreative Kommunikation. (USA)

■ **20** Einladung zur Feier des 5. Geburtstages der Werbeagentur Fallon McElligott. (USA)

■ **18** Invitation d'une entreprise de construction à une fête célébrant l'achèvement des travaux. (USA)

■ **19** Annonce d'un pique-nique estival de la Société de communcations créatives de Fort Worth, au Texas. (USA)

■ **20** Invitation à la célébration du 5e anniversaire de l'agence de publicité Fallon McElligott. (USA)

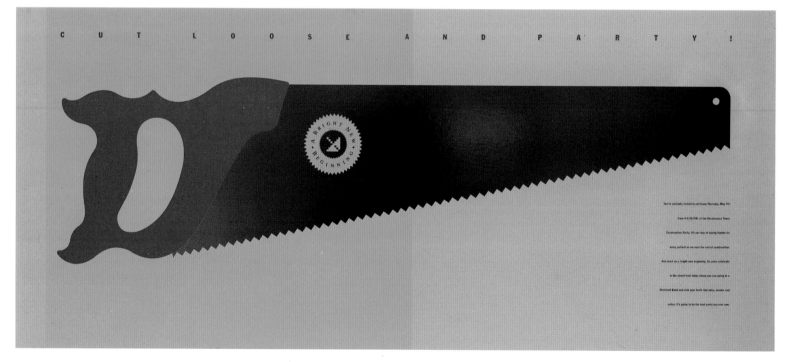

ART DIRECTOR:
JUDY DOLIM

ARTIST:
JUDY DOLIM

AGENCY:
SIBLEY PETEET DESIGN, INC.

CLIENT:
LASALLE PARTNERS

■ **18**

Fallon McElligott
Celebrates Five
To The
Manhattan Transfer's
Syncopated Jive
Rupert's
August 25
1986
V

Dip into summer. The 1986 FWSCC Summer Picnic. Saturday, June 28, at Twin Points Resort on Eagle Mountain Lake. 11:00 a.m. Bring your own food and drinks. We'll provide the fun and sun. At $3.50 per person, it promises to be a flavorful day. All in good taste.

ART DIRECTOR:
John Cooper

ARTIST:
Mike Hodges

STUDIO:
Mike Hodges

CLIENT:
*Fort Worth Society
of Graphic Communications*

■ **19**

ART DIRECTOR:
Joe Duffy

ARTIST:
Joe Duffy

STUDIO:
The Duffy Design Group

CLIENT:
Fallon McElligott

■ **20**

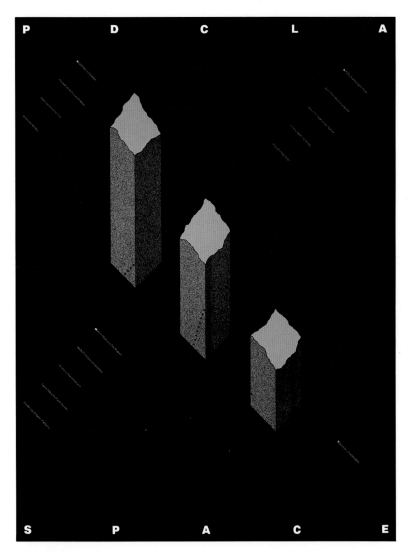

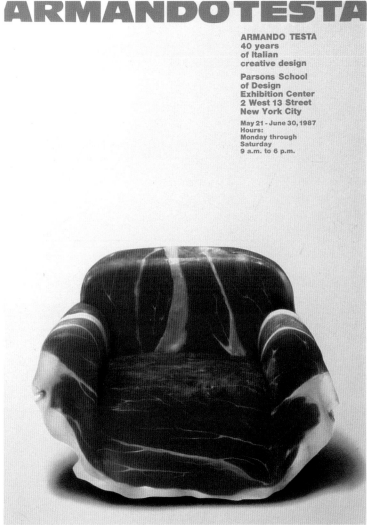

ARMANDO TESTA

ARMANDO TESTA
40 years
of Italian
creative design

Parsons School
of Design
Exhibition Center
2 West 13 Street
New York City
May 21 - June 30, 1987
Hours:
Monday through
Saturday
9 a.m. to 6 p.m.

ART DIRECTOR:
Michael Vanderbyl
DESIGNER:
Michael Vanderbyl
AGENCY:
Vanderbyl Design
CLIENT:
Modern Mode, Inc.
■ **21**

ART DIRECTOR:
Armando Testa
DESIGNER:
Franco Del Rosso/
Antonio Pepe
PHOTOGRAPHER:
Nino Chironna
AGENCY:
Armando Testa S.P.A.
CLIENT:
Armando Testa S.P.A.
■ **22**

ART DIRECTOR: ▶
Jim Newbury/
Steve Newton
DESIGNER:
Jim Newbury
ARTIST:
Bill Mayer
CLIENT:
Ad II
■ **23**

■ **21** For the opening of a new showroom of Modern Mode, Inc. in the Pacific Design Center in Los Angeles. (USA)

■ **22** Invitation to an exhibition of works by designer Armando Testa at the Parsons Gallery, New York. (USA)

■ **23** For an advertising auction in Atlanta. (USA)

■ **21** Ankündigung zur Eröffnung neuer Showrooms von Modern Mode, Inc. im Pacific Design Center in Los Angeles. (USA)

■ **22** Einladung zu einer Ausstellung des Designers Armando Testa in der Parsons Galerie in New York. (USA)

■ **23** Für eine Werbeauktion in Atlanta. (USA)

■ **21** Avis d'inauguration de nouveaux locaux de présentation de Modern Mode, Inc. au Pacific Design Center de Los Angeles. (USA)

■ **22** Invitation au vernissage d'une exposition du designer Armando Testa à la Galerie Parsons de New York. (USA)

■ **23** Pour une vente aux enchères publicitaire à Atlanta. (USA)

JOIN THE PARTY. ★

At the Atlanta Ad Auction. Mix. Mingle. And sip a couple of White Russians (or whatever your favorite cocktail). Then capitalize on the revolutionary bargains. We'll have everything from media space to VCRs on the auction block. And they'll go for prices even a peasant can afford. You could also win the door prize: a Caribbean cruise for two. (Sorry, no stopovers in Cuba).

The perfect way to get ready for May Day. And it all starts at 6:00 pm, Tuesday, April 29. Hyatt Regency Ravinia at Atlanta's Perimeter. Be there. Or be red with embarrassment.

Art Direction: Kim Neinburg, Steve Neelen Copywriting: Ken Lewis, Corinne Mitchell Illustration: Bill Mayer Printing: Graphic Ads Inc. Production: Glad Grey Typography: Type Designs Inc.

ART DIRECTOR:
Finn Nygaard

DESIGNER:
Finn Nygaard

ARTIST:
Finn Nygaard

AGENCY:
Finn Nygaard

CLIENT:
Kieler Stadtmuseum

■ **24–27**

ARTIST:
Günther Uecker
CLIENT:
MUDA 2 Galerie
■ **28**

ARTIST:
Wolf Vostell
CLIENT:
MUDA 2 Galerie
■ **29**

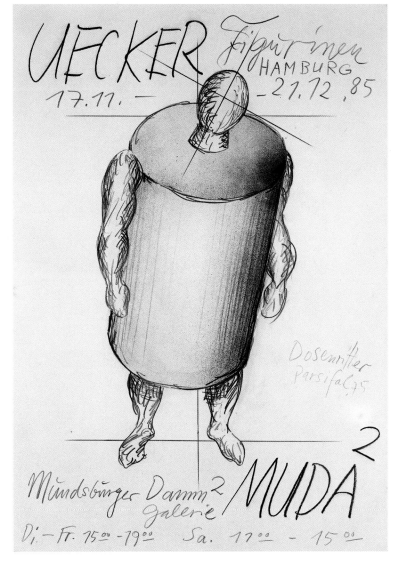

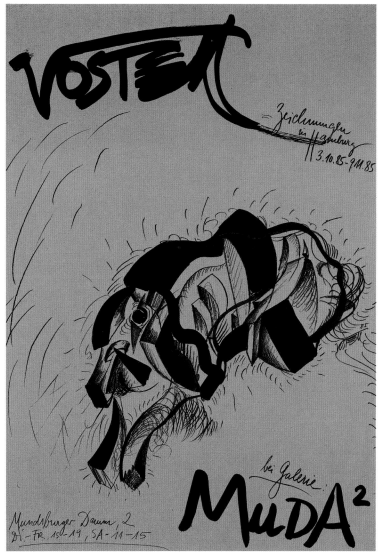

■ **24–27** Series of posters for an exhibition on the theme of "space", held at the Kiel City Museum. (GER)

■ **24–27** Serie von Plakaten für eine Ausstellung im Kieler Stadtmuseum, die dem Thema Raum gewidmet ist. (GER)

■ **24–27** Série d'affiches pour une exposition du Musée municipal de Kiel (RFA) sur le thème de l'Espace. (GER)

■ **28** For an exhibition of figurines by Günther Uecker at the Muda 2 Gallery in Hamburg. (GER)

■ **28** Für eine Ausstellung der Figurinen von Günther Uecker in der Galerie Muda 2 in Hamburg. (GER)

■ **28** Pour une exposition des figurines de Günther Uecker à la Galerie Muda 2 de Hambourg. (GER)

■ **29** "Concrete Pekinese" – for the exhibition of drawings by Wolf Vostell at the Muda 2 Gallery in Hamburg. (GER)

■ **29** »Pekinese in Beton« – für die Ausstellung von Zeichnungen von Wolf Vostell in der Galerie Muda 2 in Hamburg. (GER)

■ **29** »Pékinois enrobé de béton« – Pour une exposition des dessins de Wolf Vostell à la Galerie Muda 2 de Hambourg. (GER)

ART DIRECTOR:
Malcolm Tarlofsky

DESIGNER:
Malcolm Tarlofsky

ARTIST:
Frank Lloyd Wright

AGENCY
Media Synthesis

PUBLISHER:
Pomegranate Publications

■ 30

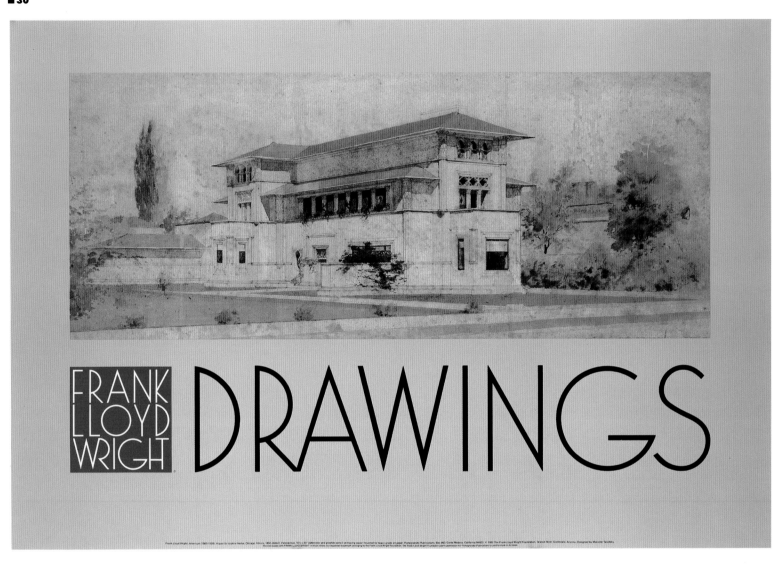

■ **30, 31** Posters issued by the Frank Lloyd Wright Foundation. Shown is a house for Isidore Heller, Chicago (1896) and a view of the bridge at the Ravine Bluffs Development (1915). The red square with white logotype is the registered trademark of the Frank Lloyd Wright Foundation (USA)

■ **32** Announcement of an exhibition of a part of the San Diego Museum of Art collection. The large illustration shows Ingres' *Study for Phidias,* 1827. (USA)

■ **30, 31** Von der Frank Lloyd Wright Foundation herausgegebene Plakate. Hier die Perspektive eines Hauses für Isidore Heller, Chicago (1896) und eine Brückenansicht (1915). Das rote Quadrat mit dem weissen Schriftzug ist das eingetragene Markenzeichen der Frank Lloyd Wright Foundation. (USA)

■ **32** Ankündigung einer Ausstellung eines Teils der Sammlung des San Diego Museum of Art. Die grosse Abbildung zeigt Ingres' *Studie für Phidias,* 1827. (USA)

■ **30, 31** Affiches publiées par la Fondation Frank Lloyd Wright: vue perspecitve d'une maison pour Isidore Heller, Chicago, 1896, et vue d'un pont, 1915. Le carré rouge où s'inscrit en blanc le nom de Frank Lloyd Wright est la marque déposée de la Fondation du même nom. (USA)

■ **32** Annonce d'une exposition consacrée à une partie des collections du Museum of Art de San Diego. L'illustration au grand format représente *L'Etude pour Phidias,* par Ingres (1827). (USA)

ART DIRECTOR:
Malcolm Tarlofsky
DESIGNER:
Malcolm Tarlofsky
ARTIST:
Frank Lloyd Wright
AGENCY
Media Synthesis
PUBLISHER:
Pomegranate Publications
■ 31

ART DIRECTOR:
David Alcorn
DESIGNER:
David Alcorn/Deena Blaylock
ARTIST:
Ingres
AGENCY:
Alcorn Visual Communications
CLIENT:
San Diego Museum of Art
■ 32

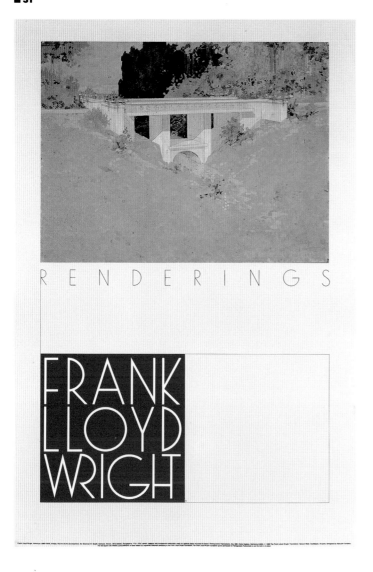

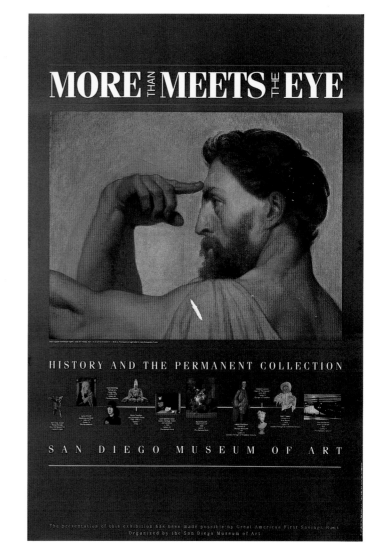

THE 12TH ANNUAL ANTIQUE MOTORCYCLE MEET

ART DIRECTOR:
Rusty Kay

DESIGNER:
Steve Curry

ARTIST:
Steve Curry

AGENCY:
Rusty Kay & Associates

CLIENT:
Antique Motorcycle Club
of America

■ 33

▶ ART DIRECTOR:
Ron Sullivan

DESIGNER:
Ron Sullivan

PHOTOGRAPHER:
Jerry Segrest

AGENCY:
Sullivan Perkins

CLIENT:
Rouse/Shops at
National Place

■ 34

■33 Announcement of the 12th annual meeting of fans of veteran motorcycles; shown is a Harley Davidson. (USA)

■34 "The National Press Building (Washington) salutes 194 years of Freedom of the Press." Poster marking the occasion of the reopening of the press building on 21 May 1985. (USA)

■33 Ankündigung des 12. Jahrestreffens der Freunde alter Motorräder; hier eine Harley Davidson. (USA)

■34 «Das National Press Building (Pressehaus in Washington) feiert 194 Jahre Pressefreiheit.» Plakat anlässlich der Wiedereröffnung des Pressehauses am 21. Mai 1985. (USA)

■33 Annonce de la 12e rencontre annuelle des amis des motos du passé. On voit ici une Harley Davidson. (USA)

■34 «Le National Press Building (Maison de la Presse à Washington) salue les 194 ans de liberté de la presse.» Affiche pour la réouverture de cette Maison de la Presse le 21-5-85. (USA)

NATIONAL PRESS CLUB
14th and F Streets, NW, Washington, DC 20045 · (202) 662-7500

The National Press Building salutes 194 years of Freedom of the Press.

Celebrate the National Press Building rededication in Washington, D.C. on May 21, 1985.

DESIGN: SULLIVAN PERKINS PHOTOGRAPHY: JERRY SEGREST

The Buffalo Fine Arts Academy, 1862

George Inness (American, 1825-94), *The Coming Storm*, 1878, Oil on canvas, 26 x 39", Collection Albright-Knox Art Gallery, Buffalo, New York, Albert H. Tracy Fund, 1900.

125

Jackson Pollock (American, 1912-56), *Convergence*, 1952, Oil on canvas, 93½ x 155", Collection Albright-Knox Art Gallery, Buffalo, New York, Gift of Seymour H. Knox, 1956.

Albright-Knox Art Gallery, 1987

Published by the Albright-Knox Art Gallery, Buffalo, New York, on the occasion of the 125th anniversary of the founding of The Buffalo Fine Arts Academy in 1862.

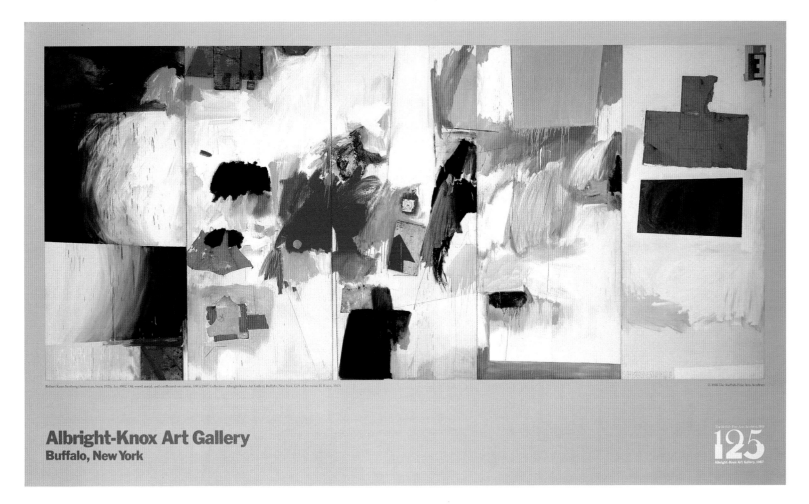

Albright-Knox Art Gallery
Buffalo, New York

125

DESIGNER:
Chermayeff & Geismar Associates
AGENCY:
Albright-Knox Art Gallery
CLIENT:
The Buffalo Fine Arts Academy/
Albright-Knox Art Gallery

■ **35, 36**

■ **35, 36** Posters to announce the 125th anniversary of the Buffalo Fine Arts Academy, the parent company of the Albright-Knox Art Gallery: *35* shows an oil painting by the American George Innes (1825-94) entitled *The Coming Storm* (1878). *36* is a painting by the contemporary American painter Robert Rauschenberg (b. 1925). Painted in 1962 in oil, wood, metal, and card-board on canvas, it is entitled *Ace.* (USA)

■ **35, 36** Plakate zur Ankündigung des 125. Geburtstags der Buffalo Fine Arts Academy, der Muttergesellschaft der Albright-Knox Art Gallery: *35* zeigt ein Ölgemälde von 1878 des Amerikaners George Innes (1825-94) mit dem Titel *The Coming Storm. 36* ist ein Gemälde des amerikanischen Malers Robert Rauschenberg (geboren 1925). Das Bild entstand 1962 und heisst *Ace.* Es handelt sich um Ölfarbe, Holz, Metall und Karton auf Leinwand. (USA)

■ **35, 36** Affiches publiées pour le 125e anniversaire de la Buffalo Fine Arts Academy, maison mère de l'Albright-Knox Art Gallery. *35* peinture à l'huile de l'Américain George Innes (1825-94), *Une Tempête se prépare* (1878). *36* tableau du peintre américain Robert Rauschenberg, né en 1925; réalisée en 1962, cette peinture, *Ace,* combine l'huile, le bois, le métal et le carton sur support de toile. (USA)

ART DIRECTOR:
*Benoit Toussaint/
Yves Hoyois*
DESIGNER:
*Benoit Toussaint/
Yves Hoyois*
ARTIST:
Jean Moebius Giraud
AGENCY:
Filigrane
CLIENT:
*Galerie Wittamer/
Schlirf Book*
■ **37**

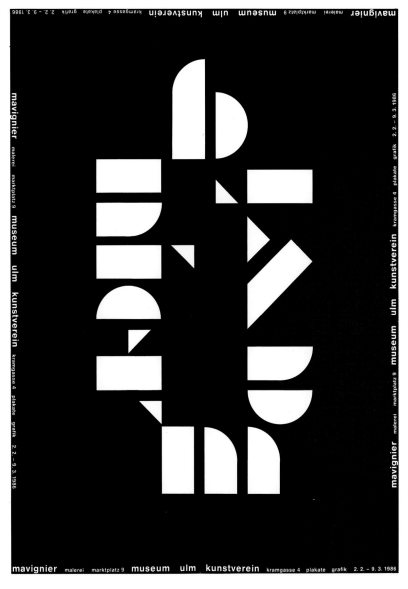

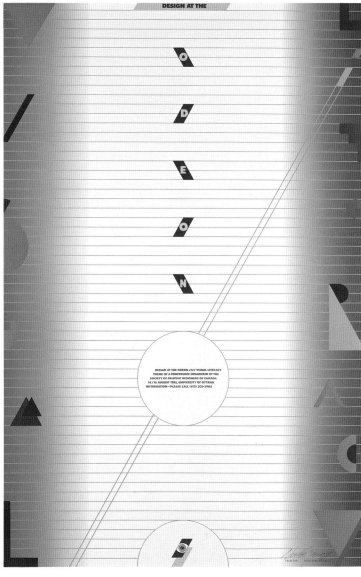

ART DIRECTOR:
Almir Mavignier

DESIGNER:
Almir Mavignier

CLIENT:
Museum und Kunstverein Ulm

■ **38**

ART DIRECTOR:
Neville Smith

DESIGNER:
Neville Smith

AGENCY:
Neville Smith Graphic Design

CLIENT:
Society of Graphic Designers of Canada

■ **39**

■ **37** To promote an exhibition by Jean Moebius Giraud at a gallery in Brussels. (BEL)

■ **38** Poster announcing an exhibition in Ulm of pictures, posters, and graphics by Almir Mavignier. (GER)

■ **39** For an exhibition and convention of the Society of Graphic Designers of Canada. (CAN)

■ **37** Ankündigung einer Ausstellung von Jean Moebius Giraud in einer Brüsseler Galerie. (BEL)

■ **38** Bilder, Plakate und Graphiken von Almir Mavignier sind Gegenstand der hier angekündigten Ausstellung in Ulm. (GER)

■ **39** Plakat für eine Ausstellung und Tagung der Society of Graphic Designers of Canada. (CAN)

■ **37** Annonce d'une exposition qu'une galerie bruxelloise consacre à Jean Moebius Giraud. (BEL)

■ **38** Les tableaux, affiches et créations graphiques d'Almir Mavignier sont au coeur de cette exposition à Ulm (RFA). (GER)

■ **39** Affiche pour une exposition organisée à l'occasion d'un congrès de la Society of Graphic Designers du Canada. (CAN)

ART DIRECTOR:
Ikko Tanaka
DESIGER:
Ikko Tanaka
AGENCY:
Ikko Tanaka Design Studio
CLIENT:
The Seibu Museum of Art
■ 40

ART DIRECTOR:
Kazumasa Nagai
DESIGNER:
Kazumasa Nagai
AGENCY:
Nippon Design Center
CLIENT:
The Museum of Modern Art, Toyama
■ 41

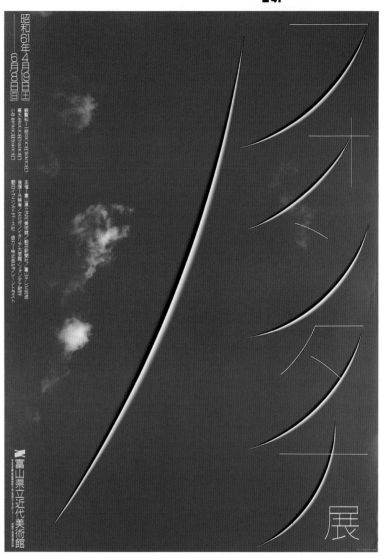

■ **40** For an exhibition at the Seibu Museum of Art. (JPN)

■ **41** Poster for an exhibition by Lucio Fontana at the Museum of Modern Art in Toyama. (JPN)

■ **42** Promotional poster for an exhibition in Seoul of Asiatic ink paintings. (KOR)

■ **43** Poster for the Museum of Modern Art in Toyama. (JPN)

■ **40** Für eine Ausstellung im Seibu Museum of Art. (JPN)

■ **41** Plakat für eine Ausstellung von Lucio Fontana im Museum of Modern Art in Toyama. (JPN)

■ **42** Asiatische Tuschmalerei ist Gegenstand der hier angekündigten Ausstellung in Seoul. (KOR)

■ **43** Plakat für das Museum of Modern Art in Toyama. (JPN)

■ **40** Annonce d'une exposition au Seibu Museum of Art. (JPN)

■ **41** Affiche pour une exposition de Lucio Fontana au Museum of Modern Art de Toyama. (JPN)

■ **42** La peinture asiatique monochrome à l'encre de Chine est le sujet de cette exposition organisée à Séoul. (KOR)

■ **43** Affiche pour le Museum of Modern Art de Toyama. (JPN)

ART DIRECTOR:
Byung Choo Suk

DESIGNER:
Byung Choo Suk

AGENCY:
LG Ad Inc.

CLIENT:
Korean Society of Fine Arts

■ **42**

ART DIRECTOR:
Kazumasa Nagai

DESIGNER:
Kazumasa Nagai

AGENCY:
Nippon Design Center

CLIENT:
The Museum of Modern Art, Toyama

■ **43**

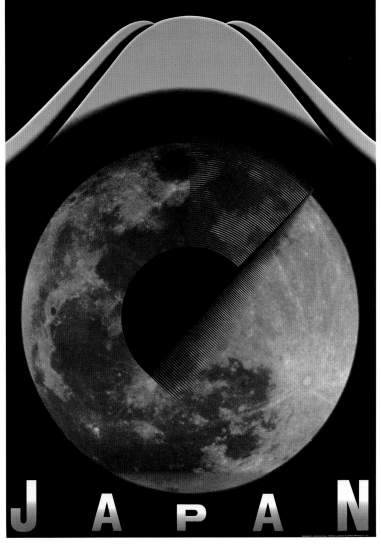

ART DIRECTOR:
Garry Emery

DESIGNER:
Garry Emery

AGENCY:
Emery Vincent Associates

CLIENT:
Continuum '85

■ 44

I N T E R C E P T I N G N A T U R E

AN EXHIBITION BY **TADAO ANDO** 10 TO 27 SEPTEMBER 1985. RMIT GALLERY 344 SWANSTON STREET MELBOURNE VICTORIA AUSTRALIA. A CONTINUUM '85 EXHIBITION WITH RMIT UNION SPONSORED BY CARRINGBUSH PTY LTD

ART DIRECTOR:
Dieter Marx

ARTIST:
Rem Koolhaas

PUBLISHER:
Edition Lidiarte

■ 45

LOS ANGELES COUNTY MUSEUM OF ART

23 NOVEMBER 1986

ART DIRECTOR:
John Coy

DESIGNER:
John Coy/
Laurie Handler

PHOTOGRAPHER:
Peter Brenner

AGENCY:
Coy

CLIENT
Los Angeles County
Museum of Art

■ 46

The Dallas Museum of Art
Sculpture Garden
Opens October 10th.

ART DIRECTOR:
Rex Peteet

DESIGNER:
Rex Peteet

ARTIST:
Rex Peteet/
Ken Shafer

AGENCY:
Sibley/Peteet Design

CLIENT:
Dallas Museum of Art

■ 47

■ **44** Intercepting Nature – for an exhibition devoted to the work of the Japanese architect Tadao Ando. (AUS)

■ **45** Delirious New York – The City of the Captive Globe, for the Office for Metropolitan Architecture, Amsterdam. (GER)

■ **46** Poster for the reopening of the Los Angeles County Museum of Art. (USA)

■ **47** To announce the festive inauguration of the Sculpture Garden of the new Dallas Museum of Art. (USA)

■ **44** »Der Natur abgelauscht« – Ankündigung einer Ausstellung, die dem japanischen Architekten Tadao Ando gewidmet ist. (AUS)

■ **45** »Wahnsinniges New York« – »Die Stadt des gefangenen Globus«. Plakat des Büros für urbane Architektur in Amsterdam. (GER)

■ **46** Plakat für die Wiedereröffnung des Los Angeles County Museum of Art. (USA)

■ **47** Ankündigung der festlichen Einweihung des Skulptur-Gartens des neuen Dallas Museum of Art. (USA)

■ **44** »A l'écoute de la nature« – annonce d'une exposition consacrée à l'architecte japonais Tadao Ando. (AUS)

■ **45** »Délire à New York« – »La ville du globe captif«. Affiche du bureau d'urbanisme et d'architecture d'Amsterdam. (GER)

■ **46** Affiche pour la réouverture du Los Angeles County Museum of Art. (USA)

■ **47** Annonce de l'inauguration en musique et théâtre du jardin des sculptures du nouveau Museum of Art de Dallas. (USA)

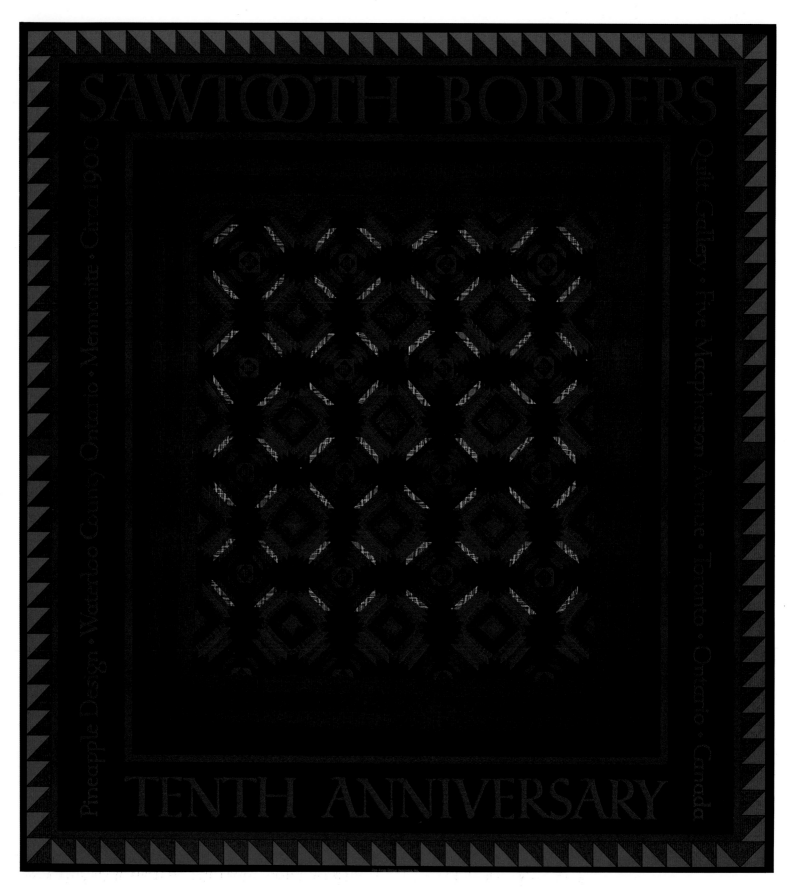

ART DIRECTOR:
ANN AMES
DESIGNER:
ANN AMES
ARTIST:
GEORGE KAY/SHIN SUGINO
AGENCY:
ANN AMES DESIGN ASSOCIATES
CLIENT:
SAWTOOTH BORDERS

■ **48**

■**48** The tenth anniversary poster for a gallery specializing in patchwork quilts. (CAN)

■**49** Announcement of an exhibition of patchwork quilts worked by members of the Amish sect. (USA)

■**50** Utensils designed and produced by the Shakers, showing their skills in simple craftsmanship, form the exhibitions that are announced on this poster. The chest of drawers and the boxes were made in 1815. (USA)

■**48** Plakat zum zehnjährigen Bestehen einer Galerie, die mit Patchwork-Decken (Quilts) handelt. (CAN)

■**49** Für eine Ausstellung von Patchwork-Decken, die von Mitgliedern der Amisch-Sekte angefertigt wurden. (USA)

■**50** Shaker-Design, schlichte, mit grossem handwerklichen Können hergestellte Gebrauchsgegenstände der Shaker-Sekte, ist das Thema der hier angekündigten Ausstellungen. Die Kommode und die Schachteln entstanden um 1815. (USA)

■**48** Affiche pour le 10e anniversaire d'une galerie spécialisée dans les couvertures en patchwork dites quilts. (CAN)

■**49** Annonce d'une exposition de couvertures en patchwork (quilts) fabriquées par des membres de la secte Amish. (USA)

■**50** Les expositions annoncées ici mettent en vedette le design des Shakers: objets utilitaires de facture simple, mais dénotant l'existence d'un artisanat d'art de grande qualité dans cette secte. La commode et les boîtes datent de 1815. (USA)

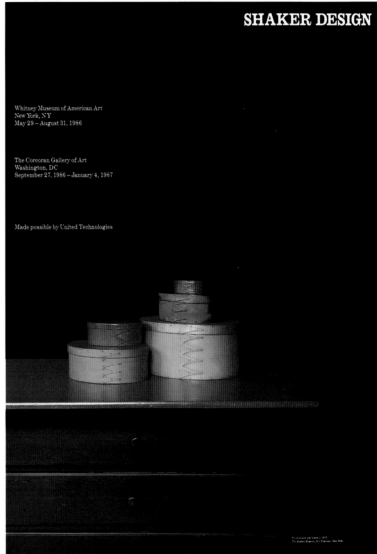

ART DIRECTOR:
ETHEL KESSLER/ELLEN ROEBUCK
DESIGNER:
MAUDE LLOYD
PHOTOGRAPHER:
JERRY IRWIN/UNIPHOTO
AGENCY:
ETHEL KESSLER DESIGN, INC.
CLIENT:
SMITHSONIAN INSTITUTION, MUSEUM SHOPS
■**49**

ART DIRECTOR:
GORDON BOWMAN/ D. BIRDSALL/R. APPLETON
DESIGNER:
ROBERT APPLETON
AGENCY:
APPLETON DESIGN, INC.
CLIENT:
UNITED TECHNOLOGIES CORP.
■**50**

■ **51** For an exhibition of German expressionist artists with items borrowed from the Ludwig (Germany) and Rosy Fischer (USA) collections. Illustrated is: *Otto and Maschka Mueller in the Study* (1911) by Ernst Ludwig Kirchner. (USA)

■ **52** Announcement of an exhibition of furniture and design by Finnish designer Alvar Aalto held at Cesano Maderno. (ITA)

■ **53** For an Oskar Kokoschka exhibition at the Kunsthaus in Zürich – the title of the picture shown is *Mandrill* (1926). (SWI)

■ **51** Plakat für eine Ausstellung deutscher Expressionisten, mit Leihgaben der Sammlungen Ludwig (Deutschland) und Rosy Fischer (USA). Abgebildet ist das Werk *Otto und Maschka Mueller im Atelier* (1911) von Ernst Ludwig Kirchner. (USA)

■ **52** Ankündigung einer Ausstellung von Möbeln und Design des Künstlers Alvar Aalto in der Gemeinde Cesano Maderno. (ITA)

■ **53** Für eine Kokoschka-Ausstellung im Kunsthaus Zürich, mit dem Bild *Mandrill* (1926). (SWI)

■ **51** Affiche pour une exposition réunissant les expressionnistes allemands des collections Ludwig (RFA) et Rosy Fischer (E.-U.). L'illustration reproduit l'œuvre qu'Ernst Ludwig Kirchner réalisa en 1911, *Otto et Machka Mueller à l'atelier.* (USA)

■ **52** Annonce d'une exposition des meubles et du design d'Alvar Aalto à la maison communale de Cesano Maderno. (ITA)

■ **53** Affiche illustrée du tableau *Mandrill* (1926) pour une exposition Kokoschka au Kunsthaus de Zurich. (SWI)

ART DIRECTOR:
SARAH LAVICKA
DESIGNER:
SARAH LAVICKA
ARTIST:
ERNST LUDWIG KIRCHNER
AGENCY:
PUBLICATIONS OFFICE OF THE
VIRGINIA MUSEUM OF FINE ARTS
CLIENT:
VIRGINIA MUSEUM OF FINE ARTS
■ **51**

ART DIRECTOR:
ROBERTO SAMBONET
DESIGNER:
ROBERTO SAMBONET
AGENCY:
ROBERTO SAMBONET
CLIENT:
AMERIGO MARIANI ARREDAMENTI
■ **52**

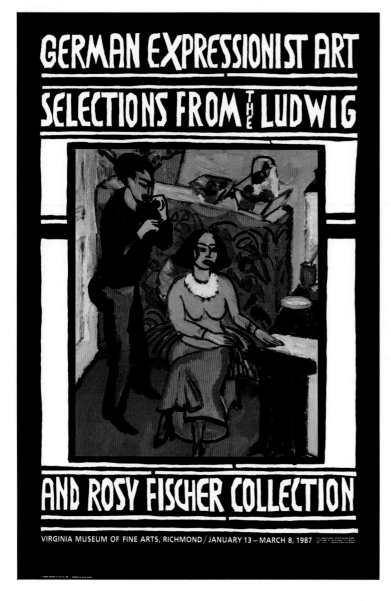

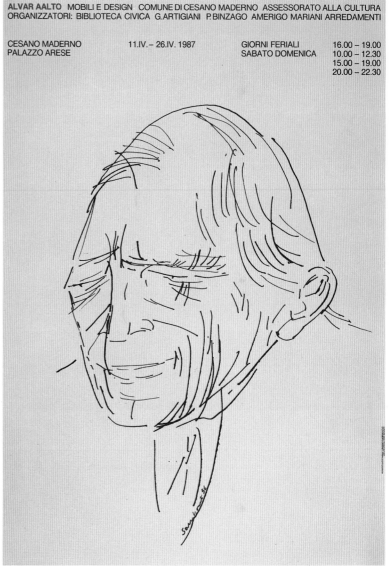

DESIGNER:
*BLUMENSTEIN +
PLANCHEREL*

ARTIST:
OSKAR KOKOSCHKA

AGENCY:
*BLUMENSTEIN +
PLANCHEREL*

CLIENT:
KUNSTHAUS ZÜRICH

■ **53**

OSKAR KOKOSCHKA

IM KUNSTHAUS ZÜRICH

5. September bis 9. November 1986

Öffnungszeiten: Montag   14–17 Uhr   Dienstag bis Freitag   10–21 Uhr   Samstag und Sonntag   10–17 Uhr.   15./21. September 1986 geschlossen

DESIGNER:
Villu Järmut/Enn Kärmas
ARTIST:
Villu Järmut/Enn Kärmas
CLIENT:
Eesti NSV Riiklik
Kunstimuuseum
■ **54**

ART DIRECTOR:
PETER POCS

ARTIST:
PETER POCS

CLIENT:
KULTURHAUS SALGOTARJAN

■ **55**

ART DIRECTOR:
PETER POCS

ARTIST:
PETER POCS

CLIENT:
STUDIO FÜR JUNGE KÜNSTLER,
BUDAPEST

■ **56**

■ **54** Poster for an exhibition of works by painter Jüri Kask at the Riiklik Museum of Art, Estonia. (USR)

■ **55** Silkscreen poster to announce an exhibition of applied art with works by young people. (HUN)

■ **56** Silkscreen poster for an exhibition of works by young artists. (HUN)

■ **54** Plakat für eine Ausstellung des Malers Jüri Kask im Riiklik Kunstmuseum, Estland. (USR)

■ **55** Ankündigung einer Kunstgewerbeausstellung mit Arbeiten junger Leute. Siebdruck. (HUN)

■ **56** Siebdruckplakat für eine Ausstellung mit Werken junger Künstler. (HUN)

■ **54** Affiche pour une exposition que le Riiklik Musée des beaux arts d'Estonie consacre au peintre Juri Kask. (USR)

■ **55** Annonce d'une exposition d'arts décoratifs réunissant les travaux de jeunes artistes. Sérigraphie. (HUN)

■ **56** Affiche sérigraphique pour une exposition consacrée à de jeunes talents. (HUN)

ART DIRECTOR:
Alain Le Quernec
DESIGNER:
Alain Le Quernec
ARTIST:
Alain Le Quernec
CLIENT:
Festival du Livre en Bretagne
■ **57**

ART DIRECTOR:
Bülent Erkmen
DESIGNER:
Bülent Erkmen
AGENCY:
Reklamevi
CLIENT:
Koleksiyon Corp.
■ **58**

■ **57** "The Words and the Tones." Silkscreen poster to announce the 7th Book Festival held in Brittany. (FRA)

■ **58** For an exhibition of Turkish avant-garde art. (TUR)

■ **59** For an exhibition showing everything connected with Hollywood and the motion-picture industry – legendary and factual. (USA)

■ **57** «Die Worte und die Töne.» Siebdruckplakat für die Ankündigung des 7. Buchfestivals in der Bretagne. (FRA)

■ **58** Für eine Ausstellung türkischer Avant-Garde-Kunst. (TUR)

■ **59** «Hollywood, Legende und Realität» ist der Titel einer Ausstellung von Gegenständen, die mit dem Film verbunden sind. (USA)

■ **57** Affiche sérigraphique bilingue français-breton pour le 7e Festival du Livre de Bretagne. (FRA)

■ **58** Pour une exposition de l'avant-garde turque. (TUR)

■ **59** «Hollywood, légende et réalité», c'est ainsi que s'intitule cette exposition d'objets et d'accessoires relatifs au cinéma. (USA)

ART DIRECTOR:
Judy Kirpich

DESIGNER:
Judy Kirpich/Claire Wolfman

ARTIST:
Doug Johnson

AGENCY:
Grafik Communications, Ltd.

CLIENT:
*Smithsonian Institution
Traveling Exhibition Service*
■ 59

Debra Norby has made some new friends.

"Debra Norby & Friends" • A show of eighteen pieces by the leading clay artist in the Northwest. • Opens February 5th, 5–9 pm. Through March 1st. • Jamison/Thomas Gallery • 217 SW First Avenue • Portland, Oregon

Poster concept and design, Warren Eakins and Pamela Sullivan. Photography, Pete Stone. Makeup, Ken Hostil. Color separation, Trade Litho. Printing, R.G. Wilks.

◄ **ART DIRECTOR:**
Warren Eakins

DESIGNER:
Warren Eeakins/
Pamela Sullivan

PHOTOGRAPHER:
Pete Stone

AGENCY:
Backwater Advertising

CLIENT:
Jamison/Thomas Gallery,
Portland

■ **60**

ART DIRECTOR:
Holger Matthies

DESIGNER:
Holger Matthies

ARTIST:
Holger Matthies

CLIENT:
Museum für Kunst und
Gewerbe Hamburg

■ **61**

GRAPHIK

■ **60** "Debra Norby has made some new friends" – literally!
Poster for an exhibition of works by this ceramic designer. (USA)

■ **61** Poster showing one of the records in an exhibition devoted
to records held at the Hamburg Museum of Arts and Crafts. (GER)

■ **60** »Debra Norby hat sich einige neue Freunde geschaffen.« Plakat für eine Ausstellung dieser Keramikerin. (USA)

■ **61** Plakat für eine der Schallplatte gewidmete Ausstellung im
Hamburger Museum für Kunst und Gewerbe. (GER)

■ **60** »Debra Norby s'est fait quelques nouveaux amis.« Affiche
pour une exposition de cette céramiste. (USA)

■ **61** Affiche pour une exposition consacrée aux pochettes de
disques par le Musée des arts décoratifs de Hambourg. (GER)

ZUR KUNST NACH KÖLN

VENEZ A COLOGNE POUR L'AMOUR DE L'ART COLOGNE – FOR ART'S SAKE

Wallraf-Richartz-Museum
Museum Ludwig

Agfa Foto-Historama
Kölner Philharmonie

Stadt Köln

ART DIRECTOR:
Graphicteam Köln
DESIGNER:
Graphicteam Köln
PHOTOGRAPHER:
Rainer Gaertner
AGENCY:
Graphicteam Köln
CLIENT:
Verkehrsamt der Stadt Köln
■ 62

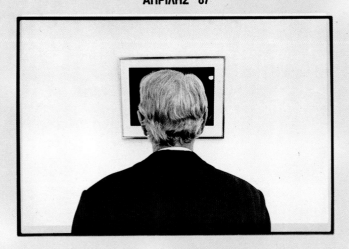

ART DIRECTOR:
Stavros Moressopulos

PHOTOGRAPHER:
Giorgos Depollas

CLIENT:
Hellenic Center of Photography

■ 63

ART DIRECTOR:
Rick Eiber

DESIGNER:
Rick Eiber

PHOTOGRAPHER:
Wah Lui

AGENCY:
Rick Eiber Design

CLIENT:
The Silver Image Gallery, Seattle

■ 64

■ **62** With the opening of the Wallraf-Richartz Museum, the city of Cologne is celebrated as an art metropolis. (GER)

■ **63** "The Month of Photography." Announcement of a photo exhibition in the Hellenic Center of Photography in Athens. (GRE)

■ **64** For an exhibition of pictures by American photographer Wah Lui. (USA)

■ **62** Mit der Eröffnung des Wallraf-Richartz-Museums wird die Stadt Köln hiermit als Kunstmetropole gefeiert. (GER)

■ **63** «Der Monat der Photographie» – Ankündiung einer Photoausstellung im Hellenic Center of Photography in Athen. (GRE)

■ **64** Für eine Ausstellung der Bilder des amerikanischen Photographen Wah Lui. (USA)

■ **62** L'inauguration du Musée Wallraf-Richartz fait de Cologne une métropole artistique célébrée sur cette affiche. (GER)

■ **63** «Le Mois de la photo» – annonce d'une exposition de photos au Centre hellénique de photographie d'Athènes. (GRE)

■ **64** Pour une exposition de l'œuvre du photographe américain Wah Lui. (USA)

ART DIRECTOR:
Judy Kirpich

DESIGNER:
Judy Kirpich

PHOTOGRAPHER:
David Sharpe

AGENCY:
Grafic Communications, Ltd.

CLIENT:
The Computer Museum,
Boston

■ 65

ART DIRECTOR:
Rosmarie Tissi

DESIGNER:
Rosmarie Tissi

AGENCY:
Odermatt & Tissi

CLIENT:
Museum für Gestaltung,
Zürich

■ 66

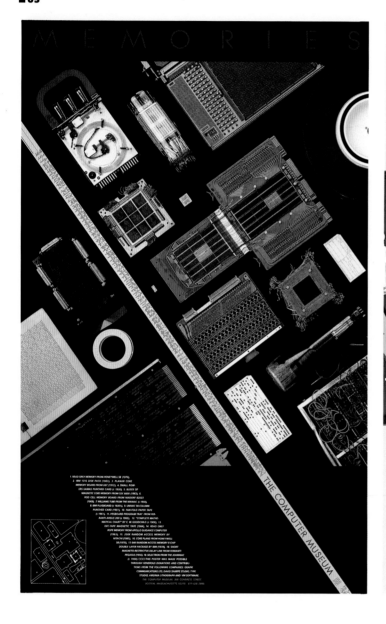

ART DIRECTOR:
Mark Richardson

DESIGNER:
Mark Richardson

PHOTOGRAPHER:
Greg Jarim

AGENCY:
DMCD, Inc.

CLIENT:
*The BMW Gallery,
New York*

■ 67

ART DIRECTOR:
Garry Emery

DESIGNER:
Garry Emery

ARTIST:
Garry Emery

AGENCY:
Emery Vincent Associates

CLIENT:
*Design Arts Board of the
Australia Council*

■ 68

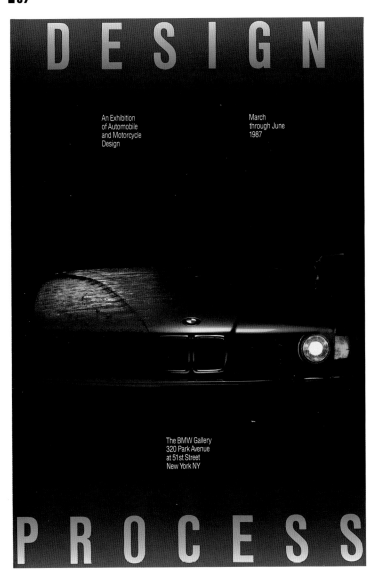

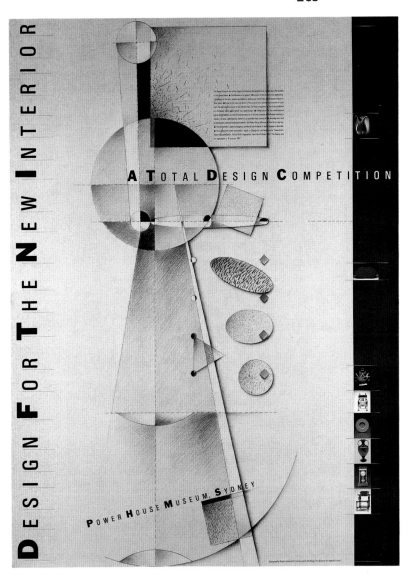

■ **65** Promotional poster for the newly opened Computer Museum in Boston. (USA)

■ **66** Poster for an exhibition of enamelled advertisement plates from a private collection, supplemented by pieces borrowed from the Museum of Design in Zürich. (SWI)

■ **67** For an exhibition at the BMW Gallery in New York devoted to the development of automobile and motorcycle design. (USA)

■ **68** Invitation to participate in the contest for designing the interior of the Power House Museum in Sydney, due to open in 1988 in celebration of Sydney's bicentennial. It is Sydney's most ambitious building construction since the Opera House. (AUS)

■ **65** Ankündigung des neu eröffneten Computer Museums in Boston. (USA)

■ **66** Plakat für eine Ausstellung über Email-Reklame-Schilder aus einer Privatsammlung, ergänzt durch Leihgaben, im Museum für Gestaltung in Zürich. (SWI)

■ **67** Für eine Ausstellung in der BMW-Galerie in New York über die Entwicklung des Auto- und Motorrad-Designs. (USA)

■ **68** Einladung zur Beteiligung am Design Wettbewerb des Power House Museums in Sydney, welches anlässlich der 200-Jahr-Feier der Stadt 1988 eröffnet wird und als grossartigstes Gebäude seit dem Bau der Oper gilt. (AUS)

■ **65** Annonce de l'inauguration du Computer Museum (Musée de l'ordinateur) de Boston. (USA)

■ **66** Affiche pour une exposition d'enseignes publicitaires émaillées provenant d'une collection privée et de divers prêts au Museum für Gestaltung de Zurich. (SWI)

■ **67** Pour une exposition à la Galerie BMW de New York: l'évolution du design des voitures automobiles et des motos. (USA)

■ **68** Appel d'envois pour le concours de design du Power House Museum of Sydney qui sera inauguré en 1988 lors du bicentenaire de la ville et passe pour être la plus formidable réalisation architecturale depuis l'Opéra de Sydney. (AUS)

ART DIRECTOR:
Kunsthaus Zürich

DESIGNER:
Egon Meichtry

ARTIST:
Gotthard Graubner

CLIENT:
Kunsthaus Zürich

■ **69**

ART DIRECTOR:
Ahn Sang-Soo

DESIGNER:
Ahn Sang-Soo

PHOTOGRAPHER:
Bae Byoung-Woo

AGENCY:
Ahn Graphics

CLIENT:
Gum Nuri

■ **70**

■ **69** Sponge-gouache by German painter and graphic designer Gotthard Graubner promoting an exhibition of his drawings and watercolors at the Kunsthaus in Zürich. (SWI)

■ **70** Poster for an exhibition of metal sculptures by Korean sculptor Gum Nuri. (KOR)

■ **71** For an exhibition of prize-winning works in the Second Canadian Competition for Furniture Design. (CAN)

■ **69** Schwammgouache des deutschen Malers und Graphikers Gotthard Graubner. Ankündigung für eine Ausstellung seiner Zeichnungen und Aquarelle im Kunsthaus Zürich. (SWI)

■ **70** Für eine Ausstellung von Metallskulpturen des koreanischen Bildhauers Gum Nuri. (KOR)

■ **71** Für die Ausstellung der prämierten Arbeiten des 2. kanadischen Wettbewerbs für Möbeldesign. (CAN)

■ **69** Gouache à l'éponge du peintre et graphiste allemand Gotthard Graubner. Annonce d'une exposition de ses dessins et aquarelles au Kunsthaus de Zurich. (SWI)

■ **70** Pour une exposition des sculptures métalliques de l'artiste coréen Gum Nuri. (KOR)

■ **71** Pour l'exposition des travaux des lauréats du 2e concours canadien de design de meubles. (CAN)

ART DIRECTOR:
Del Terrelonge
DESIGNER:
Del Terrelonge
PHOTOGRAPHER:
Ron Baxter Smith
AGENCY:
Terrelonge Design
CLIENT:
Virtu Forum & Function
■ 71

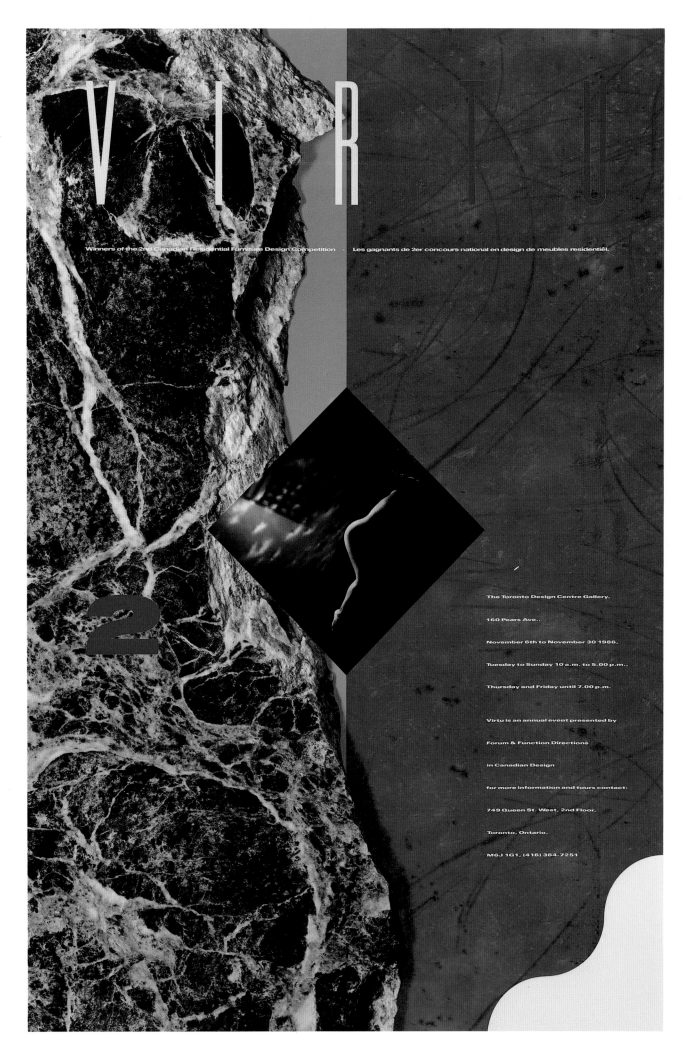

Winners of the 2nd Canadian Residential Furniture Design Competition · Les gagnants de 2er concours national en design de meubles residentiél.

The Toronto Design Centre Gallery,

160 Pears Ave.,

November 6th to November 30 1986,

Tuesday to Sunday 10 a.m. to 5.00 p.m.,

Thursday and Friday until 7.00 p.m.

Virtu is an annual event presented by

Forum & Function Directions

in Canadian Design

for more information and tours contact:

749 Queen St. West, 2nd Floor,

Toronto, Ontario,

M6J 1G1, (416) 364-7251

◄ ART DIRECTOR:
Garth Bell
DESIGNER:
Garth Bell
PHOTOGRAPHER:
Garth Bell
AGENCY:
Bell & Co.
CLIENT:
Lahti Poster Biennale
■ 72

DESIGNER:
Michel Leonardi
PHOTOGRAPHER:
Damien Hustinx
PUBLISHER:
Cops Photo, Liege
■ 73

ART DIRECTOR:
Joao Machado
DESIGNER:
Joao Machado
ARTIST:
Joao Machado
CLIENT:
Joao Machado
■ 74

■ **72** "The Right to One's Own Culture." Poster designed by artist Garth Bell after his entry to the Poster Biennale in Lahti, Finland, was withheld by the French customs. The official decree is the centerpoint of this poster. (FRA)

■ **73** For an exhibition of works by photographer Damien Hustinx in Liège. (BEL)

■ **74** Announcement of an exhibition of posters by artist João Machado in Portugal. (POR)

■ **72** »Das Recht auf eine eigene Kultur« ist der Titel dieses Plakates, welches der Künstler Garth Bell gestaltete, nachdem seine Einsendung für die Posterbiennale in Lahti, Finnland, vom französischen Zoll zurückbehalten wurde. (FRA)

■ **73** Für eine Ausstellung der Bilder des Photographen Damien Hustinx in Liège. (BEL)

■ **74** Ankündigung einer Ausstellung der Plakate des Künstlers João Machado in Portugal. (POR)

■ **72** »Le Droit à la propre culture« est le titre de l'affiche que l'artiste Garth Bell réalisa après que son envoi destiné à la Biennale de l'affiche de Lahti (Finlande) eut été interdit à l'exportation par les autorités douanières françaises. (FRA)

■ **73** Pour une exposition à Liège de l'œuvre du photographe Damien Hustinx. (BEL)

■ **74** Annonce d'une exposition des créations affichistes de João Machado au Portugal. (POR)

ART DIRECTOR:
Marshall Harmon
DESIGNER:
Edward Boria
PHOTOGRAPHER:
Scott Chaney
AGENCY:
Harmon Kemp Inc.
CLIENT:
Italian Trade Commission
■ **75**

ART DIRECTOR:
Christo Aleksiev
DESIGNER:
Christo Aleksiev
ARTIST:
Christo Aleksiev
AGENCY:
*Verband der bulgarischen
Künstler*
CLIENT:
Literaturmuseum Sofia
■ **76**

■ **75** For the promotion of Italian quality tiles. The poster is targeted at architects and interior designers. (USA)

■ **76** Poster issued by the Literature Museum in Sofia to mark the occasion of the centenary of the birth of Bulgarian poet Dimtscho Debeljanov, born on March 28, 1887 and killed in World War I in 1916. He was regarded as a "semi"-symbolist. (BUL)

■ **77** Poster entitled "The Golden Beacon" - for a residential and office high-rise building project designed in 1956 by the famous American architect Frank Lloyd Wright. (USA)

■ **75** Für die Förderung von italienischen Qualitätskacheln. Das Plakat ist an Architekten und Innendekorateure gerichtet. (USA)

■ **76** Plakat des Literaturmuseums von Sofia anlässlich des 100. Geburtstages des bulgarischen Dichters Dimtscho Debeljanov, der am 28. März 1887 geboren wurde und 1916 im 2. Weltkrieg gefallen ist. Er galt als »Halb«-Symbolist. (BUL)

■ **77** »Der goldene Leuchtturm« - Plakat eines Wohn- und Bürohochhaus-Projekts, welches 1956 vom berühmten amerikanischen Architekten Frank Lloyd Wright entworfen wurde. (USA)

■ **75** Pour la promotion des carreaux de qualité fabriqueés en Italie. Affiche destinée aux architectes et ensembliers. (USA)

■ **76** Affiche du Musée littéraire de Sophia à l'occasion du 100e anniversaire du poète bulgare mi-symboliste Dimtcho Debeljanov, né le 28 mars 1887, mort en 1916 sur l'un des fronts de la Première Guerre mondiale. (BUL)

■ **77** »Le Phare doré« - affiche pour un projet de gratte-ciel à usage de bureaux et d'appartements conçu par le grand architecte américain Frank Lloyd Wright en 1956. (USA)

ARTIST:
Frank Lloyd Wright

PUBLISHER:
The Frank Lloyd Wright Foundation

■ **77**

Frank Lloyd Wright   Project: "Golden Beacon", Office and Apartment Tower, Chicago, Illinois, U.S.A., 1956   23"×42 1/2"   Copyright © The Frank Lloyd Wright Foundation 1959   GA Drawings No.3   Copyright © A.D.A. EDITA Tokyo Co., Ltd. 1984   Printed in Japan

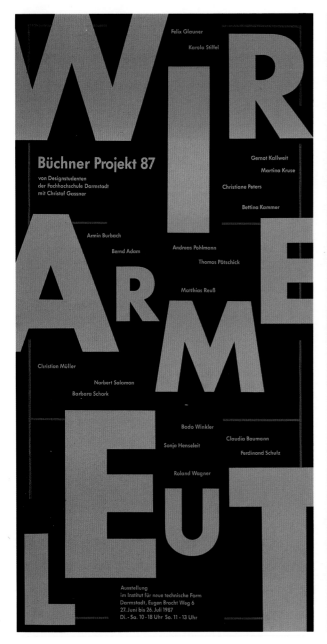

ART DIRECTOR:
Christof Gassner
DESIGNER:
Christian Müller
CLIENT:
*Fachhochschule
Darmstadt*
■78

ART DIRECTOR:
Michel Bouvet
DESIGNER:
Michel Bouvet
PHOTOGRAPHER:
Francis Laharrague
AGENCY:
Michel Bouvet
CLIENT:
Ville de Montluçon
■79

ART DIRECTOR:
Judy Kirpich/Susan English

DESIGNER:
Judy Kirpich/Susan English/
Daniel Pelavin

ARTIST:
Daniel Pelavin

AGENCY:
Grafic Communications, Ltd.

CLIENT:
Smithsonian Institution
Traveling Exhibition Service

■ **80**

ART DIRECTOR:
David Lance Goines

DESIGNER:
David Lance Goines

ARTIST:
David Lance Goines

AGENCY:
St. Heironymous Press

CLIENT:
Alain Weill

■ **81**

■ **78** Poster for the "Büchner Project" – issued by the Technical University in Darmstadt. Design students were asked to visualize the work and quotations of Georg Büchner in commemoration of the 150th year of his death. (GER)

■ **79** For an exhibition of regional collections of French faiences at the Lyre Museum of Montluçon. (FRA)

■ **80** Poster for an art nouveau exhibition at the Smithsonian Institution which also emphasizes the influence of Siegfried Bing on the development of this movement. (USA)

■ **81** "The Month of the Poster" – for a poster exhibition in Bordeaux. (FRA)

■ **78** Plakat zu einem Büchner-Projekt der Fachhochschule Darmstadt. Die Designstudenten hatten die Aufgabe, Zitate von Georg Büchner, dessen 150. Todestag 1987 gefeiert wurde, zu visualisieren. (GER)

■ **79** Für eine Ausstellung der regionalen Sammlung und französischer Fayencen im Leiermuseum von Montluçon. (FRA)

■ **80** Plakat für eine Ausstellung der Smithsonian Institution, über Jugendstilmöbel und -gegenstände und über den Einfluss Siegfried Bings auf die Entwicklung dieser Bewegung. (USA)

■ **81** «Der Monat des Plakates» – für eine Plakatausstellung in Bordeaux. (FRA)

■ **78** Affiche pour un projet Georg Büchner lancé par la Fachhochschule de Darmstadt (RFA). Les étudiants en design avaient pour tâche de visualiser des citations du grand auteur dramatique allemand mort il y a 150 ans. (GER)

■ **79** Pour une exposition des collections régionales et des faïences françaises du Musée de la Vielle de Montluçon. (FRA)

■ **80** Affiche pour une exposition de la Smithsonian Institution réunissant des meubles et objets modern style et démontrant l'influence que Siegfried Bing exerça sur ce mouvement. (USA)

■ **81** «Le Mois de l'affiche» – Pour une exposition d'affiches organisé à Bordeaux. (FRA)

ART DIRECTOR:
GRAPHITI/LIMITE
DESIGNER:
FABIO CHIANTINI/
STEFANO ROVAI
ARTIST:
FABIO CHIANTINI/
STEFANO ROVAI
AGENCY:
GRAPHITI/LIMITE
CLIENT:
MEDIATECA REGIONALE
TOSCANA
■82

ART DIRECTOR:
LUPE GARCIA/MARK WILCOX/
CHERI GROOM
DESIGNER:
LUPE GARCIA/MARK WILCOX/
CHERI GROOM
PHOTOGRAPHER:
OSCAR WILLIAMS
AGENCY:
ATKINS & ASSOCIATES, INC.
CLIENT:
TEXAS FILM FESTIVAL
■83

■82 Announcement of an international round of discussions about the survival chances of Italian and European films to the year 2000. (ITA)

■83 Poster for the first annual Texan film festival in San Antonio after a video-film and script contest. (USA)

■84 Poster for the first Czechoslovakian showing of the American film "Tarzan" with Christopher Lambert in the title role. (CSR)

■82 Ankündigung einer internationalen Gesprächsrunde über die Überlebenschancen des italienischen/europäischen Films bis zum Jahr 2000. (ITA)

■83 Plakat für das erste texanische Filmfestival in San Antonio, nach einem Videofilm- und Drehbuch-Wettbewerb. (USA)

■84 Für die tschechische Vorführung des amerikanischen Filmes «Tarzan» mit Christopher Lambert in der Titelrolle. (CSR)

■82 Annonce d'une table ronde internationale où seront mises en discussion les chances de survie du cinéma italien et européen d'ici à la fin du siècle. (ITA)

■83 Affiche du premier Festival du cinéma texan à San Antonio à la suite d'un concours de films et scénarios vidéo. (USA)

■84 Pour la projection en Tchécoslovaquie du film «Tarzan» avec Christopher Lambert dans le rôle du héros de la jungle. (CSR)

ART DIRECTOR:
Zdenek Ziegler
DESIGNER:
Zdenek Ziegler
ARTIST:
Zdenek Ziegler
CLIENT:
UPF Praha
■ 84

TAR ZAN

Britský film
Známá legenda
o pánu opic
Režie: Hugh Hudson

V hlavní úloze Christopher Lambert

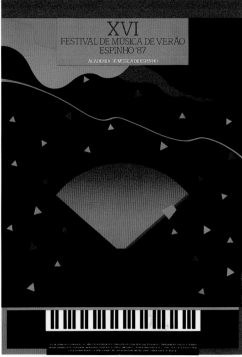

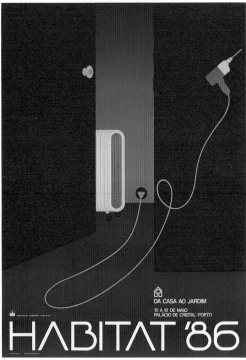

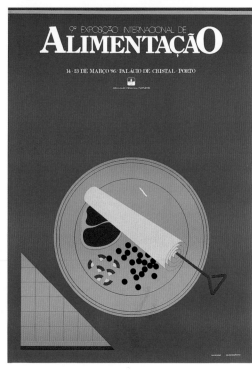

ART DIRECTOR:
Joao Machado

DESIGNER:
Joao Machado

ARTIST:
Joao Machado

CLIENT:
Associacao Industrial Portuense

■ **85, 87–90**

ART DIRECTOR:
Joao Machado

DESIGNER:
Joao Machado

ARTIST:
Joao Machado

CLIENT:
Academia de Musica de Espinho

■ **86**

ART DIRECTOR:
Joao Machado

DESIGNER:
Joao Machado

ARTIST:
Joao Machado

CLIENT:
Porto 6 Fotografos

■ **91**

■ **85–91** From a series of posters by Portuguese artist João Machado: *85* is for an exhibition about building materials, *86* announces a music festival, *87* is for an automobile salon, *88* promotes an exhibition on homes/interior design, *89* is for an exhibition on camping, *90* is for an exhibition on food, and *91* for a photo exhibition. (POR)

■ **85–91** Aus einer Serie von Plakaten des portugiesischen Künstlers João Machado: *85* für eine Ausstellung über Baumaterialien, *86* für ein Musikfestival, *87* für einen Autosalon, *88* promotes an Ausstellung über Wohnen '86 und *89* Camping '86, *90* für eine Ausstellung über Nahrungsmittel und *91* Ankündigung einer Photoausstellung. (POR)

■ **85–91** Exemples d'affiches réalisées par l'artiste portugais João Machado: *85* pour une exposition de matériaux de construction, *86* pour un festival de musique, *87* pour un salon de l'auto, *88* pour une exposition de l'habitat en 1986, *89* pour le camping en 1986, *90* pour une exposition alimentaire, *91* pour une exposition photo. (POR)

ART DIRECTOR:
Bülent Erkmen

DESIGNER:
Bülent Erkmen

PHOTOGRAPHER:
Tülin Altılar

AGENCY:
Reklamevi

CLIENT:
Mozaik Music Group

■92

ART DIRECTOR:
Bob Wilcox

DESIGNER:
Bob Wilcox

ARTIST:
Bob Wilcox

AGENCY:
Bob Wilcox

CLIENT:
Music Gallery, Toronto

■93

ART DIRECTOR:
Tom Aumayr
DESIGNER:
Paul Zwirchmayr
ARTIST:
Michael Seeger
AGENCY:
Schelter & Giesecke
CLIENT:
Kulturzentrum Wels
■ 94

ART DIRECTOR:
Günther Kieser
DESIGNER:
Günther Kieser
AGENCY:
*Hessischer Rundfunk/
Abt. Publizistik*
CLIENT:
Hessischer Rundfunk
■ 95

■ 92 Announcement of a concert entitled "Time Gives us a Break" by the Turkish group Mozaik. (TUR)

■ 93 To promote the Music Gallery, a center for experimental music in Toronto. (CAN)

■ 94 For a jazz concert in Wels, Austria. The letters were cut out by hand (papercuts). (AUS)

■ 95 Announcement issued by the radio and TV station of Hessen during the holiday period. (GER)

■ 92 Ankündigung eines Konzerts unter dem Namen «Time gives us a break» der türkischen Gruppe Mozaik. (TUR)

■ 93 Zur Förderung der Music Gallery, einem Zentrum für Experimentalmusik in Toronto. (CAN)

■ 94 Für ein Jazzkonzert in Wels, Österreich. Die Buchstaben wurden von Hand ausgeschnitten (Papierschnitt). (AUT)

■ 95 Bekanntgabe der Radio- und Fernseh-Sendungen des Hessischen Rundfunks während der Feiertage. (GER)

■ 92 Annonce d'un concert du groupe turc Mozaik intitulé «Le temps nous procure une pause créatrice». (TUR)

■ 93 Pour la promotion de la Music Gallery, un centre de musique expérimentale sis à Toronto. (CAN)

■ 94 Pour un concert de jazz organisé à Wels, en Haute-Autriche. Lettres en papier découpées à la main. (AUT)

■ 95 Annonce des émissions de radio et de télévision du Hessischer Rundfunk durant les fêtes de fin d'année. (GER)

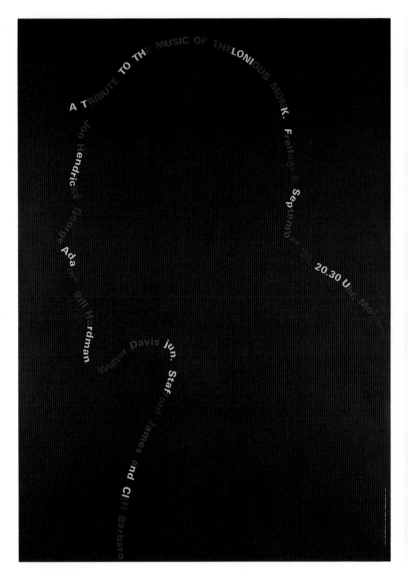

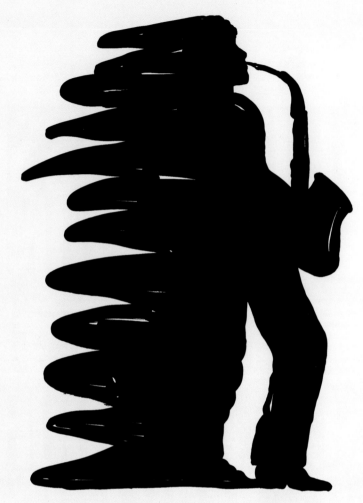

ART DIRECTOR:
Niklaus Troxler

DESIGNER:
Niklaus Troxler

ARTIST:
Niklaus Troxler

STUDIO:
Niklaus Troxler

CLIENT:
Jazz in Willisau

■ **96, 98**

ART DIRECTOR:
Niklaus Troxler

DESIGNER:
Niklaus Troxler

ARTIST:
Niklaus Troxler

STUDIO:
Niklaus Troxler

CLIENT:
Verkehrsverein Brunnen

■ **97**

■ **96** To promote a jazz concert in honor of Thelonious Monk during the jazz festival at Willisau. (SWI)

■ **97** Silkscreen poster to announce an exhibition of jazz posters by Niklaus Troxler. (SWI)

■ **98** Poster for a concert given by two jazz bands at Willisau during the jazz festival. (SWI)

■ **96** Ankündigung eines Jazz-Konzertes zu Ehren von Thelonious Monk im Rahmen des Jazz-Festivals von Willisau. (SWI)

■ **97** Siebdruckplakat für die Ankündigung einer Ausstellung der Jazz-Plakate von Niklaus Troxler. (SWI)

■ **98** Plakat für ein Konzert von zwei Jazz-Bands anlässlich des Jazz-Festivals in Willisau. (SWI)

■ **96** Annonce d'un concert de jazz en l'honneur de Thelonious Monk organisé durant le Festival de jazz de Willisau. (SWI)

■ **97** Affiche sérigraphique annonçant une exposition des affiches de jazz créées par Niklaus Troxler. (SWI)

■ **98** Affiche pour un concert de deux jazz-bands dans le cadre du Festival de jazz de Willisau, en Suisse. (SWI)

Faust I
Johann Wolfgang von Goethe
Inszenierung: Günter Krämer
Ausstattung: Andreas Reinhardt
Musik: Konstantin Wecker

Das Käthchen von Heilbronn
oder Die Feuerprobe
Heinrich von Kleist
Inszenierung: Torsten Fischer
Ausstattung: Bernd Damovsky

Dantons Tod
Georg Büchner
Inszenierung: Günter Krämer

BREMER THEATER
85/86

ART DIRECTOR:
HOLGER MATTHIES
DESIGNER:
HOLGER MATTHIES
ARTIST:
HOLGER MATTHIES
CLIENT:
BREMER THEATER
■99

■ **99** Poster announcing the performance schedule of the Bremer Theater for the 85/86 season. (GER)

■ **100** Advising completion of building construction of the Osnabrück City Theater. (GER)

■ **101** To publicize a performance of Puccini's opera *La Bohème* sung in English. (USA)

■ **99** Plakat für die Ankündigung des Spielplans des Bremer Theaters für die Saison 85/86. (GER)

■ **100** Information über die Beendigung der Bauarbeiten für die städtischen Bühnen Osnabrück. (GER)

■ **101** Ankündigung einer Aufführung der Oper *La Bohème* in englischer Sprache. (USA)

■ **99** Affiche annonçant le programme du Théâtre de Brême (RFA) pour la saison 1985/86. (GER)

■ **100** Information quant à l'achèvement des travaux de construction dans les théâtres municipaux d'Osnabrück. (GER)

■ **101** Annonce d'une représentation de l'opéra *La Bohème* en version anglaise. (USA)

ART DIRECTOR:
Holger Matthies
DESIGNER:
Holger Matthies
ARTIST:
Holger Matthies
CLIENT:
Städtische Bühnen Osnabrück
■ **100**

ART DIRECTOR:
Carlos Caicedo
PHOTOGRAPHER:
Frank White
AGENCY:
Ogilvy & Mather
CLIENT:
Texas Opera Theater, Houston
■ **101**

ART DIRECTOR:
Charles Spencer Anderson
DESIGNER:
Charles Spencer Anderson
ARTIST:
Charles Spencer Anderson
AGENCY:
The Duffy Design Group
CLIENT:
Gilbert & Sullivan Opera
■ 102

▶ ART DIRECTOR:
Paul Koeleman
DESIGNER:
Paul Koeleman
ARTIST:
Paul Koeleman/
Gerhard Jaeger
AGENCY:
Paul Koeleman
CLIENT:
Het Publiekstheater
■ 103

■ **102** Poster to promote a Gilbert & Sullivan opera performance in Minneapolis. (USA)

■ **103** Poster for a performance in Amsterdam of the play "A Filling Station" by Gildas Bourdet. (NLD)

■ **102** Ankündigung der Aufführung einer Oper von Gilbert & Sullivan in Minneapolis. (USA)

■ **103** Plakat für eine Amsterdamer Inszenierung des Stückes «Eine Tankstelle» von Gildas Bourdet. (NLD)

■ **102** Annonce de la mise en scène d'un opéra de Gilbert et Sullivan à Minneapolis. (USA)

■ **103** Affiche pour la représentation de la pièce «Une Station-service» de Gildas Bourdet sur une scène d'Amsterdam. (NLD)

een pompsttation

MET

Hedda Andriessen

Margo Dames

Ann Hasekamp

Guusje van Tilborgh

Eric van der Donk

Hein van der Heyden

Gijs de Lange

Sjoerd Pleysier

Laurens Spoor

Frans Vorstman

GILDAS

BOURDET

dekor	Barbara Kroon
kostuums	Merel van Meurs
lichtontwerp	Steve Kemp
vertaling	Frans van Woerden
bewerking/regie	Ton Lutz

PUBLIEKSTHEATER

Paul Kesteman

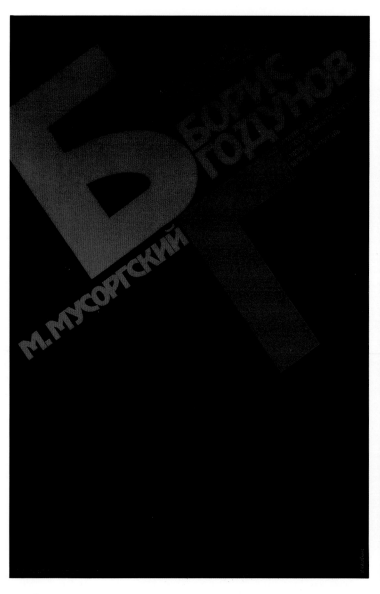

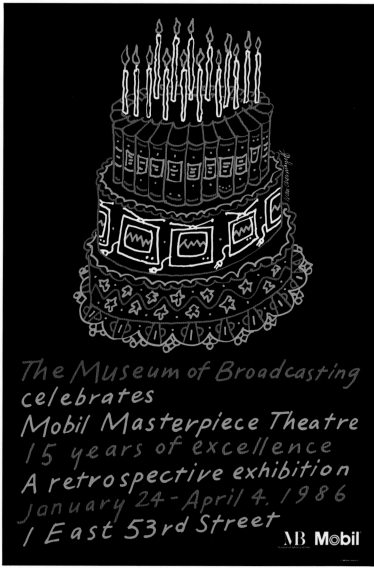

The Museum of Broadcasting
celebrates
Mobil Masterpiece Theatre
15 years of excellence
A retrospective exhibition
January 24 – April 4, 1986
1 East 53rd Street

DESIGNER:
Vytautas Kausinis

ARTIST:
Vytautas Kausinis

CLIENT:
Mintis Edition

■104

ART DIRECTOR:
Ivan Chermayeff

DESIGNER:
Ivan Chermayeff

ARTIST:
Ivan Chermayeff

AGENCY:
Chermayeff & Geismar Associates

CLIENT:
Mobil Oil Corporation

■105

■**104** Poster for a performance of Mussorgsky's folk opera *Boris Godunov.* (USR)

■**105** For an exhibition in the Museum of Broadcasting that documents 15 years of successful television productions of theater classics (sponsored by *Mobil).* (USA)

■**106** Announcement of Shakespeare's *Comedy of Errors* at the Theater in der Josefstadt, Vienna. (AUT)

■**104** Plakat für eine Aufführung von Mussorgskijs Volksoper *Boris Godunow.* (USR)

■**105** Für eine Ausstellung im Museum für Radio und Fernsehen, die 15 Jahre erfolgreicher Fernsehproduktionen klassischer Theaterstücke (unterstützt von *Mobil)* dokumentiert. (USA)

■**106** Ankündigung einer Shakespeare-Inszenierung im Theater in der Josefstadt, Wien. (AUT)

■**104** Affiche pour la représentation de l'opéra populaire *Boris Godounov* de Moussorgski. (USR)

■**105** Pour une exposition au Museum of Broadcasting (radio/TV) documentant 15 années de productions télévisées de pièces de théâtre classiques, un succès financé par *Mobil.* (USA)

■**106** Annonce de la représentation d'une pièce de Shakespeare au Théâtre In der Josefstadt, Vienne. (AUT)

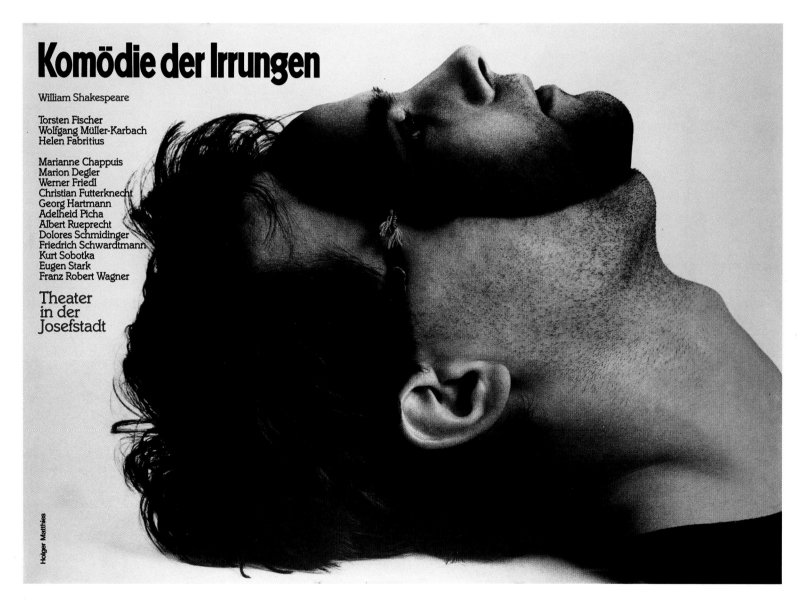

ART DIRECTOR:
HOLGER MATTHIES
DESIGNER:
HOLGER MATTHIES
PHOTOGRAPHER:
HOLGER MATTHIES
CLIENT:
THEATER IN DER JOSEFSTADT, WIEN
■**106**

ART DIRECTOR:
Paul Matthaeus

DESIGNER:
Paul Matthaeus

PHOTOGRAPHER:
Dale DeGabriele

AGENCY:
Sharp Hartwig, Inc.

CLIENT:
Seattle Opera

■107

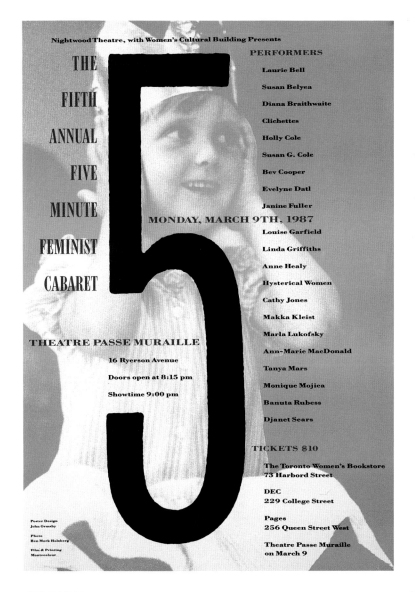

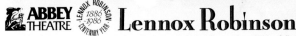

ART DIRECTOR:
JOHN ORMSBY
DESIGNER:
JOHN ORMSBY
PHOTOGRAPHER:
BEN MARK HOLZBERG
AGENCY:
JOHN ORMSBY DESIGN
CLIENT:
NIGHTWOOD THEATRE,
TORONTO
■**108**

ART DIRECTOR:
BRENDAN FOREMAN
DESIGNER:
BRENDAN FOREMAN
ARTIST:
BRENDAN FOREMAN
CLIENT:
ABBEY THEATRE
■**109**

■**107** To publicize Wagner's *The Ring of the Nibelungen* at the Seattle Opera. (USA)

■**108** Poster for the 5th annual female cabaret with 5 minute performances. (CAN)

■**109** For a performance of *The Far Hills* by Irish dramatist Lennox Robinson. (IRE)

■**107** Für die Ankündigung von Wagners *Der Ring der Nibelungen* an der Oper von Seattle. (USA)

■**108** Plakat für die 5. jährliche Frauen-Kabarett-Veranstaltung mit 5minütigen Beiträgen. (CAN)

■**109** «Die fernen Hügel» ist der Titel des hier angekündigten Stückes des irischen Dramatikers Lennox Robinson. (IRE)

■**107** Pour l'annonce de *l'Anneau du Nibelung* de Wagner joué à l'opéra de Seattle. (USA)

■**108** Affiche pour la 5e réunion annuelle des chansonnières canadiennes, chacune disposant du 5 min pour son sketch. (CAN)

■**109** Annonce d'une pièce de théâtre due à un dramaturge irlandais: «Les Collins lointaines» de Lennox Robinson. (IRE)

ART DIRECTOR:
Art Chantry
DESIGNER:
Art Chantry
AGENCY:
Art Chantry Design
CLIENT:
*The Center on
Contemporary Art, Seattle*
■ 110

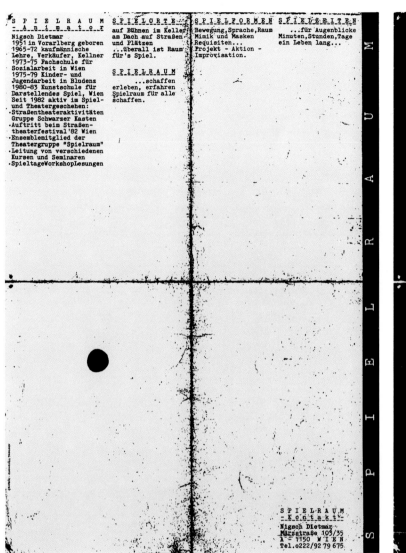

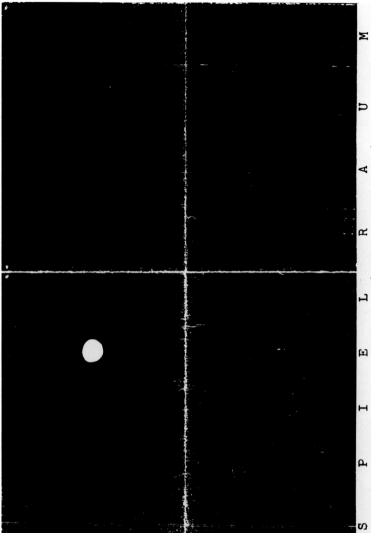

ART DIRECTOR:
Kornelius Tarmann
DESIGNER:
Kornelius Tarmann
ARTIST:
Kornelius Tarmann
CLIENT:
Dietmar Nigsch
■ **111, 112**

■ **110** To announce a literary cabaret. (USA)

■ **111, 112** Silkscreen poster on the topic "ellbow-room" for Dietmar Nigsch, a "ellbow-room animator", and who, among others, is a member of the theater group "Spielraum". (AUT)

■ **110** Für die Ankündigung eines literarischen Kabaretts. (USA)

■ **111, 112** Siebdruckplakate zum Thema «Spielraum» für Dietmar Nigsch, einen «Spielraum-Animator», der u.a. Mitglied der Theatergruppe «Spielraum» ist. (AUT)

■ **110** Annonce d'un cabaret littéraire. (USA)

■ **111, 112** Affiches sérigraphiques sur le thème de l'espace de jeu pour Dietmar Nigsch, qui anime des «espaces de jeux» et fait partie du groupe de théâtre «Espace de jeu». (AUT)

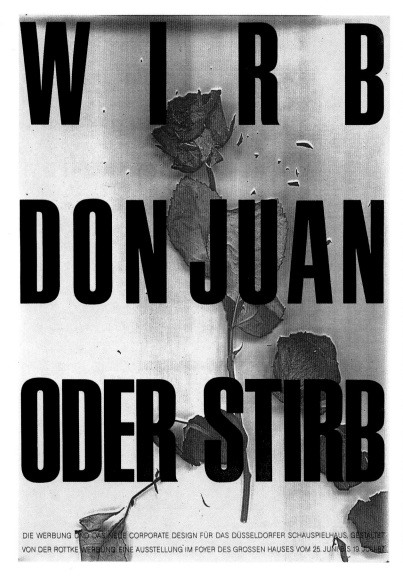

WIRB

DON JUAN

ODER STIRB

DIE WERBUNG UND DAS NEUE CORPORATE DESIGN FÜR DAS DÜSSELDORFER SCHAUSPIELHAUS, GESTALTET
VON DER ROTTKE WERBUNG. EINE AUSSTELLUNG IM FOYER DES GROSSEN HAUSES VOM 25. JUNI BIS 19. JULI 87

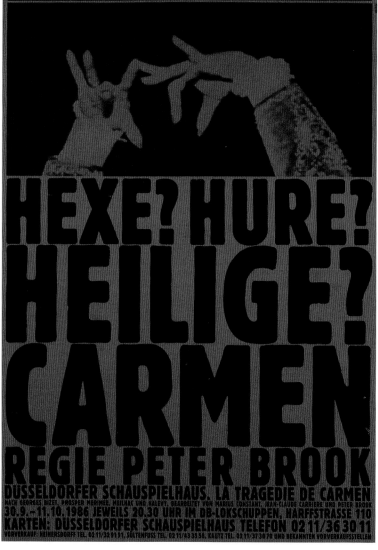

HEXE? HURE?
HEILIGE?
CARMEN
REGIE PETER BROOK
DÜSSELDORFER SCHAUSPIELHAUS. LA TRAGEDIE DE CARMEN
NACH GEORGES BIZET, PROSPER MERIMEE, MEILHAC UND HALEVY, BEARBEITET VON MARIUS CONSTANT, JEAN-CLAUDE CARRIERE UND PETER BROOK
30.9. – 11.10. 1986 JEWEILS 20.30 UHR IM DB-LOKSCHUPPEN, HARFFSTRASSE 110
KARTEN: DÜSSELDORFER SCHAUSPIELHAUS TELEFON 02 11/36 30 11
VORVERKAUF: MEINERSDORFF TEL. 02 11/32 91 51, SÜLTENFUSS TEL. 02 11/43 33 58, KAUTZ TEL. 02 11/37 30 70 UND BEKANNTEN VORVERKAUFSSTELLEN

ART DIRECTOR:
Helmut Rottke
DESIGNER:
Helmut Rottke
ARTIST:
Helmut Rottke
AGENCY:
Rottke Werbung
CLIENT:
Rottke Werbung
■ 113

ART DIRECTOR:
Helmut Rottke

DESIGNER:
Helmut Rottke

ARTIST:
Helmut Rottke

AGENCY:
Rottke Werbung

CLIENT:
Düsseldorfer Schauspielhaus
■ 114–116

■ **113** For an exhibition on advertising and the new corporate design of the Düsseldorf Theater. (GER)

■ **114–116** From a series of posters for a *Carmen* performance at the Düsseldorf Theater. *114:* "Witch, Whore, Saint?", *115:* "Düsseldorf men, leave your wives and visit Carmen", *116:* "Düsseldorf women, you can learn something from this broad". (GER)

■ **113** Für eine Ausstellung über die Werbung und das neue Corporate Design des Düsseldorfer Schauspielhauses. (GER)

■ **114–116** Beispiele aus einer Reihe von Plakaten, die mit ausgefallenen Texten für eine *Carmen*-Aufführung *(La Tragédie de Carmen,* nach Georges Bizet) am Düsseldorfer Schauspielhaus werben. (GER)

■ **113** Pour une exposition du Schauspielhaus de Düsseldorf sur la publicité et la nouvelle publicité institutionnelle. (GER)

■ **114–116** Pour une *Carmen* à Düsseldorf: *115:* «Hommes de Düsseldorf, quittez vos femmes, allez voir Carmen», *116:* «Femmes de Düsseldorf, ce sacré bout de femme peut vous apprendre pas mal de choses». (GER)

■ **117** "Floral Games" is the title of the poetry festival in Barcelona announced on this poster. (SPA)

■ **118** Announcement of a performance of Verdi's *Otello* at the Connecticut Opera. (USA)

■ **119** For the performance of a play entitled "The Delinquent Woman". The photo shows Annie Oakley in a guest appearance at Buffalo Bill's Wild West Show in Rome, 1890. (CAN)

■ **117** »Blumenspiele« ist der Titel des hier angekündigten Poesie-Festivals in Barcelona. (SPA)

■ **118** Ankündigung einer Aufführung von Verdis *Othello* an der Oper von Connecticut. (USA)

■ **119** Für die Aufführung eines Stückes mit dem Titel »Die ge-strauchelte Frau«. Die Aufnahme zeigt Annie Oakley bei einer Gast-vorstellung von Buffalo Bill's Wild West Show in Rom, 1890. (CAN)

■ **117** Annonce d'un festival de poésie catalane organisé à Barce-lone sous le titre moyenâgeux de «Jeux floraux». (SPA)

■ **118** Annonce d'une représentation de l'*Otello* de Verdi à l'opéra du Connecticut. (USA)

■ **119** Pour la représentation d'une pièce intitulée «La Délin-quante». La photo montre Annie Oakley dans le show du far-ouest que Buffalo Bill monta à Rome en 1890. (CAN)

ART DIRECTOR:
ROBERT APPLETON
DESIGNER:
ROBERT APPLETON
ARTIST:
ROBERT APPLETON
AGENCY:
APPLETON DESIGN
CLIENT:
THE CONNECTICUT OPERA, HARTFORD
■**118**

ARTIST:
PERET
AGENCY:
PERET ASOCIADOS
CLIENT:
AJUNTAMENT DE BARCELONA
■**117**

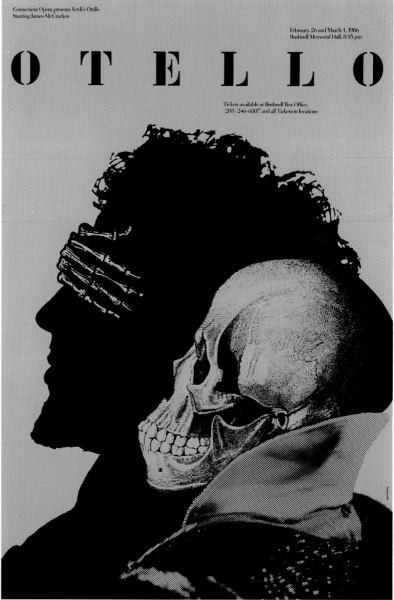

ART DIRECTOR:
Martha Fleming/
Lyne Lapointe

DESIGNER:
Martha Fleming/
Lyne Lapointe

CLIENT:
Les Petites Filles
aux Allumettes, Inc.

■ 119

ART DIRECTOR:
Masakazu Tanabe

DESIGNER:
Masakazu Tanabe

PHOTOGRAPHER:
Toshiyuki Ohashi

AGENCY:
Meitetsu Advertising, Inc.

CLIENT:
Takayama City

■120

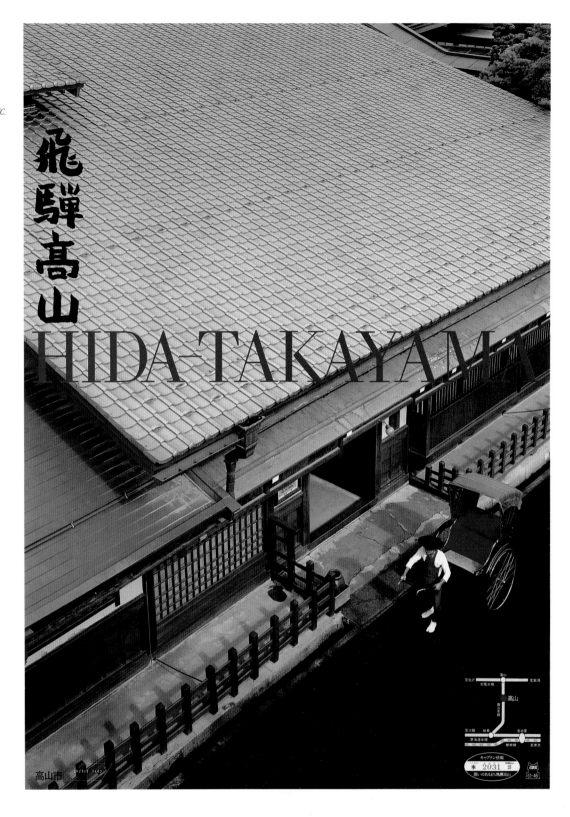

■**120** From a series of advertising posters issued by the Japanese railways. Shown is a popular tourist area of the city of Hida-Takayama. (JPN)

■**120** Werbeplakat der japanischen Eisenbahngesellschaft, auf dem ein von Touristen häufig besuchter Teil der Stadt Hida-Takayama abgebildet ist. (JPN)

■**120** Affiche publicitaire de la Société nationale des chemins de fer japonais. On y voit un quartier de la ville de Hida-Takayama très prisé des touristes. (JPN)

ART DIRECTOR:
Ikko Tamaka

DESIGNER:
Ikko Tamaka

PHOTOGRAPHER:
Irving Peng

AGENCY:
Ikko Tanaka Design Studio

CLIENT:
Issey Miyake International

■ **121–125**

ISSEY   MIYAKE   1987

ISSEY   MIYAKE   1987

ISSEY   MIYAKE   1987

ISSEY   MIYAKE   1987

■ **121–125** Posters from an advertising campaign for luxury clothing by the famous Japanese fashion designer Issey Miyake. (JPN)

■ **121–125** Plakate aus einer Kampagne für extravagante Kleidung des berühmten japanischen Modeschöpfers Issey Miyake. (JPN)

■ **121–125** Affiches pour une campagne publicitaire du grand couturier japonais Issey Miyake: vêtements extravagants. (JPN)

ISSEY　　　　　MIYAKE　　　　　1987

ART DIRECTOR:
Gene Mydlowski

DESIGNER:
Gene Mydlowski

PHOTOGRAPHER:
Gene Mydlowski

AGENCY:
Gene Mydlowski
Art Direction

CLIENT:
Pucci International

■126

ART DIRECTOR:
Pierre Neumann

DESIGNER:
Pierre Neumann

PHOTOGRAPHER:
Magalie Koenig

AGENCY:
Pierre Neumann

CLIENT:
Noblesse Oblique

■127

■**126** Poster for a new collection of window display dummies by French designer Andrée Putman. Two-color print: silver tone with black overprint. (USA)

■**127** Advertising poster for contemporary jewelry at the Boutique *Noblesse Oblique* in Lausanne. (SWI)

■**128, 129** Shop poster issued by *Levi Strauss* for their faded women's jeans, and also to promote their fashion style "Culture Clash", – a fashion in which various patterns and colors are allowed. (USA)

■**126** Plakat für eine neue Kollektion von Schaufensterpuppen der französischen Designerin Andrée Putman. Zweifarbendruck: Silberton mit schwarzem Überdruck. (USA)

■**127** Werbeplakat für zeitgenössischen Schmuck der Boutique *Noblesse Oblique* in Lausanne. (SWI)

■**128, 129** Ladenplakate der Firma *Levi Strauss* für ihre ausgewaschenen Damen-Jeans und den von ihnen propagierten Modestil «Culture Clash», bei dem verschiedene Muster und Farben erlaubt sind. (USA)

■**126** Affiche pour une nouvelle collection de mannequins d'étalages conçue par la décoratrice française Andrée Putman. Bichromie: ton argenté, surimpression en noir. (USA)

■**127** Affiche publicitaire pour les bijoux contemporains de la boutique lausannoise *Noblesse Oblique*. (SWI)

■**128, 129** Affiches intérieures de la société *Levi Strauss* pour ses jeans dames délavés et le style qu'ils propagent: «Culture Clash» (conflit de civilisations), autorisant divers dessins et coloris. (USA)

ART DIRECTOR:
Jennifer Morla
DESIGNER:
Jennifer Morla
PHOTOGRAPHER:
Matthew Rolston
AGENCY:
Morla Design, Inc.
CLIENT:
Levi Strauss & Co.
■**128**

ART DIRECTOR:
Jennifer Morla
DESIGNER:
Jennifer Morla
PHOTOGRAPHER:
Brad Mollath
AGENCY:
Morla Design, Inc.
CLIENT:
Levi Strauss & Co.
■**129**

ART DIRECTOR:
H. Ross Feltus

DESIGNER:
H. Ross Feltus

ILLUSTRATOR:
Rolf Isken/Margret Gnoth

PHOTOGRAPHER:
H. Ross Feltus

STUDIO:
H. Ross Feltus Photography

CLIENT:
Ton sur Ton

■ 130–138

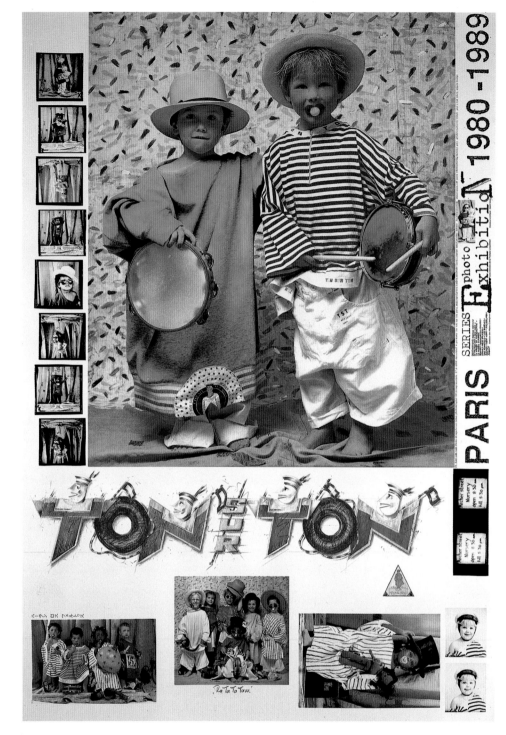

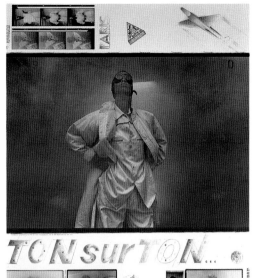

■ **130–138** Examples from a series of posters distributed worldwide with hand colored, sepia-toned black-and-white photographs for sports fashions by *Ton sur Ton*. The posters *130, 133, 135* and *137* are H. Ross Feltus' contribution to a touring exhibition on the fashions of 1980 to 1989, under the auspices of the French Ministry for Foreign Affairs.

■ **130–138** Beispiele aus einer Serie von weltweit verwendeten Plakaten mit handkolorierten, sepia-getönten Schwarzweiss-Aufnahmen für sportliche Mode der Firma *Ton sur Ton*. Die Plakate *130, 133, 135* und *137* sind der Beitrag von H. Ross Feltus zu einer Wanderausstellung über Mode zwischen 1980 und 1989 unter dem Patronat des französischen Aussenministeriums.

■ **130–138** Diverses affiches figurant dans une série diffusée dans le monde entier pour les modes sports de la société *Ton sur ton*. Photos noir et blanc teintées sépia, coloriées main. Les affiches *130, 133, 135, 137* représentent la contribution de H. Ross Feltus à une exposition itinérante de la mode entre 1980 et 1989 organisée sous le patronat des Affaires étrangères.

shu uemura cosmetics inc
5-7-17 Minami Aoyama, Minato-ku, Tokyo
107, Japan Tel 03(407)3421

パントマイムも、シャンソンも習った。だが、人前で演じるのは、恥かしい。

ART DIRECTOR:
Daisuke Nakatsuka

DESIGNER:
Yuko Suzuki/Masato Isobe

PHOTOGRAPHER:
Yoichi Nagata

AGENCY:
Nakatsuka Daisuke Inc.

CLIENT:
Shu Uemura Cosmetics Inc.

■ **139–143**

■ **139–143** The cosmetic company *Shu Uemura* promotes its products on these posters with the strange silhouettes of women enveloped in fabrics and with very unusual slogans: *139* "I studied pantomime and singing, but I am ashamed to appear in public." *140* "I always wanted to be a revolutionary, now I am a cosmetician." *141* "I own boutiques in Paris, New York, Aoyama and Kumamoto. Guess who I am." *142* "I was a new film discovery, but before I was aware of it I was a makeup artist." *143* "I have made up many Hollywood stars, but to make up an ordinary face is more difficult." (JPN)

■ **139–143** Mit eingepackten Frauenkörpern wirbt die Firma *Shu Uemura* für ihre Kosmetikprodukte: *139* «Ich habe Pantomime und Gesang studiert, aber ich schäme mich, in der Öffentlichkeit aufzutreten.» *140* «Ich wollte immer Revolutionärin werden, und nun bin ich Kosmetikerin geworden.» *141* «Ich habe Boutiquen in Paris, New York, Aoyama und Kumamoto. Raten Sie mal, wer ich bin.» *142* «Ich war eine Neuentdeckung beim Film, und ehe ich mich versah, war ich Maskenbildnerin.» *143* «Ich habe viele Gesichter von Hollywood-Stars geschminkt, aber ein gewöhnliches Gesicht zu schminken, ist schwieriger.» (JPN)

■ **139–143** La société *Shu Uemura* utilise pour sa publicité des nus féminins sous emballage: *139* «J'ai étudié la pantomime et le chant, mais j'ai honte de me produire en public.» *140* «J'ai toujours voulu être révolutionnaire, et me voilà esthéticienne.» *141* «J'ai des boutiques à Paris, New York, Aoyama et Kumamoto. Devinez qui je suis.» *142* «J'ai été découverte au cinéma, et avant que je m'en sois rendu compte, j'ai pris le chemin d'une nouvelle profession: celle de maquilleuse.» *143* «J'ai maquillé pas mal de vedettes à Hollywood, mais je vous assure qu'il est bien plus difficile de maquiller un visage ordinaire.» (JPN)

ART DIRECTOR:
Leslie Barnett

PHOTOGRAPHER:
Oliviero Toscani

AGENCY:
Esprit Design Studio

CLIENT:
Esprit De Corp.

■**144, 145**

ART DIRECTOR:
Leslie Barnett
PHOTOGRAPHER:
Oliviero Toscani
AGENCY:
Esprit Design Studio
CLIENT:
Esprit De Corp.
■**146, 147**

■**144–147** Examples from a poster campaign for *Esprit* sports fashions. *144, 146* and *147* bear the slogan "Holiday '86", *145* shows an example from the fall collection. (GER)

■**144–147** Beispiele aus einer Plakatkampagne für sportliche Mode der Firma *Esprit. 144, 146* und *147* stehen unter dem Motto «Ferien '86», *145* zeigt ein Beispiel aus der Herbstkollektion. (GER)

■**144–147** Affiches figurant dans une campagne de la société *Esprit* en faveur de ses vêtements de sport. *144, 146, 147* pour les «Vacances 86», *145* pour la collection d'automne. (GER)

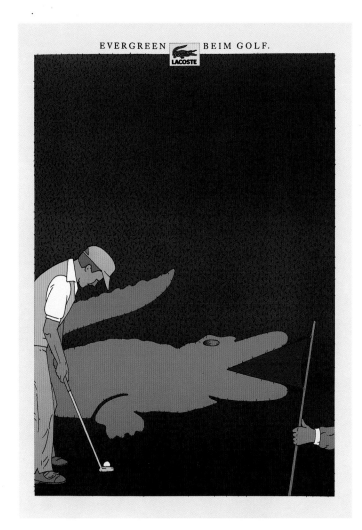

EVERGREEN BEIM GOLF.

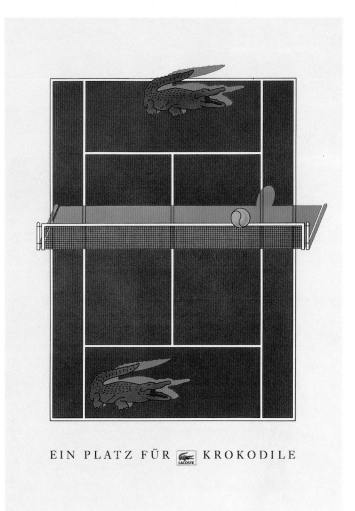

EIN PLATZ FÜR KROKODILE

ART DIRECTOR:
Dietrich Ebert

DESIGNER:
Dietrich Ebert/Carl Fritz

ARTIST:
Dietrich Ebert

AGENCY:
Alain Fion

CLIENT:
Yello Sport GmbH

■ 148—150

DAS VORBILD

■**148–150** *Lacoste* promotes its golf, tenniswear and shirts on these posters. (GER)

■**151** "Unfortunately, there are some running problems even the *Brooks Kinetic Wedge* can't solve." Advertising poster for a sports shoe. (USA)

■**148–150** Mit diesen Plakaten wirbt die Firma *Lacoste* für ihre Golf- und Tennisbekleidung sowie für ihre Hemden. (GER)

■**151** «Leider gibt es immer noch einige Situationen, die sogar ein *Brooks-Kinetic-Wedge*-Schuh nicht lösen kann.» Plakat für einen Sportschuh. (USA)

■**148–150** Affiches *Lacoste* pour des tenues de golf et de tennis *(149* «De la place pour les crocodiles») et des chemises. (GER)

■**151** «Il y a malheureusement encore des problèmes de course que même des chaussures *Brooks-Kinetic-Wedge* ne sauraient résoudre.» Affiche pour des chaussures de sport. (USA)

ART DIRECTOR:
HOUMAN PIRDAVRI
PHOTOGRAPHER:
STEVE UMLAND
AGENCY:
FALLON MCELLIGOTT
CLIENT:
BROOKS
■**151**

Unfortunately, there are some running problems even the Brooks Kinetic Wedge can't solve.

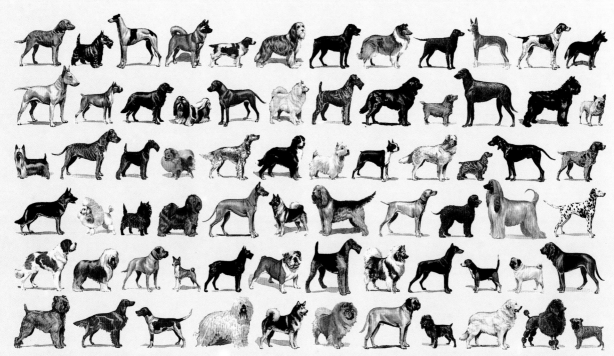

Now Hush Puppies come in just as many styles and sizes.

In 1958, Hush Puppies introduced a comfortable, basic suede shoe. It was a big hit. In fact, so big that thirty years later a lot of people still think of that shoe when they think of Hush Puppies. In reality, there are over 130 other Hush Puppies styles. Some just as traditional as the original, others more contemporary. There are stylish heels and classic business pumps for women. Dressy loafers and power wing tips for men. Even a full line of children's shoes. Look for us at the National Shoe Fair and FFANY. See what good breeding has done for the Hush Puppies line. Men's Line: Booth 2818, Jacob Javits Center. Women's Line: Hush Puppies Showroom, 717 5th Ave. at 56th Street.

ART DIRECTOR:
Mark Johnson
ARTIST:
E. M. Stevenson
AGENCY:
Fallon McElligott
CLIENT:
Hush Puppies
■**152**

■**152** "Now *Hush Puppies* come in just as many styles and sizes." Poster for a national shoe exhibition issued by the shoe company *Hush Puppies*. (USA)

■**153–155** Examples from a poster series for *Hush Puppies*. The company's canine symbol demonstrates in his own manner the particular characteristics of the various models. *153* is for a light office shoe for men, *154* pumps for the discerning and *155* ventilated sports shoes. (USA)

■**152** «Sehen Sie selbst, was dank guter 'Zucht' aus den *Hush-Puppies*-Modellen geworden ist» – Plakat der Schuhfirma *Hush Puppies* zur nationalen Schuhausstellung. (USA)

■**153–155** Beispiele aus einer Plakatserie für *Hush Puppies*. Das «Firmensymbol» demonstriert auf seine Weise die besonderen Eigenschaften der verschiedenen Modelle: *153* Hier der leichte Herrenschuh fürs Büro, *154* der Pumps für Anspruchsvolle und *155* der luftige Freizeitschuh. (USA)

■**152** «Les *Hush Puppies* existent maintenant en autant de styles et pointures différentes» – Affiche du chausseur *Hush Puppies* à l'occasion de l'exposition nationale de la chaussure. (USA)

■**153–155** Echantillons d'une série d'affiches *Hush Puppies*. L'animal emblématique démontre les qualités des différents modèles: *153* le soulier léger pour ces messieurs les ronds-de-cuir, *154* l'escarpin pour élégantes sophistiquées, *155* la chaussure de loisirs aérée à souhait. (USA)

Corporate Hush Puppies.

Dress Lites with our super-lightweight soles. They'll make someone at the office drool.

Sophisticated Hush Puppies.

Our classic pumps. For those with a nose for the finer things.

Ventilated Hush Puppies.

Will people ever stop panting over these shoes? Cool mesh casuals, in colors and tropical prints.

ART DIRECTOR:
Bob Barrie
PHOTOGRAPHER:
Rick Dublin
AGENCY:
Fallon McElligott
CLIENT:
Hush Puppies
■ 153–155

ART DIRECTOR:
Cheryl Heller

DESIGNER:
Cheryl Heller/
Nick Kaldenbaugh

PHOTOGRAPHER:
Annie Leibovitz

AGENCY:
Heller Breene

CLIENT:
Weebok

■**156, 157**

ART DIRECTOR:
Cheryl Heller
DESIGNER:
Cheryl Heller/
Nick Kaldenbaugh
PHOTOGRAPHER:
Annie Leibovitz
AGENCY:
Heller Breene
CLIENT:
Weebok
■**158, 159**

■**156–159** Posters from an advertising campaign by *Reebok* for their *Weebok* baby shoes recommended for babies of every race and color. The slogan "Baby, we're with you every step of the way" appears throughout the campaign. (USA)

■**156–159** Plakate aus einer Werbekampagne von *Reebok* für ihre Babyschuhe *Weebok*, die für alle Babys dieser Welt empfohlen werden. «Wir begleiten Dich auf all Deinen Wegen», verspricht der Slogan. (USA)

■**156–159** Affiches pour une campagne *Reebok* mettant en vedette les chaussures de bébé *Weebok* pour les bébés de toutes les races. «Nous t'accompagnons à chacun de tes pas dans la vie», telle est la promesse figurant sur chaque affiche. (USA)

shu uemura cosmetics inc

女性の数だけ、色がある。わたしの名は、シュウ ウエムラ。

shu uemura cosmetics inc

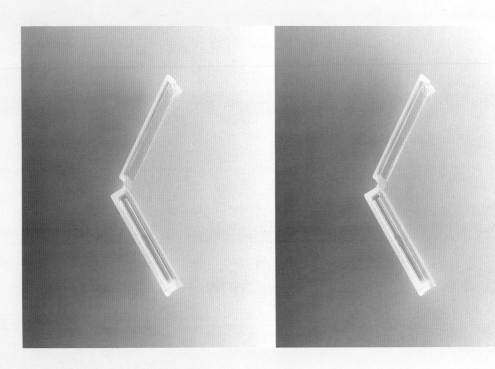

言葉よりまえに、色がある。わたしの名は、シュウ ウエムラ。

有名です。シュウ ウエムラの洗顔オイル。

名作です。シュウ ウエムラの洗顔オイル。

◄ **ART DIRECTOR:**
Daisuke Nakatsuka

DESIGNER:
Masato Isobe/Sonomi Sato/
Masako Ikumi

PHOTOGRAPHER:
Shozo Nakamura

AGENCY:
Nakatsuka Daisuke Inc.

CLIENT:
Shu Uemura Cosmetics Inc.

■ **160, 161**

ART DIRECTOR:
Daisuke Nakatsuka

DESIGNER:
Masato Isobe/Masako Ikumi

PHOTOGRAPHER:
Shozo Nakamura

AGENCY:
Nakatsuka Daisuke Inc.

CLIENT:
Shu Uemura Cosmetics Inc.

■ **162, 163**

■**160–163** Several examples from a series of posters by the Japanese cosmetic firm *Shu Uemura. 160* "Every woman can find her color here, and my name is *Shu Uemura." 161* "Before the word was the idea, and the idea was *Shu Uemura." 162* "It's a masterpiece, *Shu Uemura* cleansing oil." *163* "It is famous, *Shu Uemura* cleansing oil." (JPN)

■**160–163** Beispiele aus einer Serie von Plakaten der japanischen Kosmetikfirma *Shu Uemura. 160* «Hier kann jede Frau ihre Farbe finden. Und ich heisse *Shu Uemura.» 161* «Vor dem Wort war die Idee. Und die Idee war *Shu Uemura.» 162* «Es ist ein Meisterwerk, *Shu Uemuras* Reinigungsöl.» *163* «Es ist berühmt, *Shu Uemuras* Reinigungsöl.» (JPN)

■**160–163** Exemples d'affiches figurant dans une série de la société japonaise de cosmétiques *Shu Uemura. 160* «Ici, chaque femme peut trouver sa couleur favorite. Et je m'appelle *Shu Uemura.» 161* «Avant le verbe, il y avait l'idée. Et l'idée s'appelait *Shu Uemura.» 162, 163* Eloge de l'huile *Shu Uemura* pour les soins de la peau, qualifiée de chef-d'œuvre. (JPN)

■**164** Promotional poster for the Italien firm *Belfe*, producer of ski and tennis clothing. (ITA)

■**165** Poster issued by a gift boutique in Vevey. (SWI)

■**166** Advertising poster for a new chair design in folded steel, by Per Arnoldi. (DEN)

■**164** Werbeplakat der italienischen Firma *Belfe*, Hersteller von Ski- und Tennisbekleidung. (ITA)

■**165** Für eine Geschenkboutique in Vevey. (SWI)

■**166** Werbeplakat für eine neue Stuhlkreation aus gefalztem Stahl von Per Arnoldi. (DEN)

■**164** Affiche publicitaire de la société italienne *Belfe*, qui fabrique des vêtements de ski et de tennis. (ITA)

■**165** Pour une boutique de cadeaux veveysanne. (SWI)

■**166** Affiche publicitaire pour un nouveau siège de Per Arnoldi réalisé en acier plié. (DEN)

ART DIRECTOR:
Peter Bulach
DESIGNER:
Reinhard Eisele
PHOTOGRAPHER:
Manfred Dilling
AGENCY:
Eisele/Bulach & Partner
CLIENT:
Belfe Sportswear
■**164**

BELFE FASHION. SKI AND TENNIS. EXCLUSIVE. MADE IN ITALY

ART DIRECTOR:
Peter Scholl

DESIGNER:
Peter Scholl

PHOTOGRAPHER:
Marco Paoluzzo

AGENCY:
Scholl's Office

CLIENT:
M. L. Gasser

■165

ART DIRECTOR:
Per Arnoldi

DESIGNER:
Per Arnoldi

PHOTOGRAPHER:
Finn Rosted

AGENCY:
Lone Michelsen
Grafisk Konsulent

CLIENT:
Kjelstrup Furniture

■166

ART DIRECTOR:
Gina Morehead
PHOTOGRAPHER:
Jimmy Williams
AGENCY:
McKinney & Silver
CLIENT:
Stevens Carpet
■**167**

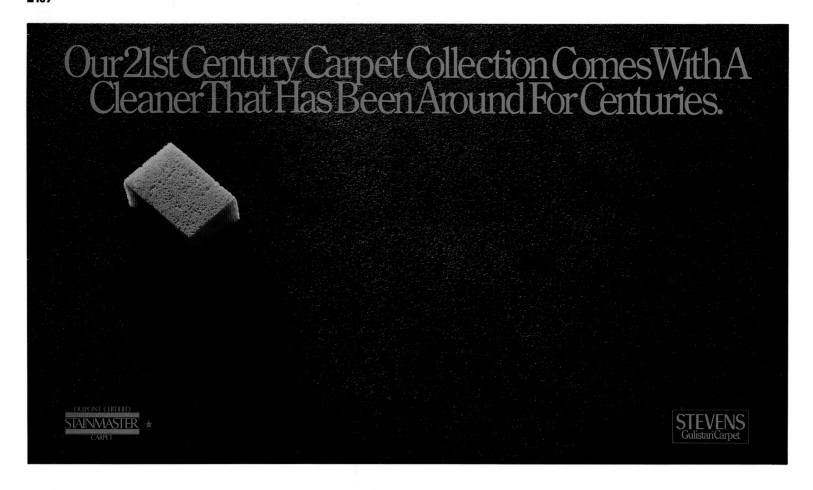

■**167** Advertising poster by *Stevens* for their dirt-resistant carpets. (USA)

■**168** "It isn't easy to kill a Pro Penn." Under this slogan *Penn* promotes its new tennis balls. (USA)

■**169** "The last thing a little girl wants to look like is a little girl." Promotional poster for children's sports clothes made by the American firm *Keds*. (USA)

■**167** Werbeplakat von *Stevens* für schmutzabstossende Teppichböden. (USA)

■**168** «Es ist nicht leicht, einen *Pro Penn* kaputt zu kriegen.» Mit diesem Slogan wirbt *Penn* für ihre neuen Tennisbälle. (USA)

■**169** «Das letzte, was sich ein kleines Mädchen wünscht, ist, wie ein kleines Mädchen auszusehen.» Werbeplakat für sportliche Kinderkleider von *Keds*. (USA)

■**167** Affiche publicitaire de *Stevens* pour des moquettes anti-poussière. (USA)

■**168** «Il n'est pas facile de venir à bout d'une *Pro Penn*.» Slogan utilisé par *Penn* pour la promotion de ses balles de tennis. (USA)

■**169** «La pire des choses, pour une petite fille, c'est d'avoir l'air d'une petite fille.» Affiche publicitaire pour les vêtements sportifs pour enfants de *Keds*. (USA)

ART DIRECTOR:
Houman Pirdavari
PHOTOGRAPHER:
Dave Jordano
AGENCY:
Fallon McElligott
CLIENT:
Penn Tennis Ball
■ **168**

ART DIRECTOR:
Beth Rokicki
PHOTOGRAPHER:
Carol Kaplan
CLIENT:
KEDS
■ **169**

◄ ART DIRECTOR:
Joe Duffy
DESIGNER:
Joe Duffyy
ARTIST:
Joe Duffy
STUDIO:
The Duffy Design Group
CLIENT:
Chaps Ralph Lauren
■**170**

ART DIRECTOR:
Cindy Lauper/
Stacy Drummond
DESIGNER:
Stacy Drummond
PHOTOGRAPHER:
Annie Leibovitz
AGENCY:
CBS Records
CLIENT:
CBS Records
■**171**

■**170** Outsize shop poster printed on packing paper to promote *Chaps* trousers by *Ralph Lauren.* (USA)

■**171** Promotional poster for Cindy Lauper's new album "True Colors". (USA)

■**170** Übergrosses Ladenplakat, auf Packpapier gedruckt, das für Hosen der Marke *Chaps* von *Ralph Lauren* wirbt. (USA)

■**171** Promotionsplakat für die neue Schallplatte «True Colors» der amerikanischen Sängerin Cindy Lauper. (USA)

■**170** Affiche intérieure surdimensionnée, sur papier d'emballage, pour les pantalons *Chaps* de *Ralph Lauren.* (USA)

■**171** Affiche promotionnelle pour le nouveau disque «True Colors» de la chanteuse américaine Cindy Lauper. (USA)

Una risposta alla crescente richiesta di cultura alimentare

Alimentazione e consumi

Le tematiche della ricerca, i contenuti, i limiti

Scienza e tecnologia

ART DIRECTOR:
Lauro Giovanetti

DESIGNER:
Lauro Giovanetti

STUDIO:
Lauro Giovanetti

CLIENT:
L'Unità

■ **172, 173**

THE SOPHISTICATED TRAVELER
PART 2 OF The New York Times Magazine

ART DIRECTOR:
Peter Schaefer

DESIGNER:
Peter Schaefer

ARTIST:
Dennis Ziemienski

CLIENT:
The New York Times

■174

■**172, 173** From a series of posters issued by the communist newspaper *L'Unità* in which they publicize their various sectors. Shown here are the posters for food and consumer goods and for science and technology. (ITA)

■**174** Advertising poster for a special supplement of the *New York Times* entitled "The Sophisticated Traveller". (USA)

■**172, 173** Aus einer Serie von Plakaten der kommunistischen Tageszeitung *L'Unità*, mit welchen sie für ihre verschiedenen Sektoren wirbt, hier für Ernährung und Konsum und für Wissenschaft und Technik. (ITA)

■**174** Werbeplakat für eine Sonderbeilage der *New York Times* unter dem Titel «der anspruchsvolle Reisende». (USA)

■**172, 173** Série d'affiches du quotidien communiste italien *L'Unità* attirant l'attention sur ses rubriques permanentes, ici les problèmes alimentaires et la consommation, la recherche scientifique et ses limites. (ITA)

■**174** Affiche publicitaire pour un supplément du *New York Times* qui s'adresse au «voyageur exigeant». (USA)

DESIGNER:
DAVID PAGE

PHOTOGRAPHER:
DAVE SIEGEL

CLIENT:
SIEGEL PHOTOGRAPHIC INC.

■176

■**175** In this tripartite poster the Swiss newspaper *Tages Anzei-ger* announces the fact that in future more articles will be devoted to art and culture. *(SWI)*

■**176** Promotion for photography and woodcuts by American Dave Siegel. (USA)

■**177** Advertising poster for the book *The Leading Edge.* (USA)

■**175** Mit diesem grossformatigen Werbeplakat weist die Schwei-zer Zeitung *Tages-Anzeiger* darauf hin, dass in Zukunft den The-men Kunst und Kultur mehr Artikel gewidmet werden. (SWI)

■**176** Werbung für Photographie und Holzschnitte des Amerika-ners Dave Siegel. (USA)

■**177** Werbeplakat für das Buch *The Leading Edge.* (USA)

■**175** Cette affiche publicitaire au très grand format permet au quotidien suisse *Tages-Anzeiger* d'informer ses lecteurs que l'art et la culture y auront désormais la part belle. (SWI)

■**176** Publicité pour les photographies et gravures sur bois de l'artiste américain Dave Siegel. (USA)

■**177** Affiche pour l'ouvrage *The Leading Edge.* (USA)

◀ **CREATIVE DIRECTOR:**
Jean Etienne Aebi
ART DIRECTOR:
Markus Stalder
ARTIST:
Markus Stalder
AGENCY:
Aebi & Partner
CLIENT:
Tages-Anzeiger AG
■**175**

ART DIRECTOR:
J. C. Suares
DESIGNER:
Gordon Harris
PHOTOGRAPHER:
Mike Fizer
AGENCY:
Stewart Tabori & Chang
CLIENT:
Stewart Tabori & Chang
■**177**

ART DIRECTOR:
Michael Mathias Prechtl
DESIGNER:
Michael Mathias Prechtl
ARTIST:
Michael Mathias Prechtl
CLIENT:
Büchergilde Gutenberg
■178

ART DIRECTOR:
Heinz Ita
DESIGNER:
Heinz Ita
CLIENT:
Diogenes Verlag
■179

■**178** Cover of *Utopia*, the most famous work by English humanist Sir Thomas More (1478-1535). Published in 1516, it describes "the best state" found on "the new isle called Utopia". From a poster series published by the Book Guild of Gutenberg. (GER)

■**179** The Swiss publisher *Diogenes* shows characters from its children's books to promote this sector of its publications. (SWI)

■**180** Promotional poster for the tenth anniversary of the book shop *Georg Büchner* in Darmstadt. (GER)

■**178** Titelbild zu dem bekanntesten Werk des englischen Staatsmannes und Humanisten Thomas Morus (1478-1535) *Utopia*, nach dem die literarische Gattung der Utopie benannt wurde. Aus einer Plakat-Edition der Büchergilde Gutenberg. (GER)

■**179** Mit Figuren aus seinen Kinderbüchern wirbt hier der Schweizer Verlag *Diogenes* für diese Buchkategorie. (SWI)

■**180** Werbeplakat zum 10jährigen Bestehen der Buchhandlung *Georg Büchner* in Darmstadt. (GER)

■**178** Illustration de couverture de l'œuvre la plus connue de l'homme d'Etat et humaniste anglais saint Thomas More (1478-1535), l'*Utopie*, qui donna son nom à tout un genre littéraire. Tiré d'un album d'affiches de la Guilde Gutenberg de Livre. (GER)

■**179** Des personnages tirés des livres d'enfants *Diogenes* servent à la promotion de cette catégorie de publications. (SWI)

■**180** Affiche publiée pour le 10e anniversaire de la librairie *Georg Büchner* de Darmstadt. (GER)

ART DIRECTOR:
Barbara & Gerd Baumann
DESIGNER:
Barbara & Gerd Baumann
AGENCY:
Baumann & Baumann
CLIENT:
Georg Büchner Buchladen
■**180**

ART DIRECTOR:
Ikko Tanaka

DESIGNER:
Ikko Tanaka/Kan Akita

AGENCY:
Ikko Tanaka Design Studio

CLIENT:
Morisawa & Co., Ltd.

■ **181, 182**

▶ **ART DIRECTOR:**
Roland Scotoni

DESIGNER:
R. Scotoni/P. Hürlimann

PHOTOGRAPHER:
Hans Feurer

AGENCY:
Young & Rubicam AG

CLIENT:
Kodak SA

■ **183–185**

■ **181, 182** Advertising poster for the neoclassic *(181)* and the ultra modern *(182)* version of the *Ryumin* lettering. (JPN)

■ **183–185** From a series of large-format advertising posters to promote *Kodacolor* Gold Film, under the slogan "It sees colors better." (SWI)

■ **181, 182** Werbeplakat für die neoklassizistische *(181)* und die ultra-moderne *(182)* Version der *Ryumin*-Schrift. (JPN)

■ **183–185** Grossformatige Werbeplakate zum Thema Farbintensität, die beim Photographieren mit *Kodacolor*-Gold-Filmen erreicht wird. (SWI)

■ **181, 182** Affiche publicitaire pour les versions néoclassique *(181)* et ultramoderne *(182)* de l'écriture *Ryumin*. (JPN)

■ **183–185** Affiches publicitaires au grand format mettant en vedette l'intensité des couleurs que l'on découvre en utilisant les films *Kodacolor* Gold. (SWI)

ART DIRECTOR:
Roland Scotoni
DESIGNER:
Roland Scotoni/
Claudia Bernet
PHOTOGRAPHER:
Christian Küenzi
AGENCY:
Young & Rubicam AG
CLIENT:
SBB/Marketing-Service
■ **186, 187**

ART DIRECTOR:
Robert Probst/
Mark Barensfeld

DESIGNER:
Robert Probst

ARTIST:
Robert Giusti

AGENCY:
Schenker, Probst,
Barensfeld

CLIENT:
Cincinnati Zoo

■ 188

■ **186, 187** Poster campaign by the Swiss Railways. *186* is to promote a special family ticket whereby children travel free and *187* is for special city tours. (SWI)

■ **188** Feline beasts – large and small – are the subject of this poster for the Cincinnati Zoo. (USA)

■ **186, 187** Beispiele aus einer Plakatkampagne der SBB (Schweizerische Bundesbahn), die hier auf verschiedene Vorteile aufmerksam macht. (SWI)

■ **188** Gross- und Wildkatzen sind das Thema dieses Plakates für den Zoo von Cincinnati. (USA)

■ **186, 187** Exemples d'affiches pour une campagne des CFF (Chemins de fer fédéraux suisses): «Le billet de famille: les enfants voyagent gratis»; «Nous entrons au cœur des villes.» (SWI)

■ **188** Les grands félins et les chats sauvages illustrent cette affiche promotionnelle pour le zoo de Cincinnati. (USA)

ART DIRECTOR:
Bob Barrie
AGENCY:
Fallon McElligott
CLIENT:
Adler Planetarium
■ 189–191

FREE MILKY WAY FOR THE KIDS.

The Adler Planetarium

SPACE AVAILABLE.

The Adler Planetarium

THE '87 NOVAS ARE HERE.

The Adler Planetarium

ART DIRECTOR:
Bob Barrie
AGENCY:
Fallon McElligott
CLIENT:
Adler Planetarium
■ 192–194

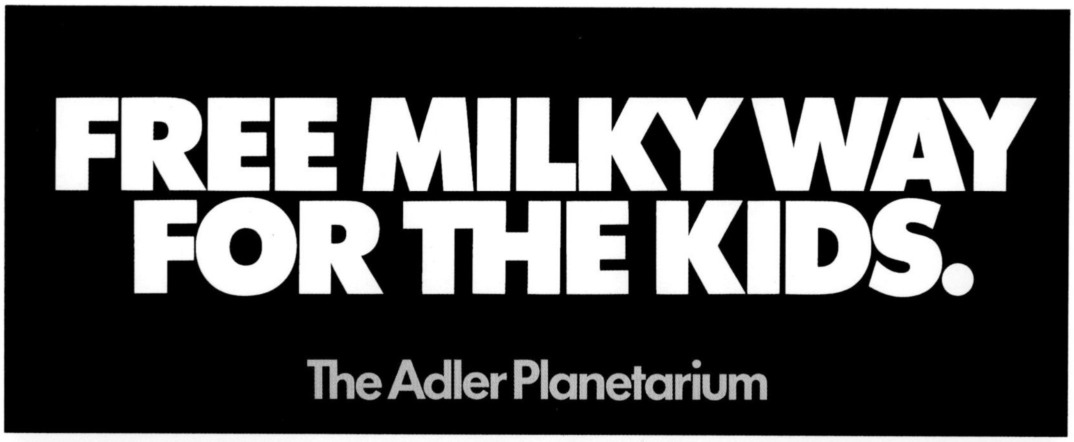

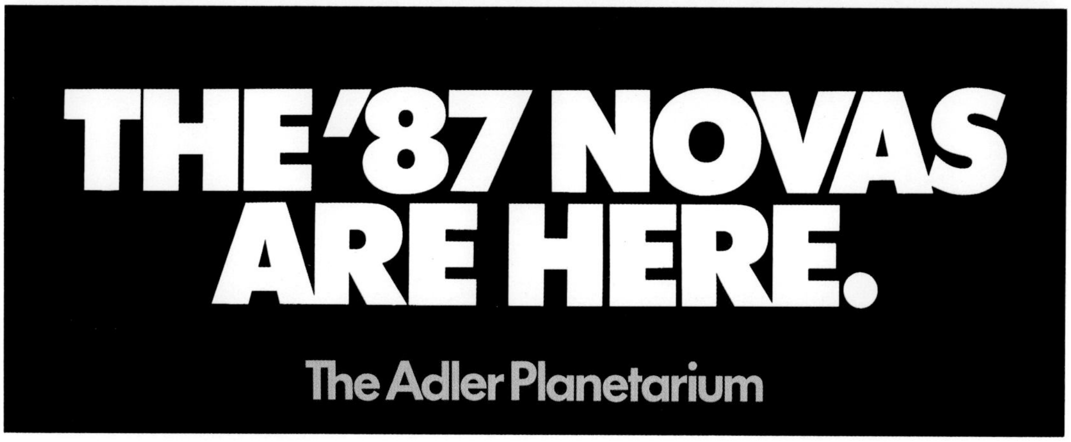

■ **189–194** Examples from a poster campaign issued by the Adler Planetarium in Chicago, Illinois, each bearing a catchy header relating to stars and space. (USA)

■ **189–194** Plakatkampagne des Adler Planetariums in Chicago, Illinois, das in populärer Werbesprache auf einige der zahlreichen Gründe für einen Besuch der Sternwarte hinweist. (USA)

■ **189–194** Exemples des affiches utilisées dans une campagne du Planétarium Adler de Chicago; jeux de mots divertissants pour vanter les charmes multiples d'une visite, (USA)

■**195** "Mirage Ahead." Real-estate agent's publicity poster to promote the sale of its waterfront homes. (USA)

■**196** With a pun in the header, this poster issued by the Minnesota Zoo announces some of its acquisitions – the North-American timber wolves. (USA)

■**197** Example from a series of advertising posters for a leisure park near New York, here with a distinct visual pun on the name of the area. (USA)

■**195** «Mirage voraus», gemeint ist der See Mirage, an dem Häuser zu verkaufen sind. Plakat für ein Maklerbüro. (USA)

■**196** Ein nordamerikanischer Timber-Wolf auf einem Plakat für den Zoo von Minnesota. Der Slogan: «Unsere neue Ausstellung ist ein Heuler.» (USA)

■**197** Beispiel aus einer Reihe von Plakaten für ein Erholungsgebiet in der Nähe von New York, hier mit deutlicher Anspielung auf den Namen der Region. (USA)

■**195** «Mirage droit devant» – soit le lac Mirage avec ses lotissements pavillonnaires. Affiche pour un courtier. (USA)

■**196** Loup gris d'Amérique du Nord sur une affiche du zoo du Minnesota: «Notre nouvelle exposition est un succès renversant» – «hurlant», dit l'affiche, car le loup *hurle*. (USA)

■**197** Affiche figurant dans une série touristique pour une aire de détente près de New York, les Catskills – nom qui contient une référence aux talents (skills) des G.O. (USA)

ART DIRECTOR:
David Gauger/Mary Orr
DESIGNER:
Mary Orr
PHOTOGRAPHER:
David Gauger
AGENCY:
Gauger & Silva, Inc.
CLIENT:
Dividend Development Corporation

■**195**

Our new exhibit is a howling success.

Timber Wolves at the Minnesota Zoo

ART DIRECTOR:
Bob Barrie
PHOTOGRAPHER:
Charles Palek
AGENCY:
Fallon McElligott
CLIENT:
Minnesota Zoo
■196

I ♥ N.Y.
CATSKILLS

ART DIRECTOR:
Milton Glaser
DESIGNER:
Milton Glaser
ARTIST:
Milton Glaser
AGENCY:
Milton Glaser, Inc.
CLIENT:
New York State Department of Commerce
■197

ART DIRECTOR:
LASSE LILJENDAHL
DESIGNER:
PETER KANDIMAA
AGENCY:
RÖNNBERG & CO
CLIENT:
VIKING LINE
■198–200

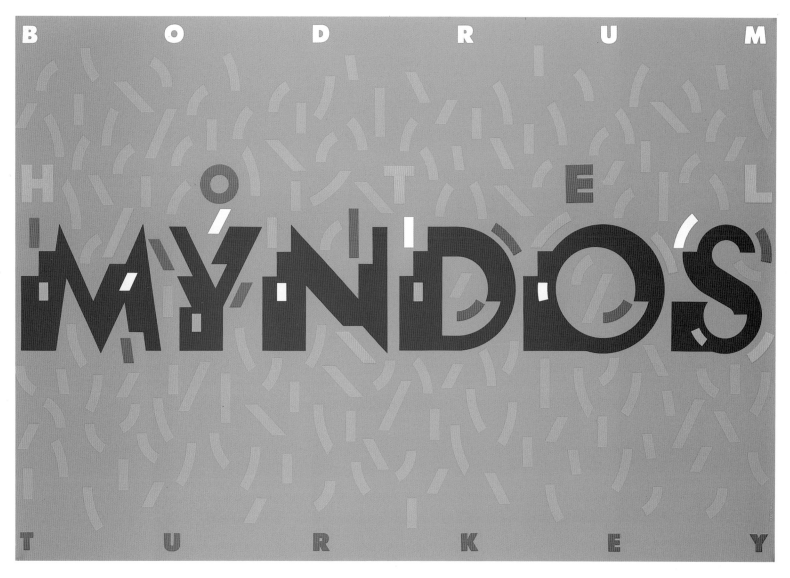

ART DIRECTOR:
BÜLENT ERKMEN
DESIGNER:
BÜLENT ERKMEN
ARTIST:
BÜLENT ERKMEN
AGENCY:
REKLAMEVI
CLIENT:
HOTEL MYNDOS
■ **201**

■ **198–200** Examples from a poster campaign for the *Viking Line* to publicize its special prices. *198:* Only by swimming to Finland would it come cheaper. *199:* The sailor semaphores the bargain rate for a family. *200:* Even for a chauffeur-driven limousine there are bargain trips. (SWE)

■ **201** Promotional poster for the Hotel Myndos in Bodrum, a well-known holiday resort in the south of Turkey. (TUR)

■ **198–200** Beispiele aus einer Plakatkampagne für die Schifffahrtslinie *Viking-Line*, die hier auf günstige Spezialtarife aufmerksam macht. *198:* Nur Schwimmen nach Finnland wäre billiger. *199* der Matrose signalisiert einen Familientarif. *200:* Auch für Überfahrten mit Auto und Chauffeur gibt es vorteilhafte Angebote. (SWE)

■ **201** Werbung für das Hotel Myndos in Bodrum, einem beliebten Ferienort im Süden der Türkei. (TUR)

■ **198–200** Examples d'affiches pour une campagne de la compagnie de navigation *Viking Line* et ses tarifs spéciaux avantageux. *198:* Aller en Finlande moins cher? Traversez à la nage. *199:* Signalisation d'un tarif de famille, *200:* Réduction même en cas de traversé en voiture avec un chauffeur. (SWE)

■ **201** Publicité pour l'hôtel Myndos de Bodrum, station balnéaire courue dans le sud de la Turquie. (TUR)

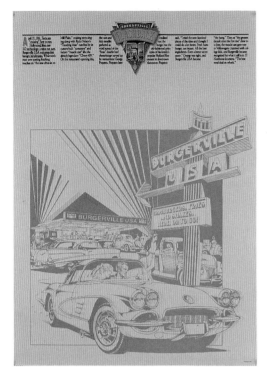

ART DIRECTOR:
Daniel Comte/
Christian Jaquet

DESIGNER:
Daniel Comte

PHOTOGRAPHER:
Bruno Bisang

AGENCY:
Atelier Jaquet AG

CLIENT:
Unifontes/Schweppes

 205

◀ **ART DIRECTOR:**
Warren Eakins
DESIGNER:
Warren Eakins
ARTIST:
*George Cheney/
Dan Mandish*
AGENCY:
*Borders, Perrin &
Norrander*
CLIENT:
Burgerville
■ **202–204**

ART DIRECTOR:
Chuck Anderson
PHOTOGRAPHER:
Rick Dublin
AGENCY:
Fallon McElligott
CLIENT:
Harry Singh's
■ **206**

The hottest dishes in town.

HARRY SINGH'S
CARIBBEAN RESTAURANT
611 W. Lake St., Minneapolis/Lake at Lyndale.

■ **202–204** To mark the occasion of its 25th anniversary the quick-snack Burgerville chain shows main events in 1961 under the header "Flashback". The pictures are three-dimensional and are only seen to the best advantage through 3-D specs. (USA)

■ **205** Tripartite poster (size 271,5 x 128 cm) to publicize *Schweppes* soft drinks. (SWI)

■ **206** "The hottest dishes in town." Poster with a real "burn hole" – unusual advertising poster for a restaurant offering Caribbean dishes. (USA)

■ **202–204** Aus Anlass ihres 25jährigen Bestehens wirbt die Schnellimbiss-Kette Burgerville auf diesen Plakaten mit Ereignissen aus dem Jahre 1961. Die Bilder sind erst durch die Brille richtig erkennbar, nämlich dreidimensional. (USA)

■ **205** Dreiteiliges Werbeplakat im Format 271,5 x 128 cm für *Schweppes*-Getränke. (SWI)

■ **206** «Die heissesten Gerichte der Stadt» – Plakat mit einem wirklichen Brandloch, eine ungewöhnliche Werbung für ein Restaurant mit Spezialitäten aus der Karibik. (USA)

■ **202–204** A l'occasion de son 25e anniversaire, la chaîne de snacks Burgerville met en scène, sur ces affiches, les événements de l'année 1961. Les lunettes spéciales jointes permettent seules de restituer l'image correcte en relief. (USA)

■ **205** Affiche publicitaire tripartite au format 271,5 x 128 cm pour les boissons *Schweppes*. (SWI)

■ **206** «Les mets les plus chauds de cette ville» – Affiche agrémentée d'un vrai trou de brûlure. Publicité insolite pour les mets épicés d'un restaurant dans le style des Caraïbes. (USA)

ART DIRECTOR:
Iwao Miyanaga/
Daisuke Nakatsuka

PHOTOGRAPHER:
Bishin Jumonji

AGENCY:
Nakatsuka Daisuke Inc.

CLIENT:
Hayashibara Biochemical
Laboratories

■ **207–210**

■ **207–210** Posters from an advertising campaign for *Prevent* sweetener. Short stories tell about the lives of the people portrayed. *207:* Hugh Hefner's bodyguard must train daily to keep his trim figure. If he stops, he'll get fat – unless he takes *Prevent. 208:* This singer constantly starved herself to keep slim before she discovered *Prevent. 209:* The two circus clowns, father and daughter, decided to go on a diet and slim down with the help of *Prevent. 210:* He says he's the son of Marilyn Monroe and Marlon Brando and doesn't worry about calories. Somebody should tell him about *Prevent.* (JPN)

■ **207–210** Aus einer Werbekampagne für *Prevent*-Süssstoff. Kurze Geschichten erzählen aus dem Leben der Abgebildeten. *207:* Dieser Leibwächter von Hugh Hefner muss täglich trainieren, um seine Figur zu erhalten. Wenn er damit aufhört, wird er dick, falls er nicht *Prevent* nimmt. *208:* Diese Sängerin hungerte dauernd, um schlank zu bleiben, bis sie eines Tages *Prevent* entdeckte. *209:* Diese beiden Zirkus-Clowns, Vater und Tochter, hoffen mit *Prevent* schlank zu werden. *210:* Er sagt, er sei der Sohn von Marilyn Monroe und Marlon Brando und kümmere sich nicht um Kalorien. Vielleicht müsste ihm jemand sagen, dass es *Prevent* gibt. (JPN)

■ **207–210** Pour une campagne publicitaire en faveur de l'édulcorant *Prevent*. Les personnes représentées ont chacune leur histoire «édulcorée» à raconter. *207:* Ce garde du corps de Hugh Hefner s'entraîne tous les jours pour garder la ligne. S'il l'oublie, seul *Prevent* peut le sauver. *208:* Cette cantatrice faisait la grève de la faim pour rester svelte, jusqu'au jour où elle découvrit *Prevent. 209:* Ces deux clowns, père et fille, décidèrent de commencer à maigrir à l'aide de *Prevent. 210:* Il prétend être le fils de Marilyn Monroe et de Marlon Brando et ne pas se soucier des calories qu'il ingurgite. Quelqu'un devrait-il lui signaler l'existence de *Prevent.* (JPN)

"If we're going to succeed, I need to know where our money is coming from and exactly where it's going."

"So where do we go from here?"

Apple
Business
Forum

Business Management Seminar
*Managing the Resources
of a Small Business*

"We should be producing a newsletter for our clients, but we don't have the time or money to do a high-quality job."

"So where do we go from here?"

Apple
Business
Forum

Desktop Publishing Seminar
*Creating High-Impact Business
Publications*

"We know what our financial picture is for the next four quarters. But we also need a plan for the next five years."

"So where do we go from here?"

Apple
Business
Forum

Desktop Productivity Seminar
*Planning, Analyzing, and
Presenting Business Projects*

"We'd like to have design workstations for all our engineers, but that's not realistic or cost-effective for our company."

"So where do we go from here?"

Apple
Business
Forum

Desktop Engineering Seminar
*Creating Professional Engineering
Designs*

ART DIRECTOR:
Ellen Romano
DESIGNER:
Ellen Romano
PHOTOGRAPHER:
Stuart Schwartz
AGENCY:
Apple Creative Services
CLIENT:
Apple Computer, Inc.
■ **211–215**

"There should be a quick, easy way
for us to get the information we
need to run our business—and to
get that information to the people
who can use it."

"So where do we go from here?"

Apple
Business
Forum

Desktop Communications Seminar
Sharing Information Among
Different Computers

■ **211–215** Series of posters for *Apple* computers in which soft-ware for *Apple MacIntosh* is offered for five different areas of business. (USA)

■ **211–215** Serie von Plakaten für *Apple* Computer, mit denen für fünf verschiedene Geschäftsbereiche Software angeboten wird, die für *Apple-MacIntosh*-Geräte erhältlich ist. (USA)

■ **211–215** Série d'affiches réalisée pour les ordinateurs *Apple*. On y offre des progiciels pour machines *Apple-MacIntosh* dans cinq domaines d'application différents. (USA)

ESB Speakers:
Unveil the Music

ESB Speakers:
Masters of Music

ART DIRECTOR:
Wynn Medinger

DESIGNER:
Wynn Medinger

ARTIST:
Mark Hess

AGENCY:
*Jones, Medinger,
Kindschi, Bushko*

CLIENT:
Mondial-Stereo

■ **216—218**

ESB Speakers:
Fidelity to Music

■ **216–218** Famous oil paintings (by Ingres, Holbein, and van Eyck) served Mark Hess as basis for this series of posters for *ESB* loudspeakers. The choice of portraits relates to the headers on each. (USA)

■ **219, 220** Advertising poster for products made by *Apple* computers. (USA)

■ **216–218** Berühmte Gemälde dienten Mark Hess als Vorlage für diese Serie von Plakaten für ESB-Lautsprecher. Die Wahl der Bilder bezieht sich auf die jeweiligen Slogans: «Enthülle die Musik», «Meister der Musik» und «Treue der Wiedergabe». (USA)

■ **219, 220** Plakatwerbung für verschiedene Geräte des Computer-Herstellers *Apple*. (USA)

■ **216–218** Mark Hess s'est inspiré de tableaux célèbres pour cette série d'affiches vantant les mérites des haut-parleurs ESB. Le choix des sujets s'inspire des slogans: «Dévoilez la musique», «Maîtres de la musique», «Fidélité de la reproduction». (USA)

■ **219, 220** Affiches pour divers ordinateurs *Apple*. (USA)

ART DIRECTOR:
Paul Pruneau
DESIGNER:
Thom Marchionna
PHOTOGRAPHER:
Tom Landecker
AGENCY:
Apple Creative Services
CLIENT:
Apple Computer, Inc.
■ **219**

ART DIRECTOR:
Paul Pruneau
DESIGNER:
Paul Pruneau
PHOTOGRAPHER:
Paul Matsuda
AGENCY:
Apple Creative Services
CLIENT:
Apple Computer, Inc.
■ **220**

It's time to change the errors of your ways.

The Apple IIc Typewriter Plus system. The better tool for typing.

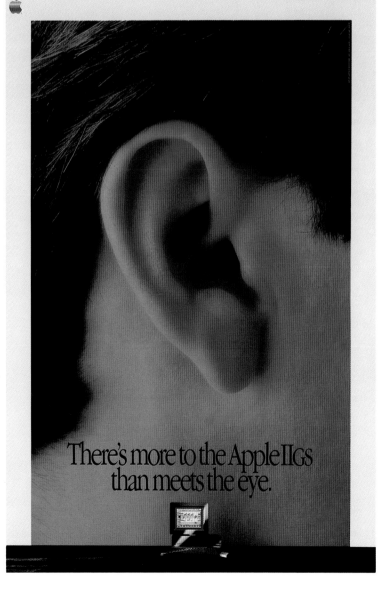

There's more to the Apple IIGS than meets the eye.

LAMBORGHINI COUNTACH 5000S

ART DIRECTOR:
David W. Bird

DESIGNER:
David W. Bird

PHOTOGRAPHER:
Neil B. Nissing

CLIENT:
Automobile Quarterly Publications

■ **221**

■ **221** One of the gallery edition posters published by the magazine *Automobile Quarterly.* (USA)

■ **222** "The Legendary Motorcycles of Germany." Poster issued by *BMW of North America.* (USA)

■ **221** Plakat aus einer von der Zeitschrift *Automobile Quarterly* herausgegebenen Galerie-Edition. (USA)

■ **222** «Die legendären Motorräder aus Deutschland.» Plakatwerbung für *BMW of North America.* (USA)

■ **221** Affiche figurant dans un portfolio d'art publié par la revue trimestrielle *Automobile Quarterly.* (USA)

■ **222** «Les motos allemandes légendaires». Affiche publicitaire pour *BMW of North America.* (USA)

THE LEGENDARY MOTORCYCLES OF GERMANY

ART DIRECTOR:
Kay Ritta

DESIGNER:
Kay Ritta

PHOTOGRAPHER:
Greg Jarim

AGENCY:
Ritta & Associates

CLIENT:
BMW of North America, Inc.

■**222**

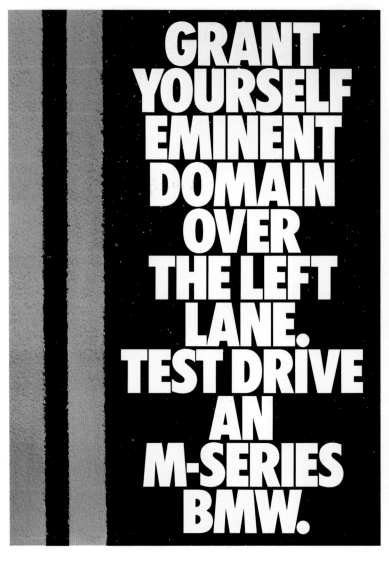

GRANT YOURSELF EMINENT DOMAIN OVER THE LEFT LANE. TEST DRIVE AN M-SERIES BMW.

FOR APPROXIMATELY THE SAME PRICE YOU CAN BUY INTO THE AUTOMOBILE'S FUTURE. OR ITS PAST.

ART DIRECTOR:
Beth Jeffe

DESIGNER:
Beth Jeffe

ARTIST:
Robert Ammirati

AGENCY:
Ammirati and Puris, Inc.

CLIENT:
BMW of North America, Inc.

■ **223**

ART DIRECTOR:
Peter Rauch

DESIGNER:
Meri Duffy

PHOTOGRAPHER:
Cailor/Resnick

AGENCY:
Ammirati and Puris, Inc.

CLIENT:
BMW of North America, Inc.

■ **224**

▶ **ART DIRECTOR:**
Jeff Vogt

DESIGNER:
Meri Duffy

PHOTOGRAPHER:
Jeffrey Zwart

AGENCY:
Ammirati and Puris, Inc.

CLIENT:
BMW of North America, Inc.

■ **225**

▶ **ART DIRECTOR:**
Peter Rauch

DESIGNER:
Beth Jeffe

PHOTOGRAPHER:
Jeffrey Zwart

AGENCY:
Ammirati and Puris, Inc.

CLIENT:
BMW of North America, Inc.

■ **226**

■ **223–226** Promotional posters intended to hang in *BMW* showrooms. *223:* A car poster without a car. The simple motif depicts the domain of the BMW, namely the passing lane. *224:* The bold diagonals – again, not the entire car – hint at the state of the art technology. *225:* The headline indicates that in a BMW-convertible there is more to enjoy than just the awareness of the road. *226:* An allusion that elegance and power can very well be combined. (USA)

■ **223–226** Für den Aushang in BMW-Showrooms bestimmte Plakate. Die Slogans: »Beherrschen Sie auch die linke Spur. Machen Sie eine Probefahrt mit einem BMW der M-Serie.« »Für ungefähr den gleichen Preis kann man sich in die Zukunft oder in die Vergangenheit des Automobils einkaufen.« »Erleben Sie ein intensiveres Gefühl für die Strasse und für alles, was darüber ist.« »Der BMW M6. Hinter seinem aristokratischen Profil verbirgt sich eine Leistungsfähigkeit von 240 km/h.« (USA)

■ **223–226** Affiches destinées à la PLV intérieure dans les locaux d'exposition BMW: »Assurez-vous la maîtrise de la piste de gauche. Essayez une BMW de la série M«. »Pour approximativement le même prix, vous pouvez vous assurer une tranche du futur ou du passé de l'automobile.« »Faites l'expérience d'un sens de la conduite plus intense et d'une perception supérieure de l'environnement.« »La BMW M6. Son profil aristocratique recouvre une puissance de 240 km/h.« (USA)

EXPERIENCE A HEIGHTENED AWARENESS OF THE ROAD. AND EVERYTHING ABOVE IT.

THE BMW 325i CONVERTIBLE

THE BMW M6. BENEATH ITS ARISTOCRATIC PROFILE LURKS A 150-MPH DISPOSITION.

BX

Nicht zu fassen.

ART DIRECTOR:
Ivica Maksimovic

DESIGNER:
Ivica Maksimovic

PHOTOGRAPHER:
Th. Herbrich/R. Jaschke

AGENCY:
RSCG Butter, Rang GmbH

CLIENT:
Citroen

■ **227**

■**227–230** A series of posters for the BX and AX series of
Citroën which aptly visualize the slogans: *227, 228, 230* – a word
play meaning "incredible" or "not able to grasp" (both touch and
comprehension) and *229* "The revolutionary *Citroën*".(GER)

■**227–230** Beispiele aus einer Serie von Plakaten für die BX-
und AX-Serie von *Citroën*, mit Interpretationen der Slogans »Nicht
zu fassen« (ergreifen und begreifen), und »Der revolutionäre
Citroën«. (GER)

■**227–230** Exemples d'affiches créées pour les séries BX et AX
de *Citroën*, interprétant les slogans »impensable/insaisissable« (jeu
de mots allemand sur 'fassen') et »La Citroën révolutionnaire« –
au pays de la révolution culturelle. (GER)

ART DIRECTOR:
IVICA MAKSIMOVIC
DESIGNER:
IVICA MAKSIMOVIC
PHOTOGRAPHER:
TH. HERBRICH/R. JASCHKE
AGENCY:
RSCG BUTTER, RANG GMBH
CLIENT:
CITROEN
■ **228**

ART DIRECTOR:
AXEL HINNEN
DESIGNER:
MICHAEL WEICKEN
PHOTOGRAPHER:
R. JASCHKE/R. WOLFF
AGENCY:
RSCG BUTTER, RANG GMBH
CLIENT:
CITROEN
■ **229**

ART DIRECTOR:
IVICA MAKSIMOVIC
DESIGNER:
IVICA MAKSIMOVIC
PHOTOGRAPHER:
TH. HERBRICH/R. JASCHKE
AGENCY:
RSCG BUTTER, RANG GMBH
CLIENT:
CITROEN
■ **230**

ART DIRECTOR:
Gary Slomka

ARTIST:
David Kimball

PHOTOGRAPHER:
Dick Voikin/Park Photo

AGENCY:
*D'Arcy Masius Benton &
Bowles*

CLIENT:
Cadillac Motor Car Division

■ **231, 232**

■ **231, 232** From a series of posters to publicize the new *Cadillac* model *Allante.* "The new spirit of *Cadillac.*" (USA)

■ **233** Poster issued by an American automobile trade magazine on behalf of *Porsche.* (USA)

■ **231, 232** Aus einer Serie von Werbeplakaten für das neue *Cadillac*-Modell *Allante.* "Der neue Geist von *Cadillac.*" (USA)

■ **233** Von einer amerikanischen Auto-Fachzeitschrift herausgegebenes Plakat für *Porsche.* (USA)

■ **231, 232** Affiches publiées dans une série publicitaire pour la nouvelle *Cadillac Allante:* «Le nouvel esprit *Cadillac.*» (USA)

■ **233** Affiche pour *Porsche* publiée par une revue professionnelle américaine de l'automobile. (USA)

ART DIRECTOR:
Richard M. Baron
DESIGNER:
Richard M. Baron
PHOTOGRAPHER:
Jeffrey Zwart
STUDIO:
Jeffrey Zwart
CLIENT:
Road & Track Specials
■ **233**

ART DIRECTOR:
Pat Burnham

PHOTOGRAPHER:
Kurt Markus

AGENCY:
Fallon McElligott

CLIENT:
US West

■ 234, 235

ART DIRECTOR:
Pat Burnham

PHOTOGRAPHER:
Jim Arndt

AGENCY:
Fallon McElligott

CLIENT:
US West

■ 236

ART DIRECTOR:
Pat Burnham
PHOTOGRAPHER:
Jim Arndt
AGENCY:
Fallon McElligott
CLIENT:
US West
■ **237**

Kick off your boots and join us at our hospitality suite.

USWEST

■ **234–237** Advertising campaign issued by *US West*, the telephone company serving the Western United States. The heritage of the hard working Westener is evoked. *237:* Invitation to *US West* employees to a reception during a conference. (USA)

■ **234–237** Aus einer Werbekampagne der amerikanischen Telephongesellschaft *US West.* «Unser Gebiet hat immer harte Arbeit bedeutet.» *237:* «Ziehen Sie Ihre Stiefel aus und seien Sie unser Gast.» Einladung an die Angestellten der *US West.* (USA)

■ **234–237** Affiches pour une campagne publicitaire de la société américaine des téléphones *US West:* «Notre territoire a toujours dû être conquis par un dur labeur.» *237:* «Otez vos bottes et venez nous rejoindre dans notre suite hospitalière.» (USA)

■**238** Poster for MCI Telecommunications. The relay runner symbolizes the firm's philosophy: spirit, determination, quality, activity, teamwork and pride. (USA)

■**239** Poster promotion for *Serien* room lighting. (GER)

■**240** Example from a poster series entitled "Famous Fools" issued by a lithographers and relating to complete devotion to the job. (USA)

■**241** Poster for Butera's restaurant in Houston. (USA)

■**238** Plakat für MCI Telecommunications, die mit diesem Staffelläufer die Firmenphilosophie versinnbildlicht: Geist, Entschlossenheit, Qualität, Aktivität, Teamwork, Stolz. (USA)

■**239** Plakatwerbung für *Serien*-Raumleuchten. (GER)

■**240** Aus einer Plakatserie unter dem Titel «Berühmte Narren» (hier Houdini) für eine Lithographenanstalt. Es geht um die vollkommene Hingabe an den Beruf. (USA)

■**241** Plakat für Butera's Restaurant in Houston. (USA)

■**238** Affiche pour MCI Telecommunications. Ce coureur de relais incarne les vertus prônées par l'entreprise: l'esprit, la détermination, la qualité, l'activité, l'équipe, la fierté. (USA)

■**239** Publicité pour les éclairages *Serien*. (GER)

■**240** Affiche publiée dans la série des «Fous célèbres» (ici, Houdini) pour un atelier de lithographie. Sont qualifiés de «fous» ceux qui s'identifient entièrement avec leur métier. (USA)

■**241** Affiche pour le restaurant Butera's de Houston. (USA)

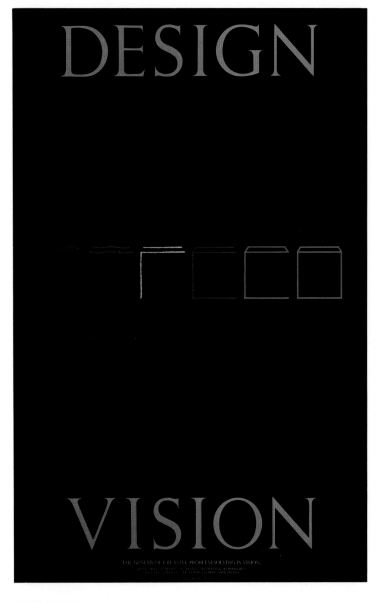

ART DIRECTOR:
Errol Beauchamp

DESIGNER:
Barry A. Merten

ARTIST:
Barry A. Merten

AGENCY:
The Beauchamp Group, Inc.

CLIENT:
The Beauchamp Group, Inc.

■ 242

ART DIRECTOR:
David Lock

DESIGNER:
Michael Adamos

ARTIST:
Michael Adamos

AGENCY:
Lock/Pettersen Ltd.

CLIENT:
IBM UK

■ 243

■ **242** "The genesis of creative problem-solving is vision." Self-promotional poster issued by the Beauchamp Group, Denver. (USA)

■ **243** Announcement poster for the *IBM* computer support service. At the touch of a finger a hardware and software information program can be called up. (GBR)

■ **244** Poster to promote music software known as the *Coda Collection,* for *Wenger Corporation.* (USA)

■ **242** «Der Ursprung kreativer Problemlösung ist Vision.» Eigenwerbung der Beauchamp Group, Inc., Denver. (USA)

■ **243** Ankündigung einer neuen IBM-Dienstleistung: Durch einen Fingerdruck auf dem Bildschirm kann ein Hardware & Software Informationsprogramm abgerufen werden. (GBR)

■ **244** Werbeplakat der *Wenger Corporation* für ihre Musik-Software, genannt *Coda Collection.* (USA)

■ **242** «La solution créatrice d'un problème naît de la vision.» Autopromotion du Beauchamp Group, Inc. de Denver. (USA)

■ **243** Annonce d'une nouvelle prestation IBM: il suffit de toucher l'écran du doigt pour que s'affiche un programme d'information sur les logiciels et matériels disponibles. (GBR)

■ **244** Affiche de la *Wenger Corporation* pour ses logiciels musicaux réunis dans la *Coda Collection.* (USA)

ART DIRECTOR:
Charles Spencer Anderson
DESIGNER:
Charles Spencer Anderson
ARTIST:
Charles Spencer Anderson
AGENCY:
The Duffy Design Group
CLIENT:
Wenger Corp.
■ 244

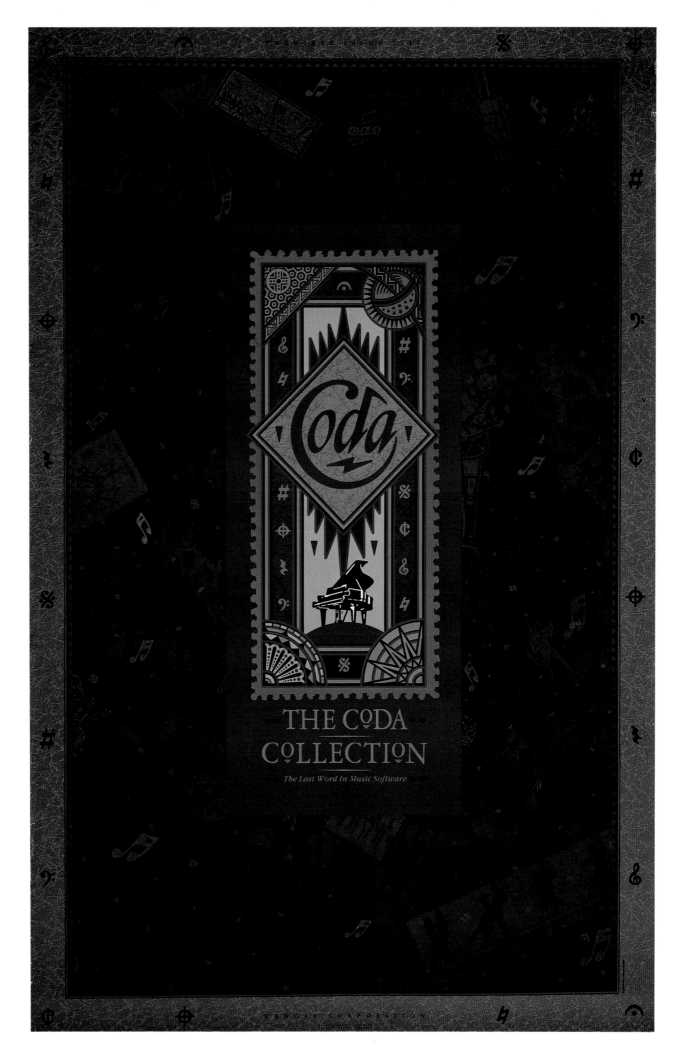

ART DIRECTOR:
Susan Berry
DESIGNER:
Susan Berry
ARTIST:
Susan Berry
AGENCY:
Boyles & Berry
CLIENT:
Ken Wray's Printing, Inc.
■**245**

ART DIRECTOR:
Mark Ashley
ARTIST:
Eric Henderson
AGENCY:
Cole Henderson Drake, Inc.
CLIENT:
Cole Henderson Drake, Inc.
■**246**

■**245** Self promotion for the printer Ken Wray. (USA)

■**246** "This year the creative director liked our Christmas card ideas so much, he decided to use them all." Season's greetings in poster size for the advertising agency Cole Henderson Drake, Atlanta. (USA)

■**247** Self-promotional poster for the German printers Ferd. Bahruth. "For people who want to see more, we print really super posters." (GER)

■**248** Three hundred and fifty-nine typefaces offered by the printers *Typeprocess* of Paris, are presented on this poster. (FRA)

■**245** Eigenwerbung der Druckerei Ken Wray. (USA)

■**246** »Die diesjährigen Vorschläge für eine Weihnachtskarte gefielen unserem Creative Director so gut, dass er beschloss, alle zu verwenden.« Weihnachts-/Neujahrsplakat der Werbeagentur Cole Henderson Drake, Atlanta, GA. (USA)

■**247** »Für Leute, die mehr sehen wollen, drucken wir richtig tolle Plakate.« Plakat für Eigenwerbung der Offsetdruckerei Ferd. Bahruth. (GER)

■**248** Mit diesem Plakat werden 359 Schrifttypen präsentiert, die die Setzerei *Typeprocess*, Paris, anbietet. (FRA)

■**245** Autopromotion de l'imprimeur Ken Wray. (USA)

■**246** »Cette année, les divers projets de carte de Noël ont tellement plu à notre directeur créatif qu'il a décidé de les utiliser tous.« Affiche de Noël et Nouvel An de l'agence de publicité Cole Henderson Drake, Atlanta, GA. (USA)

■**247** »Pour les gens qui veulent en voir pour leur argent, nous imprimons des affiches vraiment sensationnelles.« Affiche autopromotionnelle de l'imprimeur offset Ferd. Bahruth. (GER)

■**248** Affiche présentant 359 types de caractères disponibles à l'atelier de composition *Typeprocess* de Paris. (FRA)

ART DIRECTOR:
Holger Matthies

DESIGNER:
Holger Matthies

ARTIST:
Holger Matthies

CLIENT:
Ferd. Bahruth
Offsetdruckerei

■ **247**

ART DIRECTOR:
Garth Bell

DESIGNER:
Garth Bell

AGENCY:
Bell & Co.

CLIENT:
Typeprocess

■ **248**

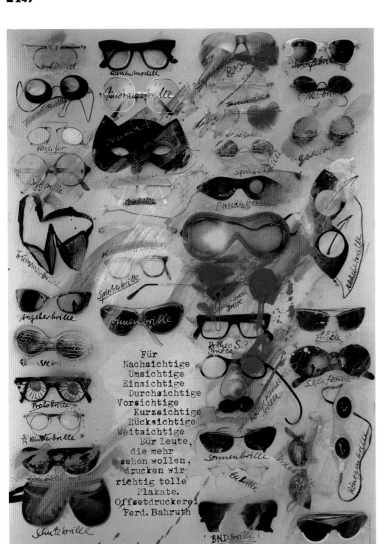

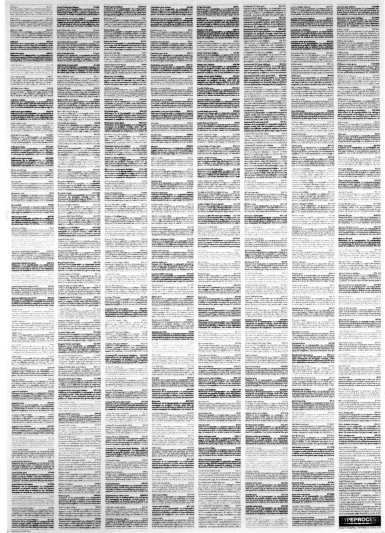

ART DIRECTOR:
Mark Anderson
DESIGNER:
Earl Gee
ARTIST:
Earl Gee/RJ Muna
STUDIO:
Mark Anderson Design
CLIENT:
AR Lithographers
■ **249**

ART DIRECTOR:
Ron Sullivan
DESIGNER:
Darrel Kolosta
ARTIST:
Darrel Kolosta
AGENCY:
Sullivan Perkins
CLIENT:
Artesian Press Inc.
■ **250**

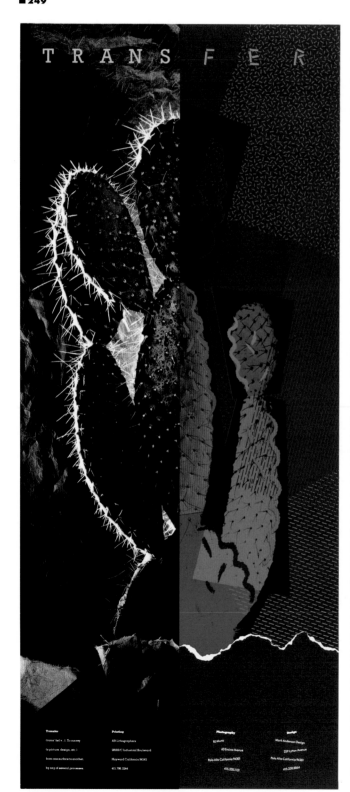

REGISTER NOW!

Are you getting out of school and trying to line up a job? Or even better, a career? One that's bright and unlimited. One where you can still work with your hands or work with computers, film, or the latest high tech machines. It pays to look into printing. See your counselor. And sign up today.

We are pleased to announce the arrival of Angela Dunkle, the first girl to be one of the guys at Fallon McElligott.

▲
▲ **DESIGNER:**
DICK MITCHELL
AGENCY:
RBMM & A/
THE RICHARDS GROUP
CLIENT:
PRINTING INDUSTRIES
ASSOCIATION
■ **251**

ART DIRECTOR:
PAT BURNHAM
PHOTOGRAPHER:
RICK DUBLIN
AGENCY:
FALLON MCELLIGOTT
CLIENT:
FALLON MCELLIGOTT
■ **252**

■ **249** Self promotion for the *AR* Lithographers *Hayward* of California. A picture or design can be transferred from one surface to another. (USA)

■ **250** Change of address for the printers Artesian Press. (USA)

■ **251** Plea to graduates to decide for a job in the printing trade. Poster issued by the Printing Industries Association. (USA)

■ **252** Poster for ad agency Fallon McElligott announcing the first girl to become "one of the guys." (USA)

■ **249** Ein Bild, Design etc. kann von einer Oberfläche auf eine andere «transferiert» werden. Eigenwerbung der AR Lithographers, Hayward, Kalifornien. (USA)

■ **250** Adressänderung der Druckerei Artesian Press Inc. (USA)

■ **251** Aufruf einer Druckerei-Vereinigung an College-Absolventen, sich für einen Beruf in ihrem Gewerbe zu entscheiden. (USA)

■ **252** Ankündigung der Werbeagentur Fallon McElligott, dass sich unter ihren «harten Typen» nun auch eine Frau befindet. (USA)

■ **249** Une image, une composition, etc. peuvent être «transférées» d'une surface à l'autre. Autopromotion d'AR Lithographers, une entreprise de Hayward, en Californie. (USA)

■ **250** Nouvelle adresse de l'imprimerie Artesian Press. (USA)

■ **251** «Annoncez-vous dès maintenant!» – Appel d'une association d'imprimeurs aux collégiens en quête d'un métier utile. (USA)

■ **252** Avis où une agence de publicité fait savoir que son équipe de «durs» compte désormais aussi une femme. (USA)

STOP

ONE FOR THE ROAD. YOU'RE INVITED TO ATTEND THE GRAND OPENING CELEBRATION OF BOARDWALK MOTOR CAR GROUPS NEW AMC/JEEP/RENAULT SHOWROOM ON THURSDAY SEPTEMBER 26 FROM 5 TO 9 PM. #1 BAIR ISLAND ROAD, REDWOOD CITY (TAKE WHIPPLE TURNOFF, EAST SIDE OF FREEWAY 101)

STOP

■ **253** Invitation by the Boardwalk Motor Car Group to the inauguration of their new exhibition rooms. (USA)

■ **254** "The decade - ComputerLand." Highlights in the ten years of this firm's history and its chain-store development are described in short sequences. (USA)

■ **253** Einladung der Boardwalk Motor Car Groups zur Einweihung ihrer neuen Ausstellungsräume. (USA)

■ **254** «10 Jahre ComputerLand» - in kurzen Sequenzen werden die Entstehungsgeschichte und die Entwicklung dieser auf Computer spezialisierten Ladenkette aufgeführt. (USA)

■ **253** Invitation des Boardwalk Motor Car Groups à l'inauguration de leurs nouvelles salles d'exposition. (USA)

■ **254** «Une décennie de ComputerLand» - bref aperçu des origines et du développement de cette chaîne de magasins spécialisés dans l'informatique et les ordinateurs. (USA)

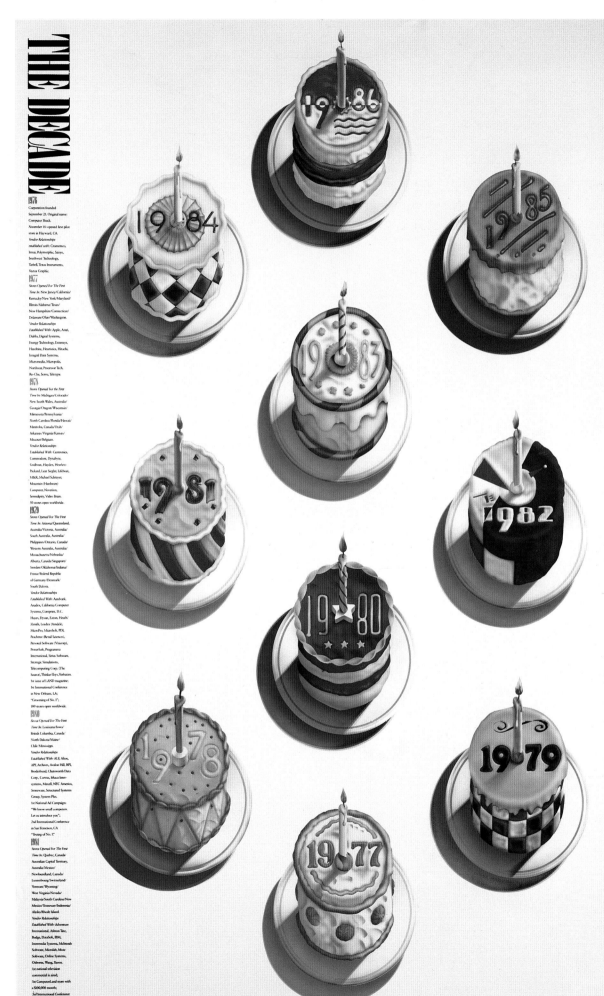

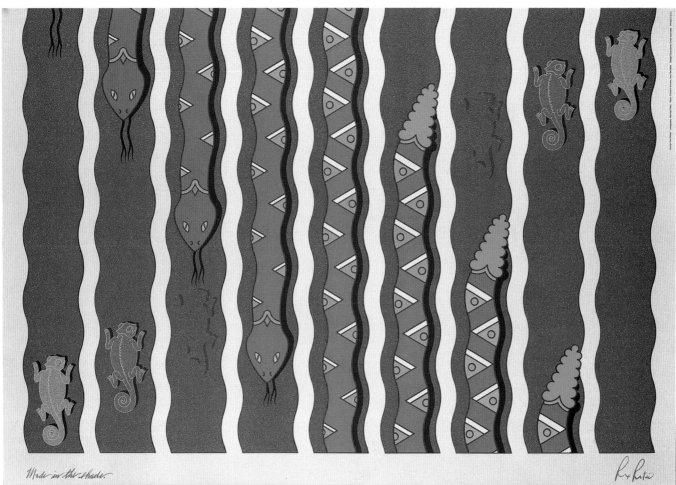

sequences

ART DIRECTOR:
James Cross
DESIGNER:
Rex Peteet
ARTIST:
Rex Peteet
AGENCY:
Cross & Associates
STUDIO:
*Sibley/
Peteet Design, Inc.*
CLIENT:
Simpson Paper Co.
■ 255

sequences

ART DIRECTOR:
*Roger Cook/
Don Shanosky*
DESIGNER:
Roger Cook
PHOTOGRAPHER:
Roger Cook
AGENCY:
*Cook and Shanosky
Assoc., Inc.*
CLIENT:
Simpson Paper Co.
■ 256

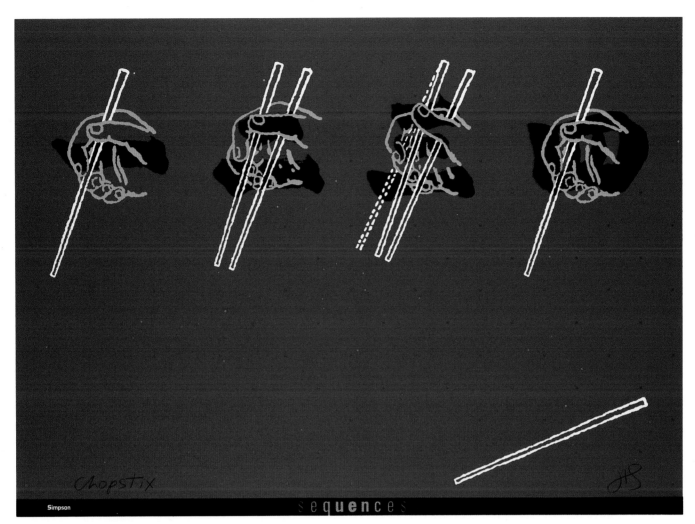

ART DIRECTOR:
JAMES CROSS/HENRY STEINER
DESIGNER:
HENRY STEINER
ARTIST:
HENRY STEINER
CLIENT:
SIMPSON PAPER CO.
■ 257

■ **255–257** Three examples from a series of posters commissioned by *Simpson* paper producers. Various renowned artists were asked to submit their ideas on the subject "sequences" to demonstrate the company's paper qualities. Shown is a sequence from nature, from life ("I was about 18"), and a sequence on the holding of chopsticks. (USA)

■ **255–257** Drei Beispiele aus einer Serie von Plakaten, die der Papierhersteller *Simpson* von verschiedenen Künstlern zum Thema «Abläufe» gestalten liess, um verschiedene Papierqualitäten zu zeigen. Hier ein Ablauf aus der Natur, der Ablauf eines Lebens («Ich war ungefähr 18») und eine Ablaufdarstellung für die Handhabung von Ess-Stäbchen. (USA)

■ **255–257** Trois exemples tirés d'une série d'affiches réalisées pour le compte du papetier *Simpson* par divers artistes sur le thème des «Processus séquentiels» pour présenter différentes qualités de papier: séquence évolutive dans la nature, processus du vieillissement («je devais avoir 18 ans»), décomposition du mouvement requis pour manger avec des baguettes. (USA)

ART DIRECTOR:
Kazumasa Nagai
DESIGNER:
Kazumasa Nagai
ARTIST:
Kazumasa Nagai
AGENCY:
Nippon Design Center
CLIENT:
Toppan Printing Co. Ltd.
■ **258, 259**

■**258–259** From a series of posters as self promotion for the Japanese printers *Toppan.* (USA)

■**260** Advertising poster of the *Shade* company for their carbon-free paper *Blackprint.* (USA)

■**258–259** Aus einer Serie von Plakaten zur Eigenwerbung der japanischen Druckerei *Toppan.* (USA)

■**260** Werbeplakat der Firma *Shade* für ihr kohlefreies Papier *Blackprint.* (USA)

■**258–259** Exemples d'affiches utilisées par l'imprimerie japonaise *Toppan* pour sa promotion. (USA)

■**260** Affiche publicitaire de la société *Shade pour son papier non carboné (Blackprint).* (USA)

DESIGNER:
Charles Spencer Anderson
ARTIST:
Joe Duffy
STUDIO:
The Duffy Design Group
CLIENT:
Shade
■260

ART DIRECTOR:
Dieter Zimmermann

DESIGNER:
Jörn Zimmermann

PHOTOGRAPHER:
Lajos Keresztes

PUBLISHER:
Art & Book Galerie Edition

■ **261–264**

■ **261–264** Posters on general sale issued by *art & book* (Gallery Edition) with photographs by Lajos Keresztes. The subject of the photographs is "Signs of Light". (GER)

■ **261–264** Im Handel erhältliche Plakate der Galerie Edition *art & book* mit Aufnahmen des Photographen Lajos Keresztes. Das Thema der Aufnahmen ist »Zeichen des Lichts«. (GER)

■ **261–264** Posters inclus dans le portfolio d'art *art & book* et représentant des œuvres du photographe Lajos Keresztes. Le thème de toutes ces photos: »Signes de lumière.« (GER)

ART DIRECTOR:
Greg Booth
DESIGNER:
Dick Mitchell
PHOTOGRAPHER:
Greg Booth
AGENCY:
RBMM & A/
The Richards Group
CLIENT:
Greg Booth/Color
Control
■265

▶ **ART DIRECTOR:**
Nancy Skolos
DESIGNER:
Nancy Skolos
PHOTOGRAPHER:
Thomas Wedell
AGENCY:
Skolos Wedell +
Raynor Inc.
CLIENT:
Berkeley Typographers
■266

GREENS AND GOLDS BY COLOR CONTROL

REDS BY GREG BOOTH

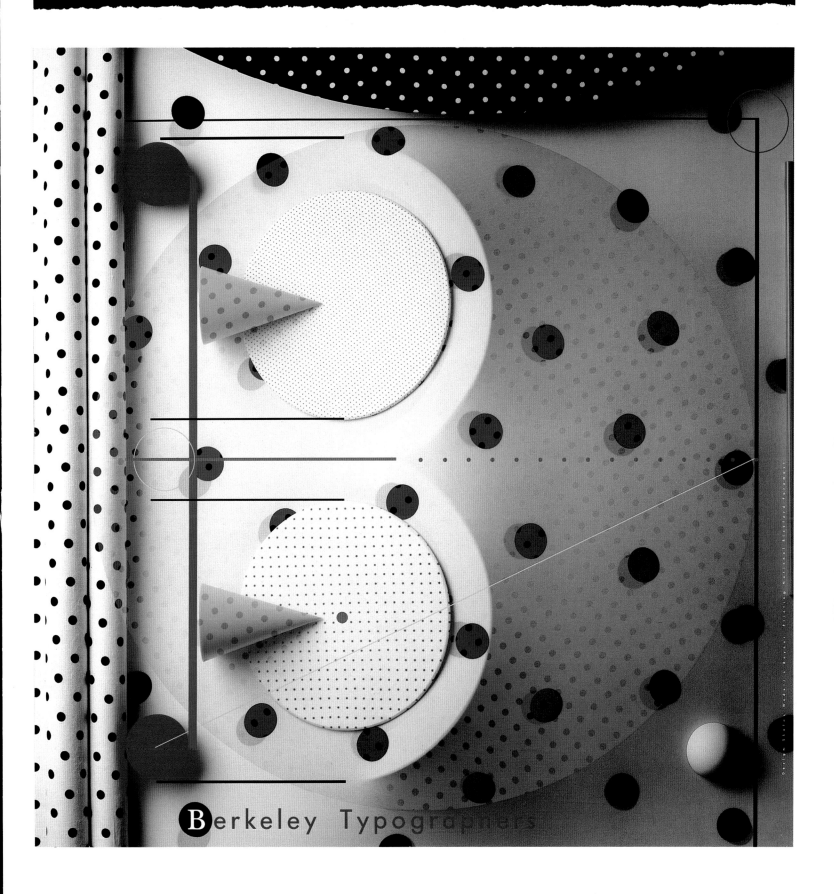

■ 265 The possibilities of color changes in the printing of photographs are shown in this poster, issued as self promotion for *Color Control* lithographers. (USA)

■ 266 Self promotion for *Berkeley Typographers*. (USA)

■ 265 Die Möglichkeiten der farblichen Veränderungen beim Druck einer Photographie zeigt dieses Plakat, welches als Eigenwerbung der Lithographenanstalt *Color Control* dient. (USA)

■ 266 Eigenwerbung der Firma *Berkeley Typographers*. (USA)

■ 265 Cette affiche montre les variations chromatiques que l'on peut obtenir en cours de reproduction d'une photo. Autopromotion de l'atelier de lithographie *Color Control*. (USA)

■ 266 Autopromotion de la société *Berkeley Typographers*. (USA)

WOLFGANG HOHNDORF, Photographer – 49211570972 – Selected Photographs published in the American Art Directors 66th Annual 1988
and shown in the American Art Directors Club New York First International Exhibition 1987:
Photos for Select Magazin: Head shot of women in trench coat / Seamed stockings, bare behind / Woman in trench coat lying down
Photos for The Manipulator: A propos / Breast, hand with glass / Bianconera / Julian and Philipp
Jury: Saul Bass, Ivan Chermayeff, Seymour Chwast, Lou Dorfsman, Wallace Elton, Gene Federico, Stephen Frankfurt, Milton Glaser, Art Kane,
Helmut Krone, Lou Silverstein, Paul Smith, Len Sirowitz, Bradbury Thompson, Massimo Vignelli, Henry Wolf, Leo Lionni.
New York   New York

ART DIRECTOR:
EVA FAYMONVILLE
PHOTOGRAPHER:
WOLFGANG HOHNDORF
CLIENT:
WOLFANG HOHNDORF
■**267**

ART DIRECTOR:
WOODY PIRTLE
DESIGNER:
*WOODY PIRTLE/
MIKE SCHROEDER*
ARTIST:
MARTHA CRUM
AGENCY:
PIRTLE DESIGN
CLIENT:
ROBERT J. HILTON CO., INC.
■**268**

■**267** Poster to publicize photographs (by German photographer Wolfgang Hohndorf) exhibited by the Art Directors Club of New York and which are also available for general sale. (USA)

■**268** «At Robert J. Hilton we've put on a brand new face.» The new company symbol shown in this poster is based on eight different typefaces. (USA)

■**269** "Two proud pasts - one glorious future." Announcement of the merger of the film giants *Metro Goldwyn Mayer* and *United Artists*. (USA)

■**267** Werbeplakat für Aufnahmen des deutschen Photographen Wolfgang Hohndorf, die in einer Ausstellung des Art Directors Club New York gezeigt wurden und auch im Handel erhältlich sind. (USA)

■**268** «Wir haben der Robert J. Hilton Co. ein neues Gesicht verpasst.» Das neue Firmensymbol wurde auf der Basis von acht verschiedenen Schrifttypen entworfen. (USA)

■**269** Ankündigung des Zusammenschlusses der Filmgesellschaften *Metro Goldwyn Mayer* und *United Artists*. «Zwei stolze Vergangenheiten, eine glorreiche Zukunft». (USA)

■**267** Pour une exposition de l'œuvre du photographe allemand Wolfgang Hohndorf organisée par l'Art Directors Club de New York. Ces photos s'obtiennent dans le commerce. (USA)

■**268** «Nous avons donné à la Robert J. Hilton Co. un nouveau visage.» Le nouvel emblème de l'entreprise a été réalisé sur la base de huit types de caractères différents. (USA)

■**269** Annonce de la fusion des deux sociétés cinématographiques *Metro Goldwyn Mayer* et *United Artists*: «Deux passés glorieux, un seul futur glorieux.» (USA)

ART DIRECTOR:
Kit Hinrichs
DESIGNER:
Kit Hinrichs/
Karen Berndt
ARTIST:
Doug Johnson
AGENCY:
Pentagram
CLIENT:
MGM/UA
Communications
■ 269

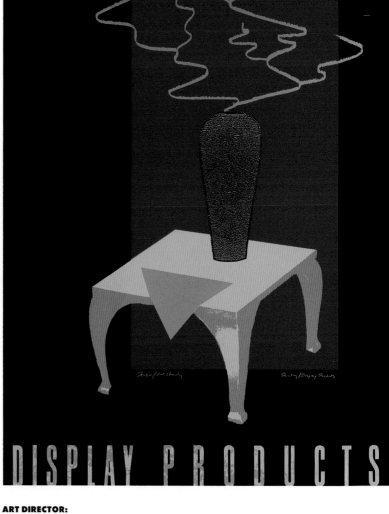

ART DIRECTOR:
Garry Emery

DESIGNER:
Garry Emery

AGENCY:
Emery Vincent Associates

CLIENT:
The Image Centre
■ **270**

ART DIRECTOR:
Art Chantry

DESIGNER:
Art Chantry

ARTIST:
Art Chantry

AGENCY:
Art Chantry Design

CLIENT:
Display Products, Inc.
■ **271**

■ **270** "Famous Fools" – the title of a poster series for the Australian lithographer *The Image Centre*. The posters are for self promotional purposes. (AUS)

■ **271** Self promotion for a company offering display products and silkscreen service. Shown here is the sophisticated effect of silkscreen printing. (USA)

■ **272** Poster to announce the change of address of the graphic design studio *Soha* to Soho, a part of Manhattan. (USA)

■ **270** »Famous Fools« ist der Titel einer Plakatreihe, unter der die Lithographenanstalt *The Image Centre* inspirierende Schöpfungen zeigt. Die Plakate dienen zur Eigenwerbung. (AUS)

■ **271** Eigenwerbung einer Firma, die Display-Produkte und einen Siebdruck-Service anbietet. Auf diesem Plakat werden die raffinierten Siebdruckmöglichkeiten demonstriert. (USA)

■ **272** Plakat für die Bekanntmachung des Umzugs des Design-Studios *Soha* in das New Yorker Quartier Soho. (USA)

■ **270** Affiche de la série des »Fous célèbres« produite par l'atelier de lithographie australien *The Image Centre* pour sa promotion, sur le thème des créations riches d'inspiration. (AUS)

■ **271** Autopromotion d'une société spécialisée dans les éléments de PLV et la sérigraphie. Cette affiche est censée démontrer les possibilités extraordinaires inhérentes à la sérigraphie. (USA)

■ **272** Affiche annonçant le déménagement du studio de design *Soha* dans le quartier new-yorkais de Soho. (USA)

ART DIRECTOR:
Michael Soha

DESIGNER:
Michael Soha/
Louis Medeiros

AGENCY:
Soha Design

CLIENT:
Soha Design

■ 272

Michael Soha, founder of Soha Design, is a second generation American descended from Polish immigrants. His grandfather, Andrew Socha, came to the U.S. in 1903, passing through the portals of Ellis Island and traveling north to Massachusetts, where he settled and worked as a shoemaker. Soon after arriving in America, he dropped the "c" in his last name to simplify pronunciation, a common practice among European immigrants of that time.

Michael Soha was born in Adams, Massachusetts in 1959. His childhood was a typical New England one, surrounded by the sounds and colors of the Berkshires, and the quiet and pervasive presence of church and history. At four, he was already showing a marked interest in art. One of his earliest recollections is an image of himself folding and cutting orange and black construction paper to form a symmetrical Halloween pumpkin—

an inkling, he says, of what would become his basic principle of approach to "design as solving a problem." His family encouraged his creative inclinations and while he was in grade school he took workshops in ceramics and drawing, then enrolled at the Charles H. McCann Technical School with aspirations toward becoming an architect.

During his high school years, he received his first taste of public

recognition. His concept for a 20 x 60 foot mural depicting 200 years of technology was accepted for the school's 1976 celebration of the Bicentennial, and in his senior year he was part of a 4-member team whose model for a domed Antarctic city received critical acclaim in the Massachusetts press and won the Charles and Helen Keller Humanities Award.

Michael first became aware of graphic design as a profession while auditing

a college-level design course in his junior year at McCann. His work on the high school yearbook fueled his interest further, and after graduating with honors, he went on to become an art major at Berkshire Community College. Impressed by his creative talent, his teachers urged him to apply to a college with a more extensive art program. He was accepted at the prestigious Pratt Institute and moved to Brooklyn in 1978. In the spring of 1979

he attended a business seminar which sparked his entrepreneurial imagination, and soon afterward Soha Design was born. Some of the clients he acquired during that time are still coming to him today.

In 1977, Michael met Leslie Chase, while they were both teaching in a summer recreational program for children in Cheshire, Massachusetts. They maintained a long-distance relationship as Leslie attended

Lesley College in Cambridge, and Pratt. They married in April, 1982. Leslie teaches first grade at a Manhattan public school and is also artistically inclined. Her watercolors on traditional landscape themes decorate the Sohas' Kensington apartment and she uses imaginative art-oriented projects to help her students learn. Michael attributes a great part of his success to her unflagging enthusiasm and encouragement.

Soha
to
Soho

Less than 20 years ago, SoHo's survival as a neighborhood hung in precarious balance as city planners and architectural preservationists waged a pitched battle to decide its fate. A 1962 study by the City Club christened Spring, Broome, Mercer and Greene Streets "commercial slum area No. 1, recommended for clearance and rebuilding." It was eyed as a possible site for a middle-income housing development and almost got bull-dozed to make way for a Lower Manhattan Expressway before it was

granted landmark status in 1973. Today, this unique area of New York is recognized for having the largest surviving collection of 19th-century cast-iron buildings in the world.

In the mid-17th century SoHo was the site of Manhattan Island's first settlement of free blacks, and remained an area of rolling farmland until the beginning of the 1800's. In the early 19th century, the rural landscape was leveled, and quickly developed into an enclave of the wealthy.

John Jacob Astor, James Fenimore Cooper, Samuel F.B. Morse and Richard Morris Hunt were only some of the noted residents of what was at that time a quiet neighborhood of genteel Federal-style brick townhouses. Then, in the 1850's, a commercial boom changed the landscape once again. Lord & Taylor, Tiffany & Co., Arnold Constable, as well as posh hotels, theatres and music halls turned the community into a bustling playground for the rich, complete with a red-light district that did a lively

business of its own. From 1860 to 1865, SoHo lost ¼ of its population as factories began to move in and the elite crowd migrated uptown.

Most of the cast-iron buildings which characterize SoHo today were erected between 1860 and 1890. Renowned architects such as John B. Snook, Isaac Duckworth, Griffith Thomas, Jarvis Morgan Slade and Henry Fernbach designed what were to become the forerunners of today's sophisticated steel and glass

skyscrapers. The elaborately detailed structures which echoed the tiered, pillared and arcaded facades of Italian Renaissance palaces, were cast in pieces in foundries and assembled on site in much the same way modern skyscrapers are built. At its height, the cast-iron architecture of SoHo incorporated such varied styles as Victorian Gothic, French Second Empire and Neo-Grec. All of the facades were cream-colored or white, in imitation of the glowing marble palaces they emulated.

From the late 19th century until well into the 20th century, SoHo remained virtually unchanged as a major center for light industry. Its flourishing artists' community is a fairly recent development in the neighborhood's rich and varied history. In the late 50's and 60's, struggling artists began to trickle in, attracted by the low rents and the airy work and living spaces of the commercial lofts. In little more than a decade, SoHo has seen a boom in galleries, boutiques and restaurants, which

often operate right alongside blue-collar pubs, textile manufacturers and nuts and bolts factories.

SoHo derives its name from its location South of Houston Street, with Canal Street, Lafayette Street and W. Broadway defining its south, east and west boundaries respectively. Greene Street, where Soha Design's new headquarters are located, is noted for its high concentration and extraordinary examples of 19th-century cast-iron architecture.

"LET'S SEE HOW IT DOES IN FOCUS GROUP."

Beware the research explosion. An onslaught of numbers we sometimes allow to make decisions for us.

Numbers can't replace a writer's wit. An art director's eye. The savvy of a media planner. Or an account executive's insight.

Research: It's a tool. Not gospel. After all, who is more qualified to make an advertising decision? Five housewives, a plumber and a night watchman. Or you?

ATLANTA AD CLUB

Concept/Copy/Layout/Production: Cole Henderson Drake, Inc. Printing: Harris Specialty Lithographers, Inc. Typography: Phototype.

"THE CLIENT LOVES EVERYTHING BUT THE HEAD."

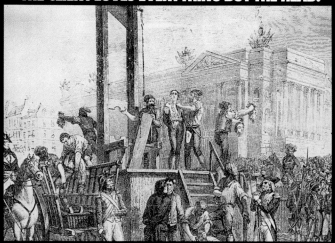

Clients and agencies should expect to frustrate one another occasionally. We work toward the same end, but from different perspectives.

The key is not letting those frustrations get the best of us. Not making compromises—born of exasperation—that may compromise the effectiveness of an idea.

If the goal is great advertising for every client, every little step in that direction is worthwhile. But let's not lose our heads.

ATLANTA AD CLUB

Concept/Copy/Layout/Production: Cole Henderson Drake, Inc. Printing: Harris Specialty Lithographers, Inc. Typography: Phototype.

"I THINK THEY'LL WANT TO SEE MORE THAN ONE EXECUTION."

Alternatives. Sometimes they're appropriate. They work. Other times, however, we seem to offer them out of habit. Choice for the sake of choice.

It's a dangerous habit. Because the best ideas aren't always safe. And quantity can hinder the cause. By confusing. And providing easier, more familiar directions.

All the back-up great ideas really need is our confidence. Then we come home saying, "We killed 'em!" Instead of, "They killed it."

ATLANTA AD CLUB

Concept/Copy/Layout/Production: Cole Henderson Drake, Inc. Printing: Harris Specialty Lithographers, Inc. Typography: Phototype.

"THE TARGET MARKET FOR THIS AD, GENTLEMEN, IS 18-34."

Traditional markets and messages are comfortable. And we sometimes fall back on them without thinking what they really mean.

Good direction, however, is essential to good advertising. Because we have to talk to people one at a time.

We can't be all things to all people. No matter how admirable the message. Just try explaining Bobby Kennedy's idealism. At a Dead Kennedy's concert.

ATLANTA AD CLUB

Concept/Copy/Layout/Production: Cole Henderson Drake, Inc. Printing: Harris Specialty Lithographers, Inc. Typography: Phototype. Photography: Eric Henderson.

ART DIRECTOR:
Jim Condit
PHOTOGRAPHER:
The Mercury News
Press 273
Minnesota Historical
Society 275
Eric Henderson 276
U. S. Air Force 277
CLIENT:
Atlanta AD Club
■ **273–277**

"THEY'LL NEVER BUY IT."

It's easier to attack than to defend. Easier to be negative than positive. Trouble is, that's how good ideas—along with bad ones—get shot down. Because the new and different make especially inviting targets.

Being positive doesn't mean always saying "yes." It means judging ads on their merits. Giving them a chance to develop. The bad ones will crash and burn along the way. While a lot more good ones get off the ground.

ATLANTA AD CLUB

Concept/Copy/Layout/Production: Cole Henderson Drake, Inc. Printing: Harris Specialty Lithographers, Inc. Typography: Phototype.

■ **273–277** With catchy headers and apt pictures the Atlanta Ad Club encourages its members to be creative, to cultivate a good relationship with the customers, to think positive rather than negative, to deliver more quality than quantity, and to test the effects of their concepts. (USA)

■ **273–277** Mit aussergewöhnlichen Bildern und Texten fordert der Atlanta Ad Club seine Mitglieder auf, kreativ zu sein, eine gute Zusammenarbeit mit dem Kunden zu pflegen, lieber positiv als negativ zu denken, mehr Qualität als Quantität zu liefern und Konzepte auf ihre Wirkung zu prüfen. (USA)

■ **273–277** C'est à travers ces textes et images insolites que l'Atlanta Ad Club invite ses membres à se montrer créatifs, à veiller à une bonne entente avec la clientèle, à cultiver la pensée positive, à fournir un travail plus qualitatif que quantitatif et à tester leurs produits quant à leur efficacité. (USA)

ART DIRECTOR:
WALT LECAT
DESIGNER:
SANDY KERMAN
PHOTOGRAPHER:
PAUL LECAT
STUDIO:
PAUL LECAT PHOTOGRAPHY
■**278**

PAUL LECAT PHOTOGRAPHY CHICAGO 312 664 7122 CALL LISA

■**278** Self promotion for photographer Paul Lecat. (USA)

■**279** With a pun on his name and ketchup (or katsup as it is sometimes called), John Katz promotes his studio. (USA)

■**280** Self promotion for photographer Dave Jordano. (USA)

■**278** Eigenwerbung des Photographen Paul Lecat. (USA)

■**279** Mit einem Wortspiel mit seinem Namen und Ketch-up wirbt der Photograph John Katz für sein Studio. (USA)

■**280** Eigenwerbung des Photographen Dave Jordano. (USA)

■**278** Autopromotion du photographe Paul Lecat. (USA)

■**279** Autopromotion de John Katz utilisant son nom pour un «Haut le Katz» homonyme de «ketchup» en anglais. (USA)

■**280** Autopromotion du photographe Dave Jordano. (USA)

KATZ UP

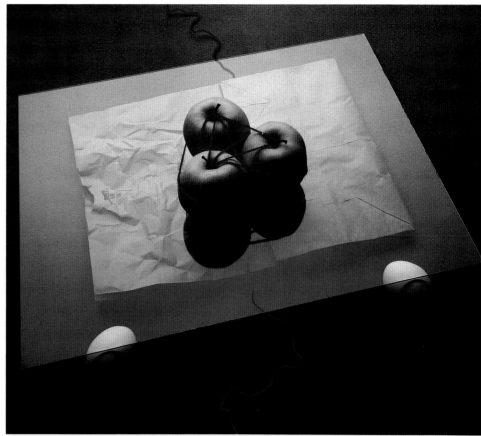

JORDANO

Dave Jordano Photography, 1335 North Wells, Chicago Illinois 60610 Represented by Vincent J. Kamin & Associates, 312.787.8834

ART DIRECTOR:
John Katz

DESIGNER:
Jack Summerford

PHOTOGRAPHER:
John Katz

AGENCY:
Jack Summerford Design

CLIENT:
John Katz Photography

■ **279**

ART DIRECTOR:
Bart Crosby

DESIGNER:
Lisa Nakamoto

PHOTOGRAPHER:
Dave Jordano

AGENCY:
Crosby Associates Inc.

CLIENT:
Dave Jordano Photography

■ **280**

ART DIRECTOR:
Monte Dolack

DESIGNER:
Monte Dolack

ARTIST:
Monte Dolack

STUDIO:
Monte Dolack Graphics

CLIENT:
Monte Dolack Graphics

■ **281**

ART DIRECTOR:
Debbie Adams

DESIGNER:
Debbie Adams/Paul Hodgson

PHOTOGRAPHER:
Derrick Carter

AGENCY:
The Spencer Francey Group

CLIENT:
Letraset Canada Ltd.

■ **282**

■ **281** Self promotional poster for Monte Dolack Graphics, Missoula, Montana, with a clear pun – literal and visual – on the word "Refridgeraiders". (USA)

■ **282** From a series of posters, available for general sale, issued by *Letraset* under the header "Word & Picture". A quotation by Karen Blixen on the subject of "passion" is blind embossed. (USA)

■ **283, 284** Self promotion for design studios Sidjakov Berman & Gomez presents the new packaging they designed for *Quaker Oats*. They were winners of the Clio Award 1986 for the best packaging design. (USA)

■ **281** Das Wortspiel »Refridgeraiders« bedeutet »Kühlschrank-Räuber«, wie auf diesem Plakat sehr deutlich dargestellt. Eigenwerbung der Monte Dolack Graphics, Missoula, MT. (USA)

■ **282** Aus einer Serie von Plakaten der Firma *Letraset* mit dem Motto »Wort & Bild«. Unter dem Thema »Leidenschaft« ist hier ein Zitat von Karen Blixen in Prägesatz gedruckt. (USA)

■ **283, 284** Eigenwerbung des Designstudios Sidjakov Berman & Gomez. *283* zeigt die von ihnen entworfene neue Packung für *Quaker Oats. 284:* Der Clio-Award wurde ihnen 1986 für das beste Packungs-Design verliehen. (USA)

■ **281** Jeu de mots qui fait de »réfrigérateurs« les »pilleurs venus du froid«. Affiche autopromotionnelle de Monte Dolack Graphics, où les pingouins jouent aux envahisseurs. (USA)

■ **282** Exemple d'affiches publiées par *Letraset* dans une série intitulée »Mot et image« et vendues également comme posters. Citation de Karen Blixen au sujet de la »passion«. (USA)

■ **283, 284** Autopromotion du studio de design Sidjakov Berman & Gomez. *283:* On y voit le nouvel emballage de *Quaker Oats* réalisé par ce groupe, ainsi que *284* le Clio, grand prix de l'emballage, reçu en 1986 pour le design d'emballage. (USA)

ART DIRECTOR:
JERRY BERMAN
DESIGNER:
JERRY BERMAN
PHOTOGRAPHER:
JOHN DEGROOT
AGENCY:
SIDJAKOV BERMAN & GOMEZ
CLIENT:
SIDJAKOV BERMAN & GOMEZ
■ **283, 284**

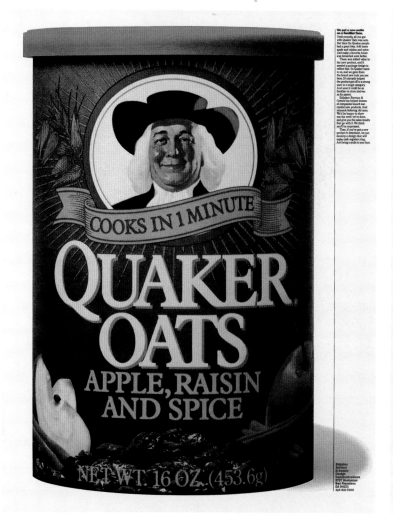

BEN VERKAAIK. REPRESENTED BY THE ART BOX AMSTERDAM / BRUSSELS

ART DIRECTOR:
Ben Verkaaik
DESIGNER:
Ben Verkaaik
CLIENT
The Art Box
■**285**

▶▲ **ART DIRECTOR:**
Dietrich Ebert
ARTIST:
Dietrich Ebert
AGENCY:
D. & I. Ebert
■**286**

▶ **ART DIRECTOR:**
Dan Krumweide
PHOTOGRAPHER:
Marvy
STUDIO:
Marvy!
Advertising Photography
■**287**

■**285** Self promotional poster for the Artbox Amsterdam, an illustrators' agency. (NLD)

■**286** New Year's card in poster size for the German graphic/illustrator team Ebert. (GER)

■**287** "Vintage ideas. Classic executions. Photography by Marvy!" Poster as self promotion for Marvy! Advertising photography. (USA)

■**285** Eigenwerbung der Artbox Amsterdam, einer Agentur zur Vermittlung von Illustratoren. (NLD)

■**286** Neujahrskarte in Plakatform des deutschen Graphiker/Illustratoren-Teams Ebert. (GER)

■**287** «Hervorragende Ideen, klassische Ausführungen, Photographie durch Marvy!» – Plakat zur Eigenwerbung der Marvy! Advertising Photography. (USA)

■**285** Affiche autopromotionnelle d'Artbox Amsterdam, agence spécialisée dans la recherche d'illustrateurs. (NLD)

■**286** Carte de Nouvel An tirée au format d'une affiche par l'équipe de graphistes et illustrateurs Ebert. (GER)

■**287** «Idées remarquables, exécutions classiques, photographies par Marvy!» Affiche autopromotionnelle de la société Marvy! Advertising Photography. (USA)

WER DEM JAHR AUF DIE SPRÜNGE HELFEN WILL, MUSS SCHON SAUMÄSSIG STARK SEIN. VIEL GLÜCK!

DIETRICH & IRMGARD EBERT
GRAFIK UND ILLUSTRATIVE DINGE
BRAIKINBACHWEG 12 · 7410 REUTLINGEN

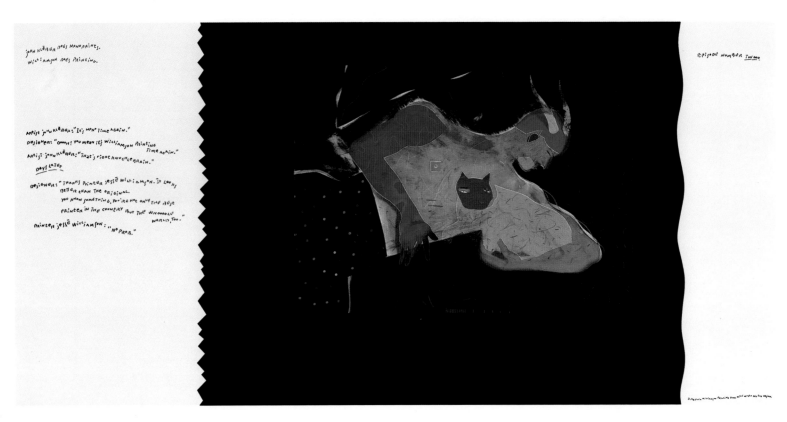

ART DIRECTOR:
Mike Mazza

DESIGNER:
Mike Mazza

ARTIST:
John Kleber

STUDIO:
Acme Studios

CLIENT:
Williamson Printing Corp.

■288

■**288, 289** Self promotion for the Williamson printers. Based on the works (mono-prints) by John Kleber, which present a great challenge in reprinting, the printers display their capabilities on these posters. (USA)

■**288, 289** Eigenwerbung der Druckerei Williamson. Anhand der Arbeiten («Mono prints») von John Kleber, die grosse Anforderungen an den Drucker stellen, soll hier die Leistungsfähigkeit unter Beweis gestellt werden. (USA)

■**288, 289** Autopromotion de l'imprimerie Williamson, qui entend démontrer ses capacités en présentant ces monotypes de John Kleber, dont la reproduction pose des problèmes particulièrement redoutables à l'imprimeur. (USA)

JOHN KLEBER DOES MONOPRINTS.
WILLIAMSON DOES PRINTING.

EPISODE NUMBER UNO.

ART DIRECTOR:
Mike Mazza

DESIGNER:
Mike Mazza

ARTIST:
John Kleber

STUDIO:
Acme Studios

CLIENT:
Williamson Printing Corp.

■289

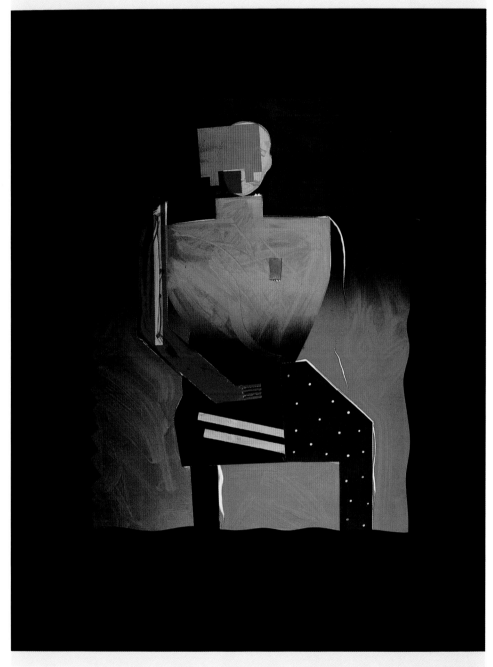

ARTIST JOHN KLEBER: "MY MONOS ARE VERY HARD TO PRINT."
DESIGNER: "YES, I KNOW."
ARTIST JOHN KLEBER: "FIND THE BEST PRINTER IN THE COUNTRY."
DESIGNER: "O.K."
                THE NEXT DAY
DESIGNER: "MR. FANCY PRINTER, CAN YOU PRINT ARTIST JOHN KLEBER'S MONOS?"
MR. FANCY PRINTER: "NO CAN DO."
                WEEKS LATER
DESIGNER: "OH NO, WILL I EVER FIND THE BEST PRINTER IN THE COUNTRY?
        WAIII'T A MINUTE, MAYBE THEY'LL FIND ME."
PHONE: "RING, RING."
PRINTER JESSE WILLIAMSON: "I CAN PRINT ARTIST JOHN KLEBER'S MONOS."
                DAYS LATER
DESIGNER: "THANKS PRINTER JESSE WILLIAMSON. IT LOOKS JUST LIKE
                                        THE ORIGINAL."
PRINTER JESSE WILLIAMSON: "PIECE O'CAKE."

ART DIRECTOR:
Michael Cronan

DESIGNER:
Linda Lawler/
Michael Cronan

ARTIST:
Linda Lawler

AGENCY:
Cronan Design

CLIENT:
Mercury Typography

■ **290**

■ **290** This silkscreen poster – as self promotion for Mercury Typography – brings to the front line the forgotten letters. A short humorous tale is related about each. (USA)

■ **291, 292** Self promotional poster for the typesetters Epitype Pty. Ltd. South Melbourne, Australia. The illustration relates to a pun on the header "Body Copy". *292* belongs to a series of posters devoted to the great type designers – this one to Frederic William Goudy. (AUS)

■ **290** Siebdruckplakat als Eigenwerbung für Mercury Typography, die sich hier vernachlässigter Buchstaben annehmen. Zu jedem wird eine kleine, humorvolle Geschichte erzählt. (USA)

■ **291, 292** Eigenwerbung für die Setzerei Epitype Pty Ltd. Die Illustrationen beziehen sich auf Wortspiele, die nur im Englischen möglich sind. Mit «Body Copy» ist der Grundtext (Brottext) gemeint. *292* gehört zu einer Reihe, die grossen Schriftentwerfern, hier Frederic William Goudy, gewidmet ist. (AUS)

■ **290** Affiche sérigraphique servant d'autopromotion à Mercury Typography, qui évoque ici des lettres bien négligées, chacune assortie d'une historiette plaisante. (USA)

■ **291, 292** Autopromotion de l'atelier de composition Epitype Pty Ltd. Les illustrations incarnent des jeux de mots typiquement anglais: body copy = caractères de labeur/«de corps»; «Goudy/doré, jamais clinquant». Série consacrée aux grands dessinateurs de caractères, ici Frederic William Goudy. (AUS)

ART DIRECTOR:
Ken Cato

DESIGNER:
Ken Cato

ARTIST:
Nigel Buchanan

AGENCY:
Cato Design Inc Pty Ltd

CLIENT:
Epitype Pty Ltd

■ **291**

ART DIRECTOR:
Ken Cato

DESIGNER:
Ken Cato

ARTIST:
Lena Gan

AGENCY:
Cato Design Inc Pty Ltd

CLIENT:
Epitype Pty Ltd

■ **292**

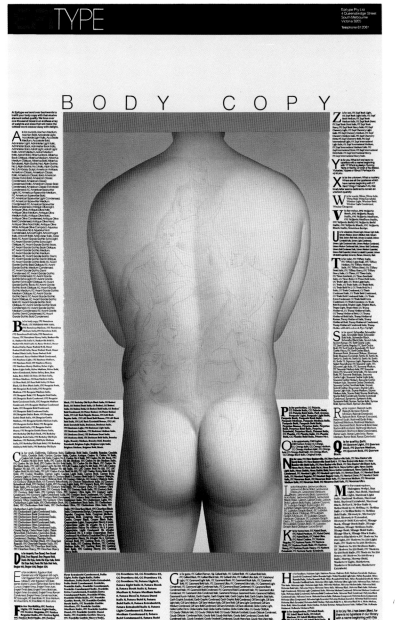

Heads turn. And in them,
jealous thoughts. That's what
England's prestigious Rolls
Royce does to people, as it
drives by. That's what Al
Pitzner's photography does,
as he drives you to perfection.
A Rolls Royce. Or cinnamon
rolls. Regardless of the shot,
a photographer-perfectionist
is who you should always
demand. Because the proof is
always in the finished prints
and transparencies.
Especially if they've been
developed at "Photo Images,"
Pitzner's own lab, which
utilizes the absolute latest
in technology to deliver a
product as perfect as Al
Pitzner demands it will be. As
perfect as you hope it will be.
If you own a Rolls Royce, you
know that driving perfection
has its own very special
rewards. If you hire Al Pitzner,
you'll soon find out that being
driven to perfection has its
own very special rewards
as well.
Number two in a series
of twelve.
Kansas City Studio:
8192 Nieman Road
Lenexa, Kansas 66214
(913) 492-0396
Color Separations:
Lasergraphics
Printing:
McGrew Color Graphics

The status is understood.
And with each, the precision
unquestioned. Germany's
Mercedes Benz is the epitomy
of quality, driving on any
road. The same can be said
of Al Pitzner's photography,
driving you to perfection.
Mercedes Benz. Or
mercerized cotton sweaters.
Regardless of the product, you
want a photographer whose
philosophy of perfection is
found in equipment as well
as attitude. That's why
Pitzner's studio is equipped
with lighting second to none
in the United States.
That's why his lab, "Photo
Images," can produce razor
sharp color prints in sizes up
to six feet by fifteen feet.
That's why Al can always
deliver a product to his
perfect standards, to mention
nothing of yours.
When you sit behind the
wheel of a Mercedes you
know that, mechanically,
you're surrounded by
perfection as you, drive. Al
Pitzner offers you that same
philosophy, photographically,
as he drives you.
Number four in a series
of twelve.
Kansas City Studio:
8192 Nieman Road Lenexa,
Kansas 66214
(913) 492-0396
Color Separations:
Lasergraphics
Printing:
McGrew Color Graphics

DESIGNER:
Mike Peterson

PHOTOGRAPHER:
Al Pitzner

AGENCY:
Sandven True Pruitt

CLIENT:
Al Pitzner Photography

■ **293–295**

■ **293–295** Three examples from a series of twelve posters as self promotion for the photo studio Al Pitzner, Lenexa, Kansas. Perfection, as shown in these automobiles, is the first rule in his work too. (USA)

■ **293–295** Beispiele aus einer Serie von 12 Plakaten als Eigenwerbung des Photostudios Al Pitzner. Perfektion, wie sie bei diesen Automodellen angeboten wird, gilt auch bei seiner Arbeit als oberstes Gebot. (USA)

■ **293–295** Trois des douze affiches autopromotionnelles du studio photographique Al Pitzner. La perfection incarnée par ces automobiles est aussi la quintessence de la recherche patiente que ce photographe poursuit à travers ses créations. (USA)

ART DIRECTOR:
DALLAS SAUNDERS
DESIGNER:
DALLAS SAUNDERS
PHOTOGRAPHER:
MARK HANAUER
AGENCY:
PORTAL PUBLICATIONS
PUBLISHER:
PORTAL PUBLICATIONS
■ **296, 297**

■ **296, 297** Poster with photographs of sports personalities, as self promotion for photographer Mark Hanauer. (USA)

■ **298** Poster promotion for an association of makeup artists and stylists in Dallas. (USA)

■ **296, 297** Plakate mit Aufnahmen von Sportlern, als Eigenwerbung des Photographen Mark Hanauer. (USA)

■ **298** Plakatwerbung für eine Vereinigung von Maskenbildnern und Stylisten in Dallas. (USA)

■ **296, 297** Affiches illustrées de photos de sportifs par Mark Hanauer, qu'il utilise pour sa promotion. (USA)

■ **298** Affiche publicitaire pour une association de maquilleurs et esthéticiens-stylistes à Dallas. (USA)

ART DIRECTOR:
Mike Schroeder
DESIGNER:
Mike Schroeder
PHOTOGRAPHER:
Geof Kern
AGENCY:
Pirtle Design
CLIENT:
*Dallas Association of
Make up Artists and Stylists*
■ 298

DALLAS ASSOCIATION OF MAKEUP ARTISTS AND STYLISTS

ART DIRECTOR:
Harvey Edwards
DESIGNER:
Harvey Edwards
PHOTOGRAPHER:
Harvey Edwards
STUDIO:
Harvey Edwards, Inc.
PUBLISHER:
*Bruce McGaw
Graphics, Inc.*
■ 299

HARVEY EDWARDS

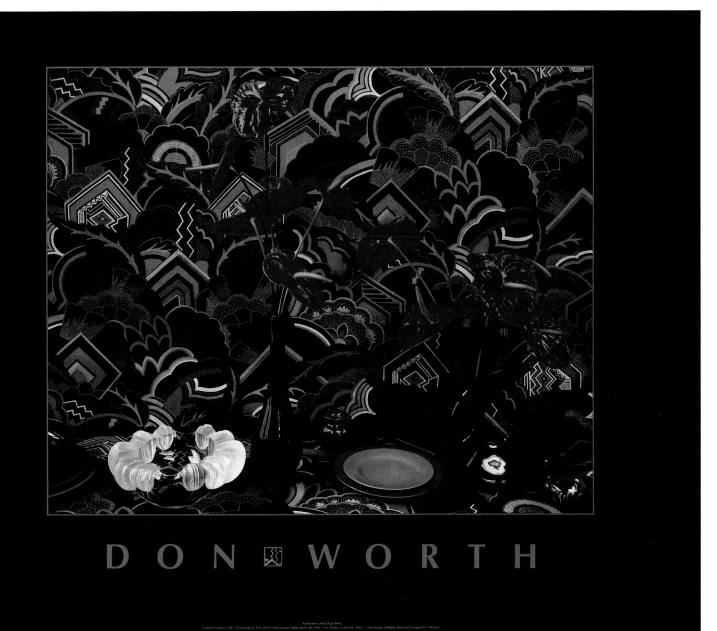

ART DIRECTOR:
Thomas F. Burke

DESIGNER:
A. M. Koury

PHOTOGRAPHER:
Don Worth

PUBLISHER:
Pomegranate Publications

■**300**

■**299** "The Black Rose" is the title of this poster that serves as self promotion for photographer Harvey Edwards and is also on general sale. (USA)

■**300** "Anthuriums and Lalique Bowl" – a six-color poster issued as self promotion for photographer Don Worth. The poster is also on general sale. (USA)

■**299** «Die schwarze Rose» ist der Titel dieses Plakates, das zur Eigenwerbung des Photographen Harvey Edwards dient und auch im Handel erhältlich ist. (USA)

■**300** «Anthuriums und Lalique Schale» – ein im Sechsfarben-Druck hergestelltes Plakat als Eigenwerbung des Photographen Don Worth. Das Plakat ist auch im Handel erhältlich. (USA)

■**299** Affiche intitulée «la Rose noire» pour la promotion du photographe Harvey Edwards, qui commercialise également son œuvre sous forme de poster. (USA)

■**300** «Anthuriums et coupe Lalique» – Affiche en six couleurs servant à l'autopromotion du photographe Don Worth. Egalement disponible sous forme de poster. (USA)

ART DIRECTOR:
Dean Hanson

PHOTOGRAPHER:
Rick Dublin

AGENCY:
Fallon McElligott

CLIENT:
Children's Defense Fund

■ **301, 302**

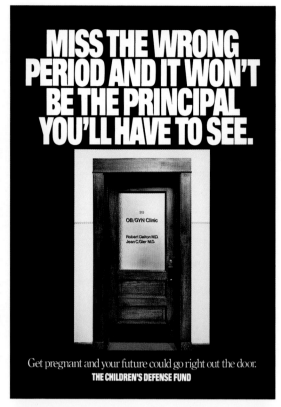

ART DIRECTOR:
Dean Hanson

PHOTOGRAPHER:
Marc Hauser

AGENCY:
Fallon McElligott

CLIENT:
Children's Defense Fund

■ **303, 304**

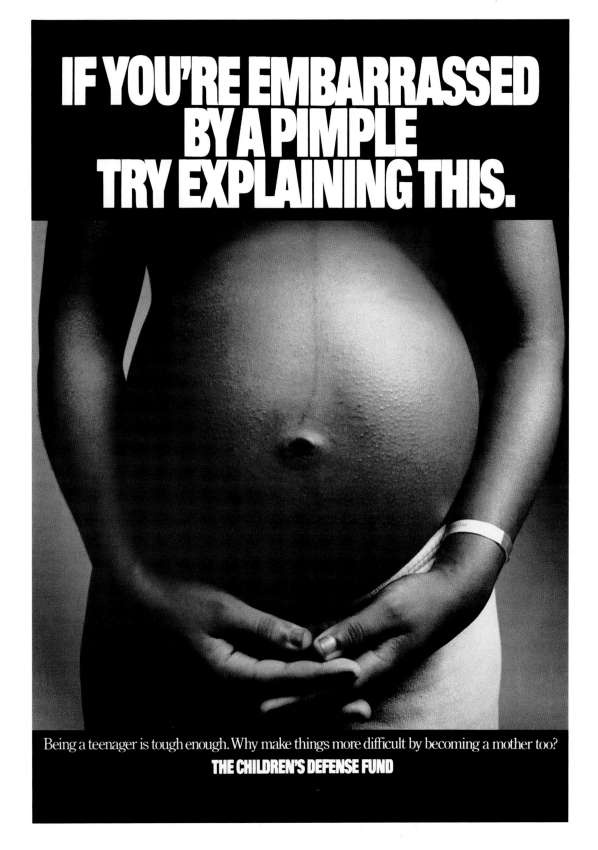

IF YOU'RE EMBARRASSED BY A PIMPLE TRY EXPLAINING THIS.

Being a teenager is tough enough. Why make things more difficult by becoming a mother too?

THE CHILDREN'S DEFENSE FUND

ART DIRECTOR:
Dean Hanson
PHOTOGRAPHER:
Rick Dublin
AGENCY:
Fallon McElligott
CLIENT:
Children's Defense Fund
■ 305

■ **301–305** Examples from a campaign for the *Children's Defense Fund* warning against teenage pregnancies. The small copy reads: *301* "If you think pregnancy would limit your wardrobe, you should see what it would do to your life." *302* "Get pregnant and your future could go right out the door." *303, 304* "Having a baby when you're a teenager... can take away your dreams." *305* "Being a teenager is tough enough. Why make things more difficult by becoming a mother too?" (USA)

■ **301–305** Beispiele aus einer Kampagne des *Children's Defense Fund* gegen Schwangerschaft bei Kindern und Jugendlichen. *301* «Werde schwanger, und Kleider sind nicht das Einzige, in das Du nicht mehr reinkommst.» *302* «Wenn Du diese Periode verpasst, ist es nicht der Schuldirektor, den Du sprechen musst.» *303, 304* «Für die nächsten 18 Jahre kannst Du Deine Träume und Deine Freiheit vergessen.» *305* «Wenn Du Dich wegen eines Pickels schämst, versuche mal dies zu erklären.» (USA)

■ **301–305** Affiches figurant dans une campagne du *Children's Defense Fund* combattant les grossesses des fillettes et des adolescentes. *301* «Enceinte, tu verras qu'il n'y a pas que les vêtements qui seront trop étroits.» *302* «Rate ta période, et ce ne pas le directeur auquel il faudra t'adresser.» *303, 304* «C'est comme si tu étais coincée pour 18 ans à venir.» *305* «Si ça t'embête déjà d'avoir des boutons, imagine un peu ce que ça te fera quand tu devras expliquer ça.» (USA)

TEN TIPS THAT COULD SAVE YOUR CHILD'S LIFE.

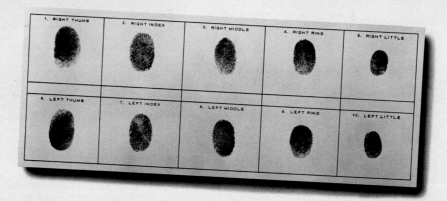

Locating a missing child can be difficult enough without having to worry about accurate identification. And the fact is, there's no more precise method for identifying your child than through fingerprints. Right now fingerprinting is available free. For more information, call the Richmond Bureau of Police, Police Community Services, at 780-4632. We're doing everything we can to ensure the safety of Richmond's children. But we can always use a hand.

THE RICHMOND POLICE

ART DIRECTOR:
JIM BROCK
DESIGNER:
JIM BROCK
PHOTOGRAPHER:
BOB JONES
AGENCY:
*FINNEGAN &
AGEE ADVERTISING*
CLIENT:
RICHMOND POLICE
■ 306

■ **306** Poster issued by the Richmond, Virginia police, requesting local parents to bring their children to the police department to be fingerprinted so that the task of identifying a missing child can be made easier. (USA)

■ **307–309** Posters from a campaign by the "Operation Crackdown" against the misuse of drugs. (USA)

■ **306** Plakat der Polizei von Richmond, Virginia, mit der Aufforderung an alle Eltern, Fingerabdrücke ihrer Kinder bei der Polizei zu hinterlegen, um die Suche nach einem vermissten Kind zu erleichtern. (USA)

■ **307–309** Kampagne gegen den Drogenmissbrauch, mit dem Slogan «Nasen sind auch nicht für Kokain bestimmt.» (USA)

■ **306** Affiche de la police de Richmond, en Virginie: «Dix tuyaux/bouts des doigts (jeu de mots) qui pourront sauver la vie de votre enfant.» Appel aux parents de faire enregistrer les empreintes digitales de leurs enfants en vue d'une disparition. (USA)

■ **307–309** Campagne contre l'abus de stupéfiants, avec ce slogan: «Le nez n'est pas fait non plus pour la cocaïne.» (USA)

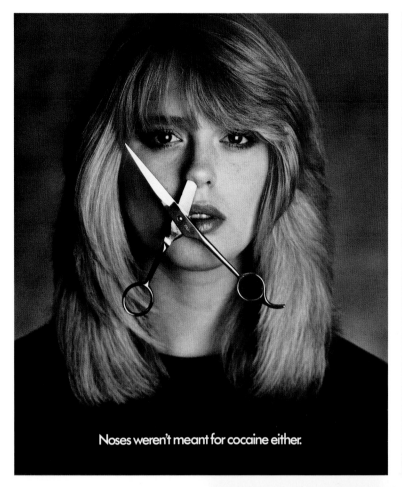

Noses weren't meant for cocaine either.

Noses weren't meant for cocaine either.

ART DIRECTOR:
J. Coby Neill
DESIGNER:
Brian Brooker
PHOTOGRAPHER:
James M. Goss
STUDIO:
Goss Photography
CLIENT:
Brooker/Neill Operation Crackdown
■ 307–309

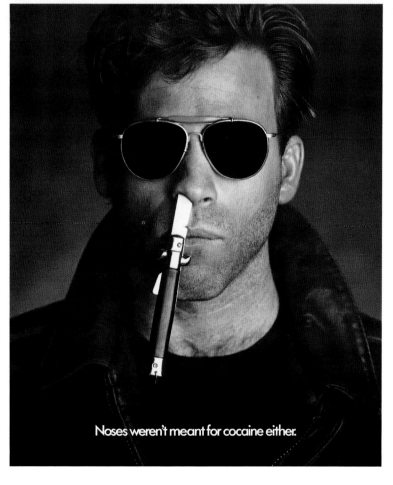

Noses weren't meant for cocaine either.

The Greatest Advertising Story Ever Told.

SCHOOL OF VISUAL ARTS

For fast, fast, fast relief take two tablets.

The Episcopal Church

ART DIRECTOR:
Richard Wilde

DESIGNER:
Richard Wilde

AGENCY:
School of Visual Arts Press

CLIENT:
School of Visual Arts

■ 310

ART DIRECTOR:
Dean Hanson

AGENCY:
Fallon McElligott

CLIENT:
The Episcopal Church

■ 311

■ **310** Graduates of the School of Visual Arts, New York, who are today counted among the most famous advertising experts of America are listed on this poster. It also appeared as a full-page ad in the *New York Times*. (USA)

■ **311, 312** Posters for the Episcopal Church. *311* illustrates the timelessness of faith as the solution to stress. *312:* God's commandments as means to soothing relief. (USA)

■ **310** Absolventen der School of Visual Arts, New York, die heute zu den bekanntesten Werbefachleuten Amerikas zählen, werden auf diesem Plakat aufgelistet. Dieses Werbeplakat erschien auch als ganzseitiges Inserat in der *New York Times*. (USA)

■ **311, 312** Plakate der Episcopal Church. *311* «Für rasche Erleichterung nehmen Sie zwei Tafeln.» *312* «Entgegen weitverbreiteter Ansicht ist Stress kein Phänomen des 20. Jahrhunderts.» (USA)

■ **310** «La plus grande histoire publicitaire jamais contée.» Liste des anciens élèves de la School of Visual Arts de New York passés aujourd'hui vedettes de l'art publicitaire américain. Affiche utilisée aussi comme annonce du *New York Times*. (USA)

■ **311, 312** Affiches de l'Episcopal Church. *311* «Pour une amélioration immédiate, prenez deux tablettes.» *312* «Contrairement à une opinion reçue, le stress n'est pas typique du XXe siècle.» (USA)

ART DIRECTOR:
DEAN HANSON
AGENCY:
FALLON MCELLIGOTT
CLIENT:
THE EPISCOPAL CHURCH
■ **312**

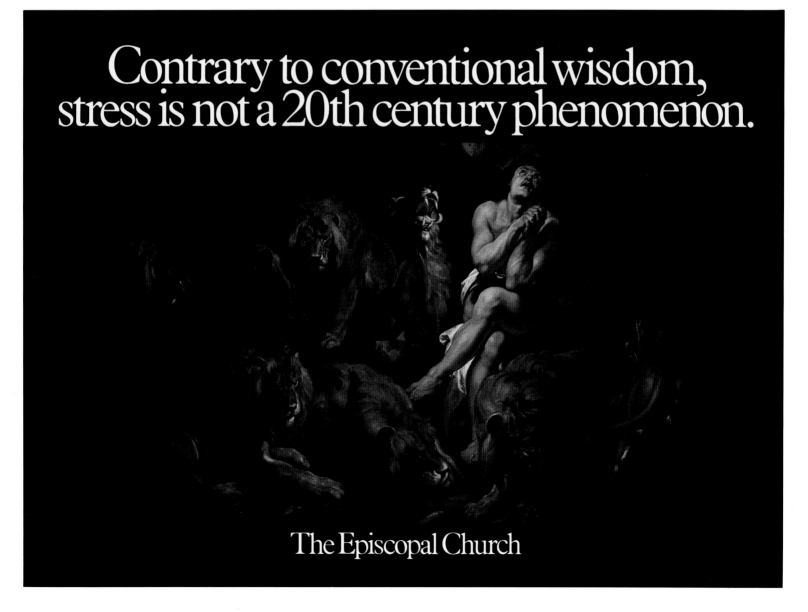

ART DIRECTOR:
John Vitro
DESIGNER:
John Vitro
AGENCY:
VW Advertising
CLIENT:
San Diego Humane Society
■ 313

WHEN YOU ADOPT A DOG,
THERE'S NO TELLING WHO THEY'LL
GROW UP TO BE.

SAN DIEGO HUMANE SOCIETY

Our special thanks to Old Yeller, Krypto, Peety, Lady, Snoopy, Asta, Astro, Lassie, Benji, Pluto, Rin Tin Tin, and Nipper.

Creative: Phillips-Ramsey; Separations: American Color; Printing: Arts & Crafts.

■**313** America's most familiar canines appeal to families to "adopt" a homeless pet. (USA)

■**313** Amerikas bekannteste Hunde appellieren an Familien, ein heimatloses Tier zu «adoptieren». (USA)

■**313** Les chiens les plus célèbres d'Amérique lancent un appel aux familles pour «l'adoption» de leurs congénères sans foyer. (USA)

SOCIETY

GESELLSCHAFT

SOCIÉTÉ

SOCIETY

GESELLSCHAFT

SOCIÉTÉ

ART DIRECTOR:
Timothy L. Eaton

DESIGNER:
Timothy L. Eaton/
Barbara Riechmann/
Philip E. Swenson

PHOTOGRAPHER:
Paul Shambroom

AGENCY:
Eaton & Associates
Design Company

CLIENT:
AIGA Minnesota

■ *314, 315*

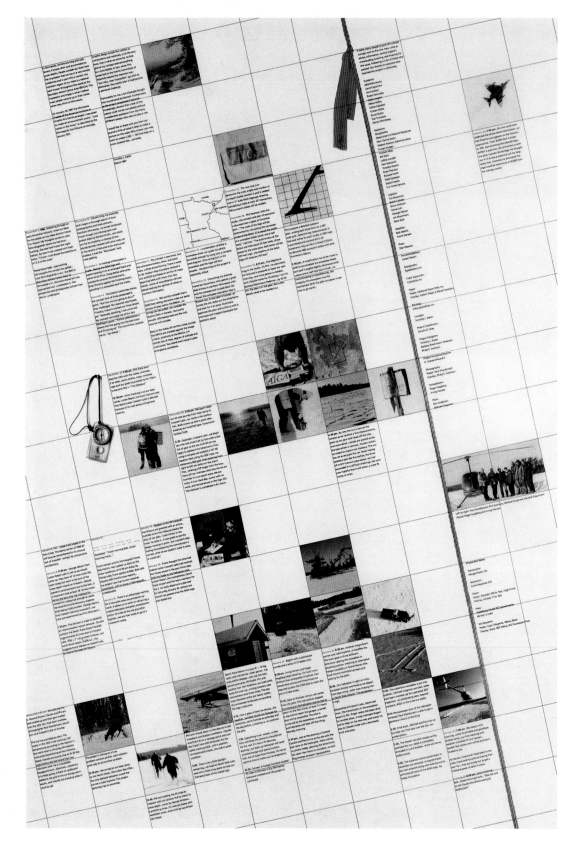

■ **314, 315** Poster for the inauguration of the AIGA chapter at Minneapolis. A sheet *(314)* gives a day-by-day account on how this vast project transpired. The idea was to "write" the AIGA logo somewhere in the snowy wilderness of the state's northern region and use a helicopter to photograph it from the air. Crescent Lake was chosen and a snowplow used for the "writing" - the logo being first marked out with surveyors' stakes. After many problems - climatic and technical - the goal was achieved. The logo, done in winter '86/'87, finally measured 200 x 760 feet. It took 22 days in all and involved 42 people. An F4D Phantom pilot, mistaking it for an SOS, zoomed down to 300 feet. He said later the logo could be read at a height of 30 000 feet. (USA)

■ **314, 315** Plakat zur Ankündigung des AIGA Stützpunktes von Minneapolis. Das Beiblatt *(314)* erklärt die Entstehungsgeschichte dieses Projekts, welches die Mitarbeit von 42 Personen in Anspruch nahm und 22 Tage von der Planung bis zur Realisation dauerte. Ort des Geschehens war der Crescent-See. Die Buchstaben wurden nach einem minuziös ausgearbeiteten Plan mit Stangen gekennzeichnet und anschliessend mit einem Schneepflug «geschrieben». Das Ergebnis wurde aus einem Helikopter photographiert. Ein Phantom-Pilot hielt das Ganze zuerst für einen Hilferuf und brachte sein Flugzeug auf eine Höhe von ca. 300 Fuss, um sich zu vergewissern. Später meinte er, der Schriftzug müsse aus einer Höhe von 30 000 Fuss immer noch gut lesbar sein. (USA)

■ **314, 315** Affiche annonçant la création de la section Minneapolis de l'AIGA documentée par cette création niviforme. La feuille jointe *(314)* retrace l'historique du projet réalisé en 22 jours par une équipe de 42 personnes au bord du lac Crescent. Les quatre lettres furent délimitées minutieusement à l'aide de perches, puis tracées à l'aide d'un chasse-neige. Le tout fut photographié depuis un hélicoptère. Réalisation qui n'alla pas sans remous. En effet, un pilote militaire survolant la scène dans son Phantom crut y lire un appel à l'aide. Descendu à quelque 300 pieds pour y regarder de plus près, il réalisa son erreur. Interrogé par la suite, il estima que l'inscription devait encore être bien lisible à une altitude de 30 000 pieds, soit 10 km. (USA)

AMERICAN INSTITUTE OF GRAPHIC ARTS
MINNESOTA CHAPTER

JANUARY 1987

■ **316** Poster to announce an experimental film series with films by Russian avant-garde artist Dziga Vertov. (GER)

■ **317** Astronomy is the subject of a lecture series which is announced on this poster. (ITA)

■ **318** Under the title "Frog" the publisher of scholastic books and educational material publicizes the best works by designers, illustrators and photographers. (USA)

■ **319** Announcement of the 10th Congress of McCormack & Dodge. (USA)

■ **316** Ankündigungsplakat zu einer Experimentalfilmreihe mit Filmen des russischen Avantgarde-Künstlers Dziga Vertov. (GER)

■ **317** Astronomie ist das Thema einer Vortragsreihe, die mit diesem Plakat angekündigt wird. (ITA)

■ **318** Unter dem Titel »Frosch« möchte der Herausgeber von Schulbüchern und Lehrmitteln die besten Arbeiten von Designern, Illustratoren und Photographen veröffentlichen. (USA)

■ **319** Ankündigungsplakat des 10. Kongresses von McCormack & Dodge. (USA)

■ **316** Affiche annonçant la projection d'une série de films expérimentaux de l'artiste russe d'avant-garde Dziga Vertov. (GER)

■ **317** Trois conférences d'astronomie sont annoncées sur cette affiche de la municipalité de Pesaro. (ITA)

■ **318** Le titre générique »Frog« sert à un éditeur de matériel pédagogique et didactique pour regrouper les meilleurs travaux de designers, illustrateurs et photographes. (USA)

■ **319** Affiche annonçant le 10e congrès de McCormack & Dodge. (USA)

ART DIRECTOR:
Andrea Hanslovsky/
Ulrich Braun/
Michael Klar
DESIGNER:
Andrea Hanslovsky/
Ulrich Braun/
Michael Klar
CLIENT:
Fachhochschule für Gestaltung,
Schwäbisch Gmünd
■ **316**

ART DIRECTOR:
Massimo Dolcini
DESIGNER:
Carlo Beccatti
ARTIST:
Carlo Beccatti
STUDIO:
Fuorischema
CLIENT:
Comune di Pesaro
■ **317**

ART DIRECTOR:
Peter Bradford/
Patricia Maka

DESIGNER:
Peter Bradford

ARTIST:
Various

AGENCY:
Peter Bradford & Associates

CLIENT:
Ginn & Company

■ **318**

ART DIRECTOR:
Beth Greely

PHOTOGRAPHER:
Lou Jones

AGENCY:
McCormack & Dodge/In House

CLIENT:
McCormack & Dodge

■ **319**

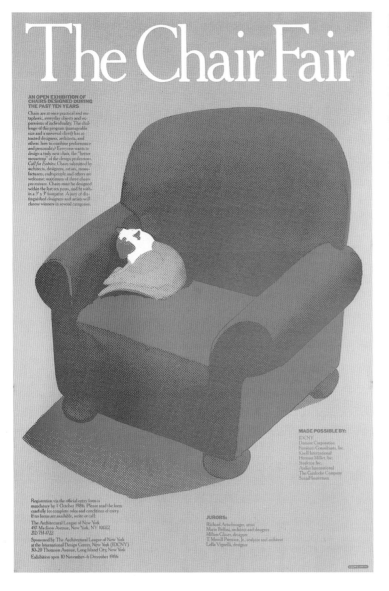

ART DIRECTOR:
Milton Glaser

DESIGNER:
Milton Glaser

ARTIST:
Milton Glaser

AGENCY:
Milton Glaser, Inc.

CLIENT:
*The Architectural League
of New York*

■ **320**

ART DIRECTOR:
Heinrich Brandt

DESIGNER:
Heinrich Brandt

AGENCY:
Atelier für Design Brandt

CLIENT:
*Kirchenkreisverband
Düsseldorf*

■ **321**

■ **320** Poster of the Architectural League of New York calling for participants to a chair design contest. (USA)

■ **321** Announcement of a Reformation commemoration under the title "What counts in the church today?". (GER)

■ **322** Poster to mark the 83rd birthday of the famous American cookery expert and cook-book author James Beard. (USA)

■ **320** Aufforderung zur Teilnahme an einem Stuhl-Design-Wettbewerb. (USA)

■ **321** Bekanntgabe einer Gedenkfeier zur Reformation unter dem Motto «Was gilt in der Kirche?». (GER)

■ **322** Plakat zum 83. Geburtstag des berühmten amerikanischen Kochpapstes und Kochbuch-Autors James Beard. (USA)

■ **320** Affiche appelant à participer à un concours de design pour la création de sièges. (USA)

■ **321** Annonce de la commémoration du début de la Réforme (les 95 thèses de Luther): «Qu'est-ce qui vaut dans l'Eglise?» (GER)

■ **322** Affiche pour le 83e anniversaire du pape de la cuisine américaine, auteur de best-sellers, James Beard. (USA)

ART DIRECTOR:
MILTON GLASER
DESIGNER:
MILTON GLASER
ARTIST:
MILTON GLASER
AGENCY:
MILTON GLASER, INC.
CLIENT:
AMERICAN EXPRESS
■322

Concept 85

Three
Designers
Talk
Design

California
College
of Arts and
Crafts

Saturday
October 19
8:30am
to 5:00pm

Speakers

Katherine McCoy, Co-Chairman of
the Department of Design, Cranbrook
Academy of Art, and partner of
McCoy & McCoy Associates began
her design career at Unimark
International. Major clients include
Chrysler Corporation, MIT Press
and Xerox Education Group. Recent
projects vary from graphic and
signage design to exhibition
and interior design for furniture
showrooms and executive offices.

Ms. McCoy is currently Chairman
of the Board of the Industrial
Designers Society of America, and a
member of the Design Arts Policy
Panel of the National Endowment for
the Arts. She is a contributing
editor of Industrial Design magazine
and was an IBM Fellow at the
1982 International Design Conference
in Aspen.

She has lectured at major design
conferences throughout the world and
has juried several exhibitions
including the AIGA Communication
Graphics Show, the STA 100, and
the 1984 Presidential Design Awards.

Stephan Geissbuhler received
his Master's degree in graphic design
from the School of Art and Design
in Basel in 1964. Prior to joining the
firm of Chermayeff Geismar &
Associates in 1978, Mr. Geissbuhler
held several positions in Switzerland
and the United States designing
and consulting for major companies
and design firms. After coming to the
U.S. he was on the faculty of
the Philadelphia College of Art, cul-
minating in his appointment as the
Chairman of the Graphic Design
Department, in 1975. Mr. Geissbuhler
became a partner at Chermayeff
& Geismar Associates.

Projects and major clients include
the bicentennial exhibit for the
Smithsonian Institution, an identity
program for the U.S. Environmental
Protection Agency, work for
Banco de Italia in Argentina, Dixon
Pacific Corporation, IBM Signage
in New York, Philip Morris, Inc. and
Chemical Bank.

Mr. Geissbuhler has served on
the board of the AIGA and
is currently a member of the faculty
for the improvement of federal
Graphics. Awards and recognition
include two First Swiss National Prizes
for Applied Art, AIGA, New York
Art Directors Club and numerous
other awards.

Paula Scher received her BFA from
Tyler School of Art in 1970. Prior to
her joining the partnership of Koppel,
Koppel & Scher, she was an art
director for CBS Records, had designed
two new magazines for Time, Inc.
and authored and designed two
books, The Honeymoon Book, and
The Brownstone.

Ms. Scher is currently on the Board
of Directors of the AIGA and teaches
a Senior Portfolio Course at the
School of Visual Arts in New York.

Awards and recognition include four
Grammy nominations for Cover of
the Year from the National Association
of Recording Arts and Sciences,
awards from CA, Graphis, AIGA, Mead
Grafanografik, The New York Art
Directors Club and Society of
Illustrators. Works are in the perma-
nent collections of the Museum
of Modern Art, The Library of Congress
and the Maryland Institute of Art.

Program

California College of Arts and Crafts
presents the sixth in a series of
one-day symposiums created to bring
students in contact with the pro-
fessional design community. The
CCAC School of Design has
previously hosted such luminaries
as Roger Black, John Cassado,
The CMG Group, April Greiman, John
Van Hamersveld, Kit Hinrichs, Alexia
Landon, Russell Leong, McKay
Maginnis, Harry Marnyn, Woody Pirtle,
Christopher Pullman, Michael
Salisbury, Steinböber Deutsch &
Gard, Deguld Stoermer, Lucille Tenazas,
Mark Trenk, and Massimo Vignelli.

Concept '85 will be held Saturday,
October 19, 1985 from 8:30am
to 5:00pm at Nahl Hall on the CCAC
campus. There is no registration
or fee. Coffee and donuts reception
at 8:30am. Speakers begin
at 9:00am. There will be a mid-day
break, please bring a bag lunch.

California College of
Arts and Crafts
5212 Broadway at College Avenue
Oakland, California 94618
For information call
415 653-8118

The School of Design at CCAC offers
programs leading to the Bachelor
of Fine Arts and Master of Fine Arts
degrees in graphic design. Studies
include exhibit design, environmental
graphics and signage, typography,
illustration, editorial design and
package design. The faculty: Doug
Akagi, Leslie Becker, Craig Bergquist,
Michael Cronan, Christina Donna,
Craig Frazier, Thomas Ingalls, Laura
Lamar, Michael Mabry, Michael
Manwaring, Melissa Matlock, Gunter
Mohr, Bonnie Russell, Tanys Stringham,
Lucille Tenazas, Michael Vanderbyl,
and department chairman Steven
Renwell, invite you to participate in
Concept '85, an opportunity
to broaden your visual vocabularies.
Produced in conjunction with
The Design Alliance, a CCAC
student organization.

■ **323** Poster for the Stanford Conference on Design. (USA)

■ **324** Announcement of a symposium of the California College of Arts and Crafts. Three well-known designers give information to the students on graphic design. (USA)

■ **325** Poster for one of the Architectural League of New York's lecture series entitled "Emerging Voices '87", aimed at young architects. (USA)

■ **323** Plakat für eine Tagung über Design. (USA)

■ **324** Ankündigung eines Symposiums des California College of Arts and Crafts. Drei bekannte Designer werden die Studenten über Graphik-Design informieren. (USA)

■ **325** Für eine von der Architectural League New York organisierte Vortragsreihe unter dem Titel «Emerging Voices '87», die an junge Architekten gerichtet ist. (USA)

■ **323** Affiche pour un colloque de design. (USA)

■ **324** Affiche annonçant un symposium du California College of Arts and Crafts, avec la participation de trois vedettes du design graphique. (USA)

■ **325** Pour un cycle de conférences organisé par l'Architectural League New York sous le titre «Emerging Voices '87», pour rendre compte des travaux des jeunes architectes. (USA)

ART DIRECTOR:
Michael Cronan
DESIGNER:
Michael Cronan
ARTIST:
Michael Cronan
AGENCY:
Cronan Design
CLIENT:
Stanford Conference on Design
■ **323**

◀ **ART DIRECTOR:**
Michael Mabry
DESIGNER:
Michael Mabry
ARTIST:
Michael Mabry
AGENCY:
Michael Mabry Design
CLIENT:
California College of Arts & Crafts
■ **324**

▶ **DESIGNER:**
Michael Bierut
AGENCY:
Vignelli Associates
CLIENT:
The Architectural League of New York
■ **325**

ART DIRECTOR:
Michael Schwab

DESIGNER:
Michael Schwab

ARTIST:
Michael Schwab

AGENCY:
Michael Schwab Design

CLIENT:
Art Directors Club of Tulsa
■ 326

ART DIRECTOR:
Frank Baseman

DESIGNER:
Frank Baseman

PHOTOGRAPHER:
William Albert Allard

AGENCY:
*Frank Baseman
Graphic Design*

CLIENT:
AIGA Philadelphia
■ 327

■ **326** For a conference of the Art Directors Club of Tulsa, at which works by illustrator and graphic designer Michael Schwab are to be shown. (USA)

■ **327** Invitation to an AIGA Philadelphia event on the subject "30 Years Design in Texas, a Retrospective". (USA)

■ **328** Announcement of a conference of the AIGA San Francisco on the theme "Fashion and Graphics". (USA)

■ **326** Für ein Treffen des Art Directors Club von Tulsa, an welchem Arbeiten des Illustrators und Graphikers Michael Schwab gezeigt werden. (USA)

■ **327** Einladung zu einem Anlass des AIGA Philadelphia unter dem Motto «30 Jahre Design in Texas, eine Retrospektive». (USA)

■ **328** Ankündigung eines Kongresses des AIGA San Francisco über das Thema «Mode und Graphik-Design». (USA)

■ **326** Pour une réunion de l'Art Directors Club de Tulsa, dans l'Oklahoma, agrémentée d'une exposition des travaux de l'illustrateur et graphiste Michael Schwab. (USA)

■ **327** Annonce d'une exposition de l'AIGA de Philadelphie consacrée à «30 années de design au Texas – une rétrospective». (USA)

■ **328** Annonce d'un congrès de l'AIGA de San Francisco axé sur «la mode et le design graphique». (USA)

ART DIRECTOR:
Jennifer Morla
DESIGNER:
Jennifer Morla
PHOTOGRAPHER:
Michelle Clement
AGENCY:
Morla Design, Inc.
CLIENT:
AIGA San Francisco
■ **328**

DESIGNER:
Craig Neuman

PHOTOGRAPHER:
Arthur Meyerson

AGENCY:
Barkley Evergreen

CLIENT:
*Kansas City
Art Directors Club*

■ 329

Arthur Meyerson in Kansas City • February 16, 1987 • Stanford and Sons Comedy House

ART DIRECTOR:
Charles Spencer Anderson/
Joe Duffy

DESIGNER:
Charles Spencer Anderson/
Joe Duffy

ARTIST:
Charles Spencer Anderson/
Joe Duffy

STUDIO:
The Duffy Design Group

CLIENT:
Sacramento Community
Center Theatre

■ **330**

■ **329** Invitation to a conference of the Art Directors Club of Kansas City at which works by photographer Arthur Meyerson are shown. (USA)

■ **330** Announcement of a design conference in Sacramento, California. (USA)

■ **329** Einladung zu einem Treffen des Art Directors Club von Kansas City, bei welchem die Arbeiten des Photographen Arthur Meyerson gezeigt werden. (USA)

■ **330** Ankündigung eines Design-Kongresses in Sacramento, Kalifornien. (USA)

■ **329** Invitation à une réunion de l'Art Directors Club de Kansas City à l'occasion d'une exposition des créations du photographe Arthur Meyerson. (USA)

■ **330** Annonce d'un congrès de design tenu dans la ville californienne de Sacramento. (USA)

■ **331** With a deliberate pun on the word "boars" this poster announces a lecture by illustrator Braldt Bralds at a conference of the Art Directors/Copywriters Club of Minneapolis. (USA)

■ **332** Invitation by the Communications Arts Society of New Mexico to a lecture by designer Chris Hill. (USA)

■ **333** Contest poster for the Toronto Art Directors Club. (CAN)

■ **331** Ankündigung eines Vortrages des Designers Braldt Bralds beim monatlichen Treffen des Art Directors/Copywriters Club von Minneapolis. (USA)

■ **332** Einladung der Communications Arts Society von New Mexiko zu einem Vortrag des Designers Chris Hill. (USA)

■ **333** Wettbewerbsplakat des Art Directors Club Toronto. (CAN)

■ **331** Annonce d'une conférence du designer Braldt Bralds à l'occasion de la réunion mensuelle de l'Art Directors/Copywriters Club de Minneapolis. (USA)

■ **332** Invitation de la Communication Arts Society du Nouveau-Mexique à une conférence du designer Chris Hill. (USA)

■ **333** Affiche-concours de l'Art Directors Club de Toronto. (CAN)

◀ **ART DIRECTOR:**
Nancy Rice

DESIGNER:
Nancy Rice

ARTIST:
Braldt Bralds

AGENCY:
Rice & Rice Advertising, Inc.

CLIENT:
*Art Directors/
Copywriter Club Minneapolis*

■ **331**

◀ **ART DIRECTOR:**
*R Vaughn/S Wedeen/
L Fuqua/M Chamberlain*

DESIGNER:
*R Vaughn/S Wedeen/
L Fuqua/M Chamberlain*

ARTIST:
S Wedeen/M Chamberlain

AGENCY:
Vaughn/Wedeen Creative, Inc.

CLIENT:
*Communication Artists
of New Mexico*

■ **332**

ART DIRECTOR:
Joe Shyllit

DESIGNER:
Joe Shyllit

PHOTOGRAPHER:
Bert Bell

AGENCY:
Kuleba Shyllit Advertising

CLIENT:
*Art Directors Club
of Toronto*

■ **333**

1 9 8 6

THE ART DIRECTORS'
CLUB OF TORONTO

CALL FOR ENTRIES · DEADLINE: FRIDAY, JULY 25, 1986.

■ **334** Poster to announce a reading by Seymour Chwast at the Tyler School of Art, the graphic-design department of Temple University. (USA)

■ **335** Park City – a newly developed skiing area in the Wasatch Mountains of Utah State – is the location for a design conference announced on this poster. (USA)

■ **336** The 37th International Designer Congress in Aspen is held under the title of this poster "Success & Failure". (USA)

■ **334** Ankündigung einer Lesung von Seymour Chwast an der Tyler School of Art, der Abteilung für graphisches Design der Temple University. (USA)

■ **335** Bekanntmachung einer Tagung für Designer in Park City, einem neu erschlossenen Skigebiet in den Wasatch-Bergen im Staate Utah. (USA)

■ **336** «Erfolg & Misserfolg» – Thema des 37. Designer-Kongresses in Aspen, der mit diesem Plakat angekündigt wird. (USA)

■ **334** Annonce d'une conférence de Seymour Chwast à la Tyler School of Art, qui constitue le département de design graphique de la Temple University. (USA)

■ **335** Annonce d'un colloque réunissant des designers à Park City, un nouveau centre de sports d'hiver aménagé dans les montagnes Wasatch de l'Utah. (USA)

■ **336** «Succès et échecs», c'est là le thème du 37e congrès international de design d'Aspen annoncé par cette affiche. (USA)

ART DIRECTOR:
Frank Baseman
DESIGNER:
Frank Baseman
ARTIST:
Frank Baseman
AGENCY:
Tyler Design Workshop
CLIENT:
Tyler School of Art/
AIGA Philadelphia
■ **334**

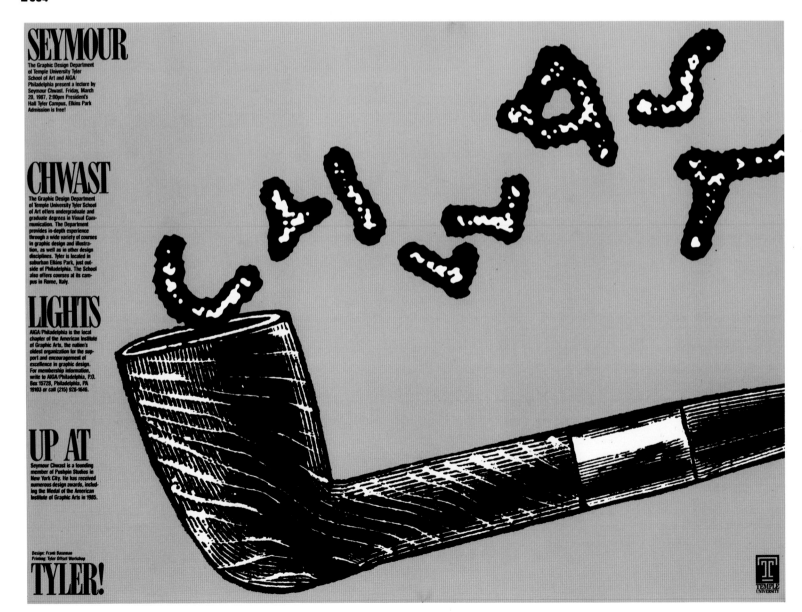

Success & Failure

37th International Design Conference in Aspen

As the world of the designer
becomes increasingly complex,
success and failure become
more difficult to assess
for ourselves, our products,
our companies, and our clients.

Sunday June 14
through Friday June 19, 1987

Conference Chairman:
Michael Crichton,
Author & Filmmaker

Topics Include:

Corporate Design for Failure
Failure as a Component of Success
Redesigning Failure
Typecasting: Price of Success?
Uses of Failure
Professional Success, Personal Failure
Professional Failure, Personal Success
Penalties of Achievement
Perfect Design
Coping with Design Conflicts
Is Fear of Failure Necessary?
Creative Risk and Creative Error
Well-designed Failure
Rewarded Inadequacies
Famous Successes Reconsidered

ART DIRECTOR:
Don Weller

DESIGNER:
Don Weller

ARTIST:
Don Weller

AGENCY:
*The Weller Institute for the
Cure of Design, Inc.*

CLIENT:
*The Design Conference that
Just Happens to be in Park City*

■335

ART DIRECTOR:
Robert Miles Runyan

DESIGNER:
Robert Miles Runyan

ARTIST:
Guy Billout

AGENCY:
*Robert Miles Runyan &
Associates*

CLIENT:
Aspen Design Conference

■336

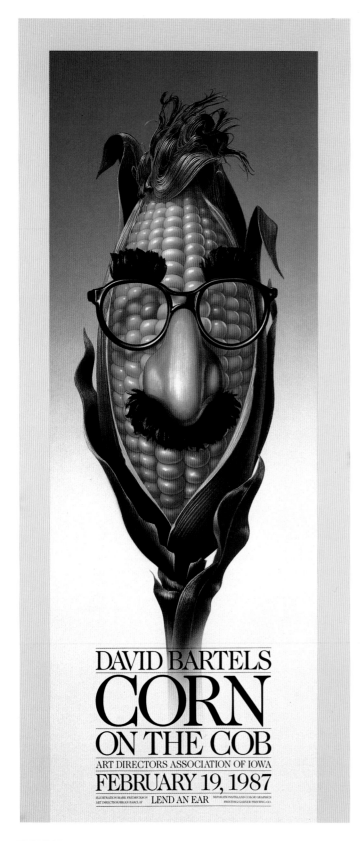

ART DIRECTOR:
Brian Barclay

DESIGNER:
Chuck Hart

ARTIST:
Mark Fredrickson

AGENCY:
Bartels & Carstens

CLIENT:
*Art Directors Association
of Iowa*

■337

ART DIRECTOR:
Ron Sullivan

DESIGNER:
Diana McKnight

PHOTOGRAPHER:
Tom Ryan

AGENCY:
Sullivan Perkins

CLIENT:
*Dallas Designers'
Chili Cook-off*

■338

■ **337** Poster for "Corn on the Cob" – an event organized by the Art Directors Association of Iowa. (USA)

■ **338** Invitation to the 6th Annual Designers Chili Cook-off (contest) in Dallas. The illustration depicts a curve template, used by graphic designers in their work. (USA)

■ **339** For a summer seminar on investor relations. (USA)

■ **337** Plakat für eine Veranstaltung der Art Directors Association von Iowa. (USA)

■ **338** Einladung zum 6. Chili-Kochwettbewerb der Designer von Dallas. Die Abbildung zeigt ein Kurven-Lineal, welches von Graphikern benutzt wird. (USA)

■ **339** Für ein Sommer-Seminar über Investor Relations. (USA)

■ **337** Affiche créée à l'occasion d'une manifestation de l'Art Directors Association de l'Iowa. (USA)

■ **338** Invitation au 6e concours annuel de plats de chili réalisés par les designers de Dallas. L'illustration représente le pistolet traceur de courbes du graphiste. (USA)

■ **339** Pour un séminaire d'été sur l'investissement. (USA)

ART DIRECTOR:
MARK FREYTAG
DESIGNER:
MARK FREYTAG
AGENCY:
THE ICON GROUP
CLIENT:
SOUTHWEST OHIO CHAPTER
■**339**

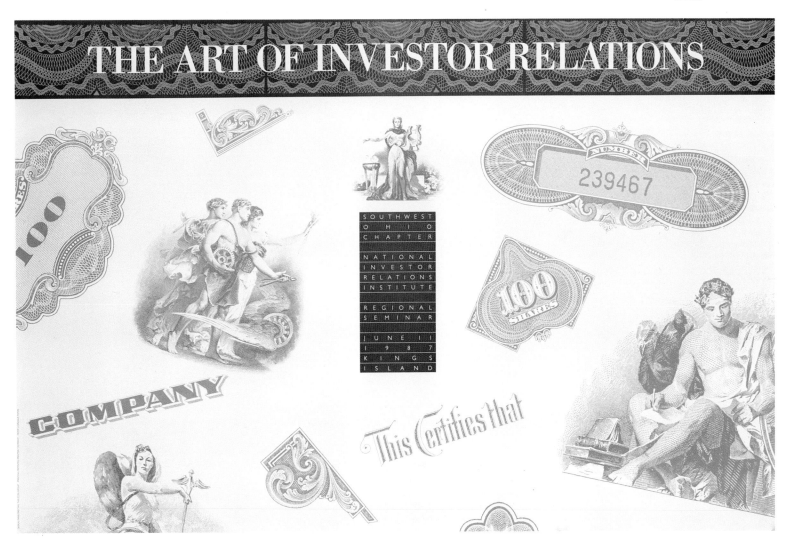

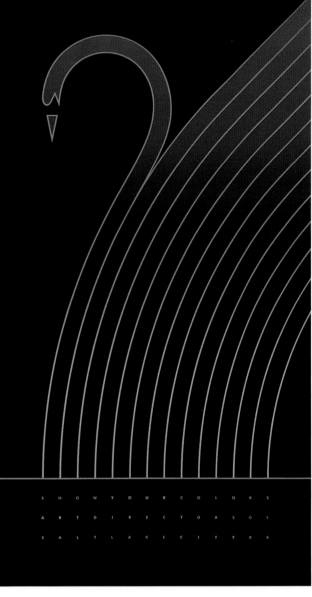

ART DIRECTOR:
Jack Anderson/Pat Hansen

DESIGNER:
Jack Anderson/Pat Hansen

ARTIST:
Jack Anderson/Pat Hansen

PHOTOGRAPHER:
James Frederick Housel

AGENCY:
*Pat Hansen Design/
Hornall Anderson
Design Works*

CLIENT:
AIGA Seattle

■ **340**

ART DIRECTOR:
McRay Magleby

DESIGNER:
McRay Magleby

ARTIST:
McRay Magleby

AGENCY:
BYU Graphics

CLIENT:
Brigham Young University

■ **341**

■ **340** Announcement of the opening of a further new chapter of the American Institute of Graphic Arts (AIGA) in Seattle. (USA)

■ **341** "Show your Colors." Invitation issued by Brigham Young University to the Art Directors of Salt Lake City to participate in a contest. (USA)

■ **342** Poster to announce a conference of the Art Directors/Copywriters Club of Minneapolis at which Seymour Chwast – the most famous left-hander of all American designers – is the guest speaker. (USA)

■ **340** Ankündigung der Eröffnung eines weiteren Stützpunktes des American Institute of Graphic Arts (AIGA) in Seattle. (USA)

■ **341** «Zeigt her Eure Farben» – Einladung der Brigham Young University an die Art Directors von Salt Lake City zur Teilnahme an einem Wettbewerb. (USA)

■ **342** Für ein Treffen des Art Directors/Copywriters Club von Minneapolis, zu dem Seymour Chwast, der als berühmtester Linkshänder unter den amerikanischen Designern gilt, als Gastredner eingeladen wurde. (USA)

■ **340** Annonce de la création d'une nouvelle section de l'American Institute of Graphic Arts AIGA à Seattle. (USA)

■ **341** «Montrez voir vos couleurs» – sur cette affiche, l'Université Brigham Young invite les directeurs artistiques de Salt Lake City à participer à un concours. (USA)

■ **342** Pour une réunion de l'Art Directors/Copywriters Club de Minneapolis rehaussée d'une conférence de Seymour Chwast, qui passe pour être le gaucher le plus célèbre parmi les designers américains. (USA)

ART DIRECTOR:
Brooke Kenney

DESIGNER:
Brooke Kenney

ARTIST:
Seymour Chwast

AGENCY:
Laughing Graphics

CLIENT:
*Art Directors/
Copywriters Club
of Minneapolis*

■ 342

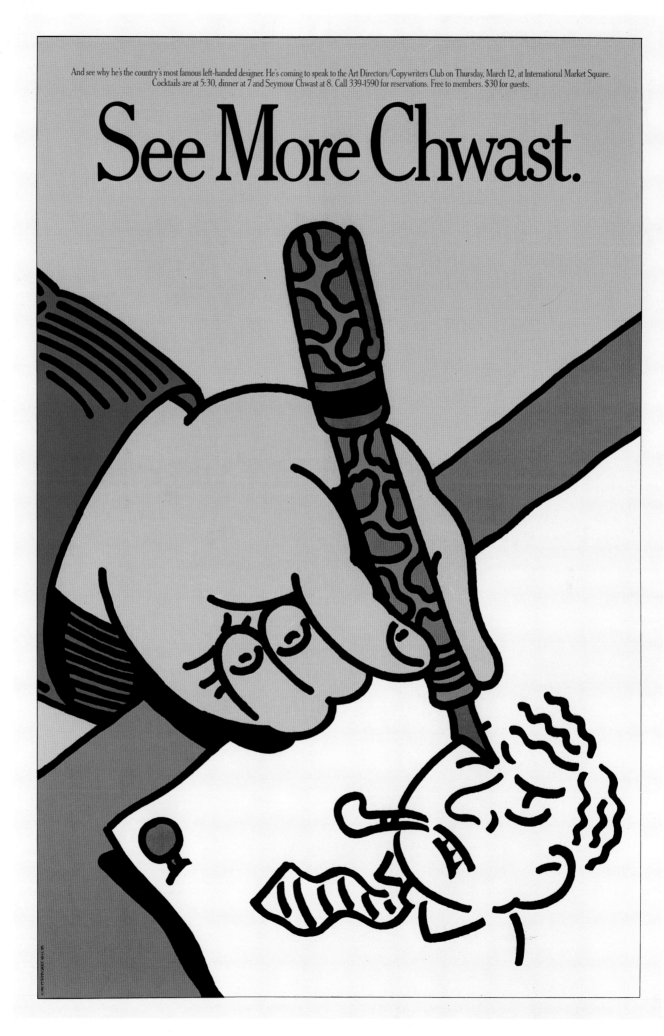

ART DIRECTOR:
Cameron Clement

DESIGNER:
Jennifer Clement

ARTIST:
Steven Guarnaccia

CLIENT:
Tulsa Art Directors Club

■ **343**

ART DIRECTOR:
Dugald Stermer

DESIGNER:
Dugald Stermer

ARTIST:
Dugald Stermer

CLIENT:
AIGA New York

■ **344**

■ **343** Poster for a conference of the Art Directors Club of Tulsa, at which the artist Guarnaccia speaks. (USA)

■ **344** Poster calling for entries from designers in America and Canada to take part in a contest for book design, organized by AIGA, New York. (USA)

■ **345** To announce a summer seminar for students at which they have a chance to watch painters, illustrators, ceramic artists, designers, and sculptors at work. (USA)

■ **346** For a convention dealing with international environmental design. (USA)

■ **343** Plakat zu einem Treffen des Art Directors Club von Tulsa, bei dem der Zeichner Guarnaccia sprechen wird. (USA)

■ **344** Aufforderung an Designer in Amerika und Kanada, sich an einem Wettbewerb für Buch-Design, ausgeschrieben vom AIGA New York, zu beteiligen. (USA)

■ **345** Für ein Sommer-Seminar für Studenten, wobei sie Gelegenheit haben werden, Maler, Illustratoren, Keramik-Künstler, Designer und Bildhauer bei der Arbeit zu beobachten. (USA)

■ **346** Für eine internationale Fachtagung über die graphische und architektonische Umweltgestaltung. (USA)

■ **343** Affiche invitant à une réunion de l'Art Directors Club de Tulsa. Conférencier invité: le dessinateur Guarnaccia. (USA)

■ **344** Appel lancé aux designers américains et canadiens désirant participer à un concours de design de livres organisé par l'AIGA de New York. (USA)

■ **345** Annonce d'un séminaire d'été destiné aux étudiants et leur offrant l'occasion d'observer des peintres, illustrateurs, céramistes, designers et sculpteurs en plein effort créatif. (USA)

■ **346** Affiche pour un congrès professionnel d'environnementalistes venus de divers pays. (USA)

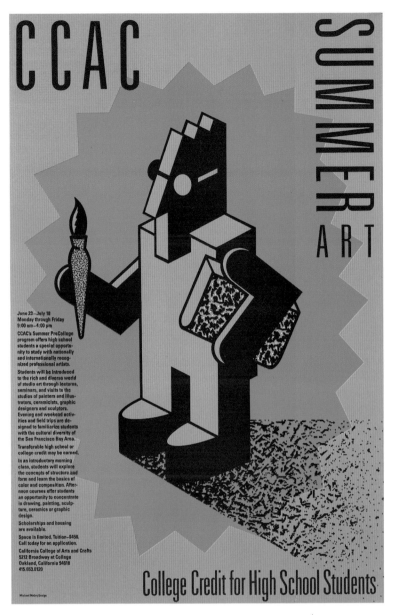

ART DIRECTOR:
Michael Mabry

DESIGNER:
Michael Mabry

ARTIST:
Michael Mabry

AGENCY:
Michael Mabry Design

CLIENT:
*California College of
Arts & Crafts*

■ **345**

ART DIRECTOR:
Alice Hecht

DESIGNER:
Alice Hecht

PHOTOGRAPHER:
Dirk Bakker

AGENCY:
Hecht Design

CLIENT:
*SEGD Society
of Environmental
Graphic Design*

■ **346**

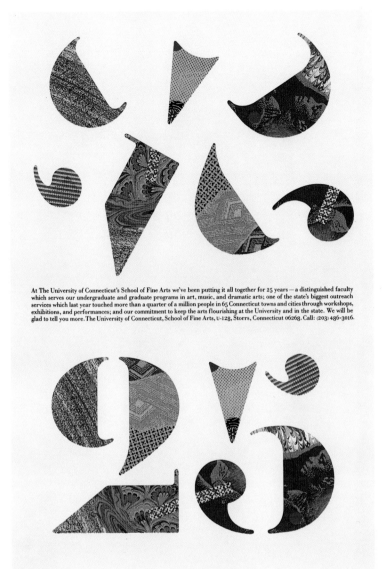

ART DIRECTOR:
Peter Good

DESIGNER:
Peter Good

ARTIST:
Peter Good

AGENCY:
Peter Good Graphic Design

CLIENT:
University of Connecticut

■348

◀ **ART DIRECTOR:**
Doug Joseph/Rik Besser

DESIGNER:
Doug Joseph

PHOTOGRAPHER:
Arthur Meyerson

AGENCY:
Besser Joseph Partners

CLIENT:
ASMP

■347

ART DIRECTOR:
Michael Vanderbyl

DESIGNER:
Michael Vanderbyl

ARTIST:
Michael Vanderbyl

AGENCY:
Vanderbyl Design

CLIENT:
Workspace

■349

■**347** For a conference of the American Society of Magazine Photographers. (USA)

■**348** Poster for various courses which the School of Fine Arts at the University of Connecticut has offered for 25 years. (USA)

■**349** For a conference on work-space and office design. (USA)

■**347** Für ein Treffen der American Society of Magazine Photographers. (USA)

■**348** Plakat für Kurse, die die School of Fine Arts der Universität von Connecticut seit 25 Jahren anbietet. (USA)

■**349** Ankündigung eines Kongresses über Bürogestaltung. (USA)

■**347** Pour une réunion de l'American Society of Magazine Photographers. (USA)

■**348** Affiche-programme des cours que la School of Fine Arts de l'Université du Connecticut organise depuis 25 ans. (USA)

■**349** Pour un congrès d'aménagement de bureaux. (USA)

S P H I N X

A bizarre synthesis of woman and animal, the sinister Sphinx besieged the city of Thebes, tormenting passersby who could not solve her dark riddle: "What creature moves on four legs in the morning, two at noon, and three in the evening?" Oedipus solved the riddle and became king of Thebes.

Don't let a bizarre schedule give you a complex. Please in your registration for Summer Term today.

M I N O T A U R

Half man, half bull, the horrible, man-eating Minotaur lurked in the passages of the infamous Labyrinth, from which no man had returned. Unwinding a ball of string to retrace his steps, the Athenian hero Theseus entered the maze, slew the odious beast, and fled Crete with his true love, Ariadne.

Don't be strung out by a beastly schedule. Wind up your registration for Spring Term today.

P E G A S U S

The wild, winged Pegasus, born of Medusa's blood, was first ridden by the Corinthian hero Bellerophon. Using a golden bridle from the goddess Athena, he mounted the magic steed and killed the Chimera—a fire-breathing monster, part lion, part goat, with the tail of a serpent.

Don't be scorched by poor class selection. Register today and fly into Spring Term with a golden schedule.

M E D U S A

One of three ghastly Gorgon sisters, the snake-haired, flying Medusa, had a lethal stare that turned onlookers into stone. The young hero Perseus, with some help from the Gods, overcame the hideous creature. Looking only at Medusa's reflection in his shield, he closed in on winged sandals and decapitated her.

Don't come face-to-face with a ghastly schedule. Complete your registration for Summer Term now.

ART DIRECTOR:
McRay Magleby

DESIGNER:
McRay Magleby

ARTIST:
McRay Magleby

AGENCY:
BYU Graphics

CLIENT:
Brigham Young University

■ **350–354**

CERBERUS

The triple-
headed hound, Cerberus,
kept an unrelenting
watch over the entrance
to the Greek underworld
of Hades. Heracles
completed his twelfth
and final labor by
going down to Hades,
subduing the vicious
canine, and bringing him
up to King Eurystheus.
Terrified, the king made
Heracles return the dog
to the underworld.

Don't
be hounded by
registration worries.
Mail in your tuition
payment for Spring Term
before the deadline—
April 15

■ **350–354** Brigham Young University of Utah reminds its students to enroll for the spring and summer terms - and to pay their fees in good time - with the aid of short episodes and scenes from Greek mythology as hints on this poster series. (USA)

■ **350–354** Mit Episoden aus der griechischen Mythologie fordert die Brigham Young University, Utah, ihre Studenten auf, die Registrierung für das Frühjahrs- respektive das Sommersemester nicht zu verpassen und die Gebühren rechtzeitig einzuzahlen. (USA)

■ **350–354** Episodes empruntés à la mythologie grecque permettent à l'Université Brigham Young de rappeler à ses étudiants l'urgence de s'immatriculer pour le semestre de printemps respectivement d'été pour ne pas rater le coche, et de verser les droits. (USA)

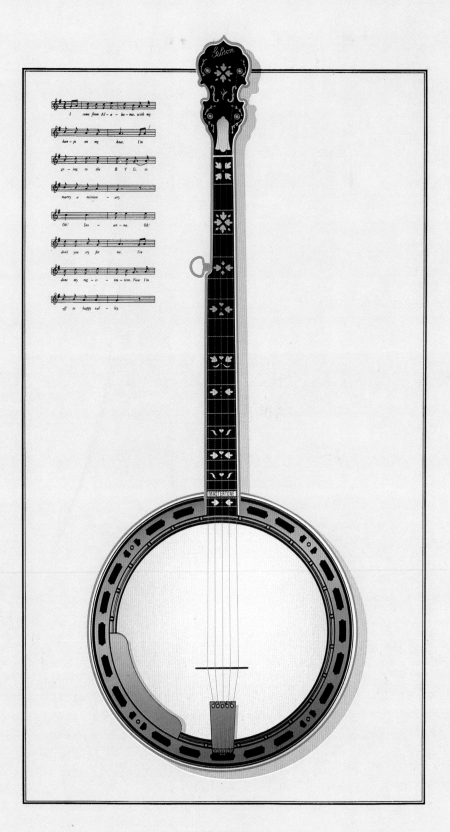

ART DIRECTOR:
McRay Magleby

DESIGNER:
McRay Magleby

ARTIST:
McRay Magleby

AGENCY:
BYU Graphics

CLIENT:
Brigham Young University

■ 355–357

■ **355–357** From a series of posters issued by Brigham Young University of Utah to remind students to enroll for the winter term in good time. Famous melodies get new lyrics – that tell of the advantages of early enrollment. (USA)

■ **355–357** Plakate, die die Studenten der Brigham Young University, Utah, daran erinnern sollen, sich rechtzeitig für das Wintersemester anzumelden. Bekannte Melodien wurden neu betextet, um auf die Vorteile einer frühzeitigen Registrierung hinzuweisen. (USA)

■ **355–357** Affiches rappelant aux étudiants de l'Université Brigham Young (Utah) les délais d'immatriculation pour le semestre d'hiver. Des textes ad hoc sur des airs anciens bien connus exposent tous les avantages d'une inscription faite à temps. (USA)

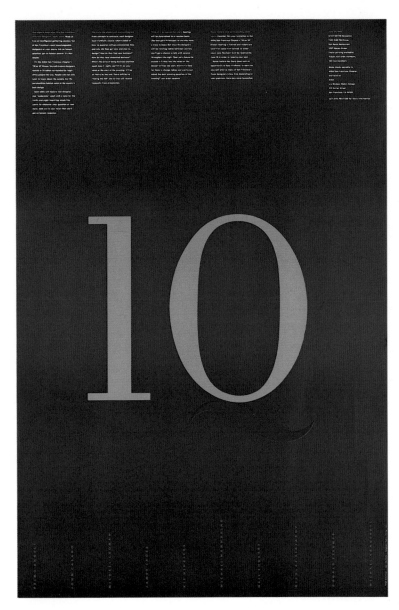

ART DIRECTOR:
Craig Frazier
DESIGNER:
Craig Frazier
AGENCY:
Frazier Design
CLIENT:
AIGA San Francisco
■358

ART DIRECTOR:
Craig Frazier
DESIGNER:
Craig Frazier
AGENCY:
Frazier Design
CLIENT:
American Assoc. of Artificial Intelligence
■359

■**358** Announcement of a discussion evening with well-known designers. (USA)

■**359** Poster for a conference of the American Association of Artificial Intelligence. (USA)

■**360** Invitation to a conference of the Dallas Society of Visual Communications. (USA)

■**361** Poster to publicize a class reunion at the Castleberry High School. (USA)

■**358** Ankündigung eines Diskussionsabends mit bekannten Designern. (USA)

■**359** Plakat für eine Tagung der American Association of Artificial Intelligence. (USA)

■**360** Einladung zu einer Tagung der Dallas Society of Visual Communications. (USA)

■**361** Bekanntgabe eines Klassentreffens der Castleberry High School. (USA)

■**358** Annonce d'une soirée-débats réunissant une série de designers de grande réputation. (USA)

■**359** Affiche pour un colloque de l'American Association of Artificial Intelligence, sur les ordinateurs «intelligents». (USA)

■**360** Invitation à une réunion de la Dallas Society of Visual Communications. (USA)

■**361** Rappel d'une réunion d'anciens élèves de la Castleberry High School. (USA)

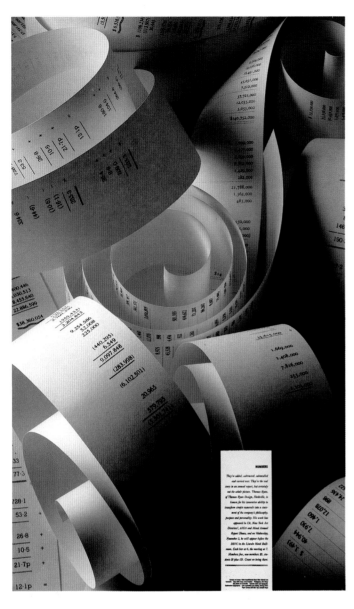

ART DIRECTOR:
ROBIN AYRES

DESIGNER:
ROBIN AYRES

PHOTOGRAPHER:
JOHN WONG/GREG BOOTH
& ASSOCIATES

AGENCY:
RBMM & A/
THE RICHARDS GROUP

CLIENT:
DALLAS SOCIETY OF VISUAL
COMMUNICATIONS

■360

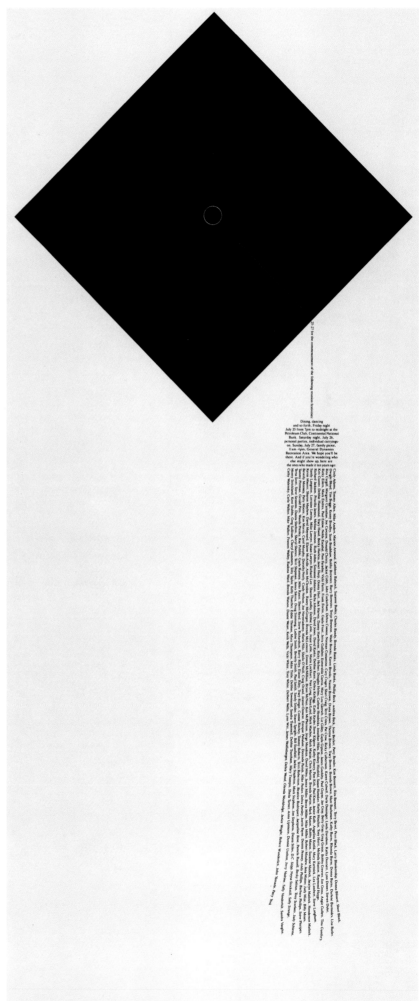

ART DIRECTOR:
D.C. STIPP

DESIGNER:
D.C. STIPP

ARTIST:
D.C. STIPP

AGENCY:
RBMM & A/
THE RICHARDS GROUP

CLIENT:
CASTLEBERRY HIGH SCHOOL
CLASS OF '76

■361

■**362–364** From a series of several posters to motivate the employees of IBM Europe. The perfection of nature is used in connection with each employee's own success and failure, effort and achievement.

■**362–364** Aus einer Plakatserie zur Motivation der Mitarbeiter von IBM-Europe. Die Perfektion in der Natur wird in Zusammenhang gebracht mit Erfolg und Misserfolg, Einsatz und Perfektion jedes einzelnen Mitarbeiters.

■**362–364** Série d'affiches censées motiver davantage les collaborateurs d'IBM Europe. Le thème de la perfection à laquelle atteint la nature sert à interroger les succès, les échecs, l'ardeur au travail et le perfectionnisme du personnel.

ART DIRECTOR:
Garth Bell

DESIGNER:
Garth Bell

PHOTOGRAPHER:
Harri Peccinotti

AGENCY:
Bell & Co.

CLIENT:
IBM Europe

■**362–364**

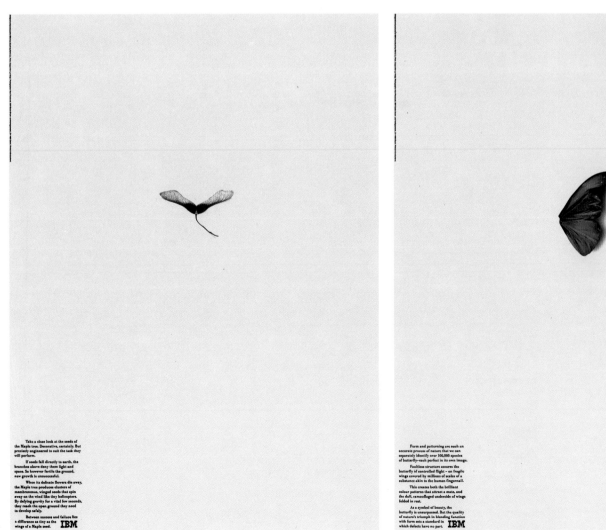

Designed and produced for IBM Asia South by Batt & Co, Paris. Copywriter Lym Hegt. Photographer Henri Pacciotti. IBM Boster Dieck- und Vertagsanstalt, CH-4002 Basel. Printed in Switzerland.

No symbol promises new life as certainly as the egg. Each egg is perfect. Each, in theory, has equal potential for growth and development. Yet without constant effort and care, the potential remains unfulfilled.

Every season, countless eggs fail to hatch. Countless chicks fail to fly. From the perfection of the egg, even the smallest error in meeting needs like warmth or safety can rob the parent birds of success.

Attention to detail, throughout the process, is the commitment that leads such a perfect beginning to perfect, soaring flight at the end.

Only positive, individual efforts can develop this full potential first time, and every time. **IBM**

ART DIRECTOR:
Charles Spencer Anderson

DESIGNER:
Charles Spencer Anderson

ARTIST:
Charles Spencer Anderson

AGENCY:
The Duffy Design Group

CLIENT:
First Bank, Minneapolis

■365

ART DIRECTOR:
John Van Dyke

DESIGNER:
John Van Dyke

PHOTOGRAPHER:
Howard Petrella

AGENCY:
Van Dyke Company

CLIENT:
Van Dyke Company

■366

■**365** Poster to promote good teamwork. (USA)

■**366** From an exhibition of posters at the AIGA San Francisco. Under the title of "Stars and Stripes" various designers offer their interpretations of the American flag. (USA)

■**367** For the 50th anniversary of the Golden Gate Bridge. (USA)

■**365** Plakat zur Förderung der Arbeit im Team. (USA)

■**366** Aus einer Ausstellung der AIGA San Francisco unter dem Titel «Stars and Stripes», an der Interpretationen der amerikanischen Flagge durch verschiedene Designer gezeigt wurden. (USA)

■**367** Zum 50jährigen Bestehen der Golden-Gate-Brücke. (USA)

■**365** Affiche pour la promotion du travail en équipe. (USA)

■**366** Interprétation du drapeau américain «Stars and Stripes» figurant dans une exposition où l'AIGA de San Francisco a réuni diverses versions design des couleurs nationales. (USA)

■**367** Pour le 50e anniversaire du pont du Golden Gate. (USA)

ART DIRECTOR:
Primo Angeli

DESIGNER:
Primo Angeli

ARTIST:
*Ian McLean/
Mark Jones*

AGENCY:
Primo Angeli Inc.

CLIENT:
*Friends of the
Golden Gate Bridge*

■ 367

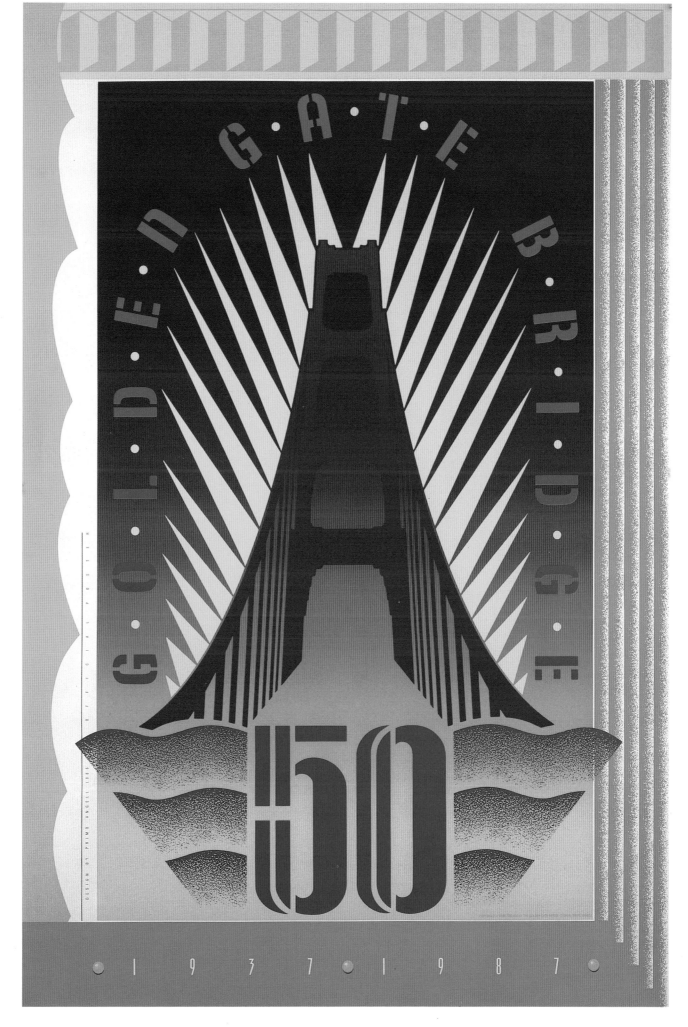

FULLY, FREELY & ENTIRELY

DELAWARE RATIFIES THE CONSTITUTION On December 7, 1787 ♦ Delaware became the first state to ratify the United States Constitution. ♦ Thirty elected delegates ♦ ten each from New Castle, Kent and Sussex counties ♦ met in Battell's Tavern in Dover ♦ and voted unanimously in favor of the Constitution. ♦ The ratification document is one of the state's historical treasures. ♦ Courtesy, Delaware State Archives. ♦

★ ★ ★ ★ ★ ★ ◆ ★ ★ ★ ★ ★ ★

We the Deputies of the People of the Delaware State, in Convention met, having taken into our serious consideration the Federal Constitution proposed and agreed upon by the Deputies of the United States in a General Convention held at the City of Philadelphia on the seventeenth day of September in the Year of our Lord One thousand seven hundred and eighty seven, Have approved, assented to, ratified, and confirmed, and by these Presents, Do, in virtue of the Power and Authority to us given for that purpose, for and in behalf of ourselves and our Constituents, fully, freely, and entirely approve of, assent to, ratify and confirm the said Constitution.

Done in Convention at Dover this seventh day of December in the Year aforesaid, and in the Year of the Independence of the United States of America the twelfth. In Testimony whereof We have hereunto Subscribed our Names.

SUSSEX COUNTY	KENT COUNTY	NEW CASTLE COUNTY
John Ingram	Nicholas Ridgely	James Latimer, Pres.*
John Jones	Richard Smith	James Black
William Moore	George Truitt	John Jones
William Roll	Richard Bassett	Gunning Bedford, Sr.
Thomas Laws	James Sykes	Kensey Johns
Isaac Cooper	Allen McLane	Thomas Watson
Woodman Stockley	Daniel Cummins, Sr.	Solomon Maxwell
John Laws	Joseph Barker	Nicholas Way
Thomas Evans	Edward White	Thomas Duff
Isreal Holland	George Manlove	Gunning Bedford, Jr.

James Latimer was elected President of the Delaware Convention

Delaware artist Robert E. Goodier recreates the scene in his painting "Delaware, The First State: Ratification of the Federal Constitution." ♦ The pictured signers are (standing left to right) Nicholas Ridgely ♦ and Gunning Bedford, Sr. ♦ (At the table seated clockwise from left) Allan McLane ♦ Gunning Bedford, Jr. ♦ James Latimer ♦ Richard Bassett ♦ Kensey Johns, the elder ♦ and James Sykes. ♦ Courtesy, Bank of Delaware. ♦

THE SIGNERS

Through LONG, PAINFUL & DISINTERESTED LABOURS these five men represented Delaware at the Convention in Philadelphia in the summer of 1787 which drafted the United States Constitution. ♦ Delawareans favored a strong national government as long as they had an equal voice in Congress. ♦ The Delaware Assembly instructed its delegates to stand firm for the provision that "each state shall have one vote." ♦ George Read reminded the Convention that Delawareans would withdraw if legislative representation was determined by the states' populations. ♦ Gunning Bedford, Jr. threatened to seek foreign allies. ♦ John Dickinson proposed the Great Compromise which gave Delaware and all the states equal representation in the Senate. ♦

★ ★ ★ ★ ★ ★ ◆ ★ ★ ★ ★ ★ ★

ART DIRECTOR:
Martha Carothers

DESIGNER:
Martha Carothers

ARTIST:
Robert Goodier

AGENCY:
The Post Press

CLIENT:
Delaware Heritage Commission
■ 369

◄ **ARTIST:**
Christer Themptander

CLIENT:
ANC Stockholm
■ 368

ART DIRECTOR:
Martha Carothers

DESIGNER:
Martha Carothers

AGENCY:
The Post Press

CLIENT:
Delaware Heritage Commission
■ 370

■ **368** "75 Years of Struggle" – poster in commemoration of the 75th anniversary of the South African freedom movement, the African National Congress. The colors of the ANC are black, green and yellow. (SWE)

■ **369, 370** Poster series to commemorate 7 December 1787 when Delaware ratified as the first state the constitution of the United States. (USA)

■ **368** «75 Jahre Kampf» – Plakat des ANC Stockholm zur Erinnerung an das 75jährige Bestehen der südafrikanischen Befreiungsbewegung African National Congress. Schwarz, Grün, Gelb sind die Farben des ANC. (SWE)

■ **369, 370** Plakatserie zum Gedenken des 7. Dezember 1787, an welchem Delaware als erster Staat die Verfassung der Union ratifizierte. (USA)

■ **368** «75 années de lutte» – affiche rappelant le 75e anniversaire du mouvement de libération noir d'Afrique du Sud, l'African National Congress ANC, qui a opté pour un drapeau tricolore noir, vert, jaune. (SWE)

■ **369, 370** Série d'affiches commémoratives de l'Etat de Delaware, qui fut le premier, le 7 décembre 1787, à ratifier la Constitution fédérale des Etats-Unis. (USA)

ART DIRECTOR:
David Hillman
DESIGNER:
David Hillman
AGENCY:
Pentagram
CLIENT:
Napoli '99 Foundation
■ 371

A poster
commissioned by 'Napoli 99 Foundation'
as a contribution towards
the cultural image of the city

GEGEN
DEN
LAUF
DER ZEIT

ART DIRECTOR:
Renate Herter
DESIGNER:
Renate Herter
ARTIST:
Renate Herter
AGENCY:
Renate Herter
■ 372

Peace.

Don't break the beautiful earth.

ART DIRECTOR:
Ivan Chermayeff

DESIGNER:
Ivan Chermayeff

PHOTOGRAPHER:
Alan Shortall

AGENCY:
Chermayeff & Geismar Associates

CLIENT:
The Shoshin Society

■ **373**

ART DIRECTOR:
Takeshi Ohtaka

DESIGNER:
Takeshi Ohtaka

PHOTOGRAPHER:
Nob Fukuda

CLIENT:
May Teck Co., Ltd.

■ **374**

■ **371** From a poster campaign on behalf of the Napoli '99 Foundation - here an appeal against air pollution. (ITA)

■ **372** "Against the Course of Time." A poster making a poetical expression against universal war and armaments. (GER)

■ **373** Poster issued by the Shoshin Society to further international peace. (USA)

■ **374** "Don't break the beautiful earth." An appeal for human reason. (JPN)

■ **371** Aus einer Plakatkampagne im Auftrag der Stiftung Napoli '99 - hier ein Aufruf gegen die Luftverschmutzung. (ITA)

■ **372** Ein in poetischer Sprache ausgedrückter Appell gegen den Krieg und die Aufrüstung in dieser Welt. (GER)

■ **373** Ein von der Shoshin-Gesellschaft herausgegebenes Plakat für den internationalen Frieden. (USA)

■ **374** «Zerbrich die schöne Welt nicht» - Appell an die Vernunft der Menschheit. (JPN)

■ **371** Extrait d'une campagne d'affiches de la Fondation Napoli 99. Sujet traité ici: la pollution de l'air. (ITA)

■ **372** Affiche au langage poétique - «contre le cours (ou canon) du temps» contre la guerre et la course aux armements. (GER)

■ **373** Affiche publiée par la Société Shoshin, plaidant pour la paix mondiale. (USA)

■ **374** «Ne brisez pas cette Terre si belle» - un appel pour que la raison l'emporte sur les passions. (JPN)

TWENTY-FIFTH ANNIVERSARY 1961-1986

AAHA
AMERICAN ASSOCIATION
OF HOMES FOR THE AGING

ART DIRECTOR:
Milton Glaser
DESIGNER:
Milton Glaser
ARTIST:
Milton Glaser
AGENCY:
Milton Glaser, Inc.
CLIENT:
AAHA American Assoc. of Homes for the Aging
■375

ART DIRECTOR:
Jerzy Wawrzak
DESIGNER:
Tadeusz Piechura
PHOTOGRAPHER:
Tadeusz Piechura
STUDIO:
Tadeusz Piechura
CLIENT:
KAW
■376

ART DIRECTOR:
Mike Peterson
DESIGNER:
Mike Peterson
PHOTOGRAPHER:
Al Pitzner
AGENCY:
Sandven True Pruitt, Inc.
CLIENT:
Advertising Club of Kansas City
■377

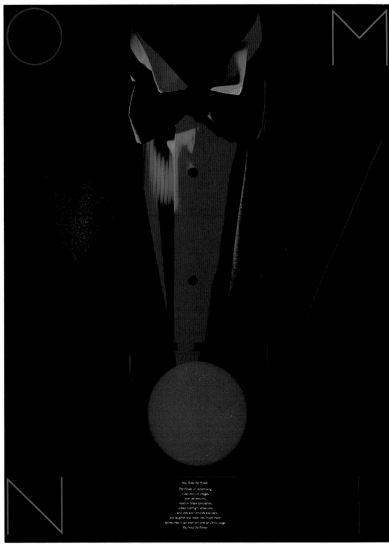

■**375** Poster to mark the 25th anniversary of the American Association of Homes for the Aging. (USA)

■**376** "Month of National Remembrance." One of the posters published every year in April in Poland in remembrance of the Polish soldiers killed in action in World War II and those who died during the German occupation. (POL)

■**377** Invitational poster issued by the Advertising Club of Kansas City to participate at the annual contest of best works in advertising. (USA)

■**375** Plakat zum 25jährigen Bestehen der amerikanischen Gesellschaft für Altersheime. (USA)

■**376** «Monat des nationalen Gedenkens.» Eines der alljährlich in Polen im April erscheinenden Plakate zum Gedenken an die polnischen Gefallenen des Zweiten Weltkrieges und an die Besetzung Polens durch die deutsche Wehrmacht. (POL)

■**377** Einladungsplakat des Advertising Club of Kansas City zur Teilnahme am jährlichen Wettbewerb der besten Arbeiten in der Werbebranche. (USA)

■**375** Affiche pour le 25e anniversaire de la Société américaine des homes pour vieillards. (USA)

■**376** «Mois du souvenir national.» L'une des affiches par lesquelles la Pologne rend hommage, chaque année en avril, à ses tués de la Seconde Guerre mondiale, tout en évoquant la sombre période de l'occupation militaire allemande. (POL)

■**377** Affiche d'invitation de l'Advertising Club de Kansas City à tous les publicitaires désirant participer au concours annuel du Club pour déterminer les meilleurs travaux de la branche. (USA)

ART DIRECTOR:
Kabel Harris

DESIGNER:
Kabel Harris

ARTIST:
Bill Mayer

AGENCY:
Lawler Ballard

■378

OUR DECISION TO STAY OPEN FOR THANKSGIVING HAS ALREADY RUFFLED A FEW FEATHERS.

Join us for dinner between noon and 8 p.m. You'll be thankful you came.

■**378** Poster issued by the Lawler Ballard ad agency by way of invitation to a traditional turkey dinner on Thanksgiving Day, with the slogan, "Our decision to stay open for Thanksgiving has already ruffled a few feathers." (USA)

■**378** «Manchem hat sich das Gefieder gesträubt über unsere Entscheidung, die Büros Thanksgiving nicht zu schliessen.» Plakat der Werbeagentur Lawler Ballard zu einem Truthahn-Festessen anlässlich des amerikanischen Erntedankfestes. (USA)

■**378** «Plus d'un a eu les plumes hérissées à la perspective de nous voir ouvrir nos bureaux le jour de Thanksgiving.» Affiche de l'agence de publicité Lawler Ballard invitant au traditionnel dîner de dindonneau célébrant la fin des moissons. (USA)

INDEX

VERZEICHNIS

INDEX

Subscription rates for one year:
USA: US$ 79.00 p.a. second
class postage paid at New York
Canada: Cdn $ 82.00
Great Britain and Eire:
£ 45.00
'All other countries: SFr. 118.–
Subscription fees include
postage to any part of the
world. (For Latin American
countries and India, please
add SFr. 12.– for registered
post.) Surcharge of SFr. 25.–
for airmail.

Single copies: US$ 15.00, Cdn
$ 16.50, £ 9.20, SFr. 24.–

SUBSCRIPTIONS AND
DISTRIBUTION:

USA and Canada: Graphis
U.S Inc., 141 Lexington Ave-
nue, New York, N.Y. 10016
Contact: Ford Pedersen
Telephone: (212) 532-9387

Address changes USA: Trans-
books Inc., 131 Varick Street,
New York, N.Y. 10013

All other countries: Graphis
Press Corp., Dufourstrasse 107,
CH-8008 Zürich, Switzerland
Contact: Hannelore Dörries
Telephone: 01/ 251 97 52
Telex: 57 222 grpc ch

SUBSCRIBE TO GRAPHIS: FOR USA AND CANADA

MAGAZINE	USA	CANADA
☐ GRAPHIS (One year/6 issues)	US$79.00	CDN$99.00
☐ 1987 Portfolio (Case holds six issues)	US$11.00	CDN$15.00

☐ Check enclosed
☐ Please bill me (My subscription will begin upon payment)
☐ Students may request a 40% discount by sending student ID.
IMPORTANT! PLEASE CHECK THE LANGUAGE VERSION DESIRED:
☐ ENGLISH ☐ GERMAN ☐ FRENCH
Subscription fees include postage to any part of the world. Latin America and India
Registered Mail: Add US$8.00 (CDN$11.00). Surcharge of US$16.00 (CDN$21.00) for Airmail.

NAME

TITLE

COMPANY

ADDRESS

CITY

STATE   POSTAL CODE

COUNTRY

PROFESSION

SIGNATURE   DATE

Please send coupon and make check payable to:
GRAPHIS US, INC. 141 LEXINGTON AVENUE, NEW YORK, NEW YORK USA 10016
Guarantee: You may cancel your subscription at any time and receive a full refund on all
unmailed copies. Please allow 6-8 weeks for delivery of first issue.

REQUEST FOR CALL FOR ENTRIES
Please put me on your "Call for Entries" list for the following title(s).
Please check the appropriate box(es).
☐ GRAPHIS PHOTO   ☐ GRAPHIS POSTER   ☐ GRAPHIS DESIGN
☐ GRAPHIS PACKAGING ☐ GRAPHIS DIAGRAM   ☐ GRAPHIS ANNUAL REPORTS
By submitting material to any of the titles listed above, I will automatically qualify for a
25% discount toward the purchase of the title.

BOOK ORDER FORM: FOR USA AND CANADA

ORDER YOUR GRAPHIS ANNUALS NOW!

BOOKS	USA	CANADA
☐ Graphis Poster 88	US$59.50	CDN$79.50
☐ Graphis Design Annual 87/88	US$59.50	CDN$79.50
☐ Photographis 87	US$59.50	CDN$79.50
☐ Graphis Posters 87	US$59.50	CDN$79.50
☐ Graphis Annual 86/87	US$59.50	CDN$79.50
☐ Photographis 86	US$59.50	CDN$79.50
☐ Graphis Posters 86	US$59.50	CDN$79.50
☐ 42 Years of Graphis Covers	US$49.50	CDN$60.00

☐ Check enclosed
☐ Please bill me (Mailing costs in addition to above book price will be charged)

NAME

TITLE

COMPANY

ADDRESS

CITY

POSTAL CODE   COUNTRY

PROFESSION

SIGNATURE   DATE

Send coupon and make check payable to:
GRAPHIS US, INC., 141 LEXINGTON AVENUE, NEW YORK, NY, 10016, USA.

REQUEST FOR CALL FOR ENTRIES
Please put me on your "Call for Entries" list for the following title(s).
Please check the appropriate box(es).
☐ GRAPHIS DESIGN   ☐ GRAPHIS POSTER   ☐ GRAPHIS PHOTO
☐ GRAPHIS PACKAGING ☐ GRAPHIS DIAGRAM   ☐ GRAPHIS ANNUAL REPORTS
By submitting material to any of the titles listed above, I will automatically qualify for a
25% discount toward the purchase of the title.

SUBSCRIBE TO GRAPHIS: FOR EUROPE AND THE WORLD

MAGAZINE	WORLD	U.K.
☐ GRAPHIS (One year/6 issues)	SFr.118.–	£45.00
☐ 1987 Portfolio (Holds six issues)	SFr. 19.–	£ 8.00

☐ Check enclosed (for Europe, please make SFr.–checks
payable a Swiss bank)
☐ Please bill me (My subscription will begin upon payment)
☐ Students may request a 40% discount by sending student ID.
IMPORTANT! PLEASE CHECK THE LANGUAGE VERSION DESIRED:
☐ ENGLISH ☐ GERMAN ☐ FRENCH
Subscription fees include postage to any part of the world. Latin America and India–
Registered Mail: Add SFr. 12.–Surcharge of SFr.25.–(£10.00) for Airmail.

NAME

TITLE

COMPANY

ADDRESS

CITY   POSTAL CODE

COUNTRY

PROFESSION

SIGNATURE   DATE

Please send coupon and make check payable to:
GRAPHIS PRESS CORP., DUFOURSTRASSE 107, CH-8008 ZÜRICH, SWITZERLAND
Guarantee: You may cancel your subscription at any time and receive a full refund on all
unmailed copies. Please allow 6-8 weeks for delivery of first issue.

REQUEST FOR CALL FOR ENTRIES
Please put me on your "Call for Entries" list for the following title(s).
Please check the appropriate box(es).
☐ GRAPHIS PHOTO   ☐ GRAPHIS POSTER   ☐ GRAPHIS DESIGN
☐ GRAPHIS PACKAGING ☐ GRAPHIS DIAGRAM   ☐ GRAPHIS ANNUAL REPORTS
By submitting material to any of the titles listed above, I will automatically qualify for a
25% discount toward the purchase of the title.

BOOK ORDER FORM: FOR EUROPE AND THE WORLD

BOOKS	WORLD	U.K.
☐ Graphis Poster 88	SFr.105.–	£42.00
☐ Graphis Design Annual 87/88	SFr.112.–	£45.00
☐ Photographis 87	SFr.112.–	£45.00
☐ Graphis Posters 87	SFr.105.–	£42.00
☐ Graphis Annual 86/87	SFr.112.–	£45.00
☐ Photographis 86	SFr.112.–	£45.00
☐ Graphis Posters 86	SFr.105.–	£42.00
☐ 42 Years of Graphis Covers	SFr .85.–	£35.00

☐ Check enclosed (For Europe, please make SFr. checks payable to a Swiss Bank)
☐ Amount paid into Graphis account at the Union Bank of Switzerland, Acct № 3620063
in Zürich.
☐ Amount paid to Postal Cheque Account Zürich 80-23071-9 (Through your local post office)
☐ Please bill me (Mailing costs in addition to above book price will be charged)

NAME

TITLE

COMPANY

ADDRESS

CITY   POSTAL CODE

COUNTRY

PROFESSION

SIGNATURE   DATE

Send coupon and make check payable to:
GRAPHIS PRESS CORP., DUFOURSTRASSE 107, CH-8008 ZÜRICH, SWITZERLAND

REQUEST FOR CALL FOR ENTRIES
Please put me on your "Call for Entries" list for the following title(s).
Please check the appropriate box(es).
☐ GRAPHIS DESIGN   ☐ GRAPHIS POSTER   ☐ GRAPHIS PHOTO
☐ GRAPHIS PACKAGING ☐ GRAPHIS DIAGRAM   ☐ GRAPHIS ANNUAL REPORTS
By submitting material to any of the titles listed above, I will automatically qualify for a
25% discount toward the purchase of the title.

GRAPHIS U.S., INC.
141 LEXINGTON AVENUE
NEW YORK, NEW YORK 10016
U.S.A.

GRAPHIS PRESS CORP.
DUFOURSTRASSE 107
CH-8008 ZÜRICH
SWITZERLAND

GRAPHIS U.S., INC.
141 LEXINGTON AVENUE
NEW YORK, NEW YORK 10016
U.S.A.

GRAPHIS PRESS CORP.
DUFOURSTRASSE 107
CH-8008 ZÜRICH
SWITZERLAND